T0202974

Communications
in Computer and Information Science   **1622**

More information about this series at https://link.springer.com/bookseries/7899

Hans-Georg Fill · Marten van Sinderen ·
Leszek A. Maciaszek (Eds.)

Software Technologies

16th International Conference, ICSOFT 2021
Virtual Event, July 6–8, 2021
Revised Selected Papers

 Springer

Editors
Hans-Georg Fill
Digitalization and Information Systems
Group
Universität Fribourg
Fribourg, Switzerland

Marten van Sinderen
Department of Computer Science
Information Systems Group
Enschede, The Netherlands

Leszek A. Maciaszek
Institute of Business Informatics
Wrocław University of Economics
Wrocław, Poland

Department of Computing
Macquarie University
Sydney, Australia

ISSN 1865-0929 ISSN 1865-0937 (electronic)
Communications in Computer and Information Science
ISBN 978-3-031-11512-7 ISBN 978-3-031-11513-4 (eBook)
https://doi.org/10.1007/978-3-031-11513-4

This Springer imprint is published by the registered company Springer Nature Switzerland AG
The registered company address is: Gewerbestrasse 11, 6330 Cham, Switzerland

Preface

The present book includes extended and revised versions of a set of selected papers from the 16th International Conference on Software Technologies (ICSOFT 2021), held as an online event due to the COVID-19 pandemic, during July 6–8, 2021.

ICSOFT 2021 received 117 paper submissions from authors in 36 countries, of which 9% were included in this book.

The papers were selected by the event chairs and their selection was based on a number of criteria that include the classifications and comments provided by the Program Committee members, and the assessments provided by the session chairs and the program chairs. The authors of selected papers were then invited to submit a revised and extended version of their papers having at least 30% innovative material. The revisions and extensions were verified by the event chairs during this final stage.

The purpose of the ICSOFT conference series, which started in 2006, is to bring together researchers, engineers, and practitioners interested in software technologies. The conference areas are "Software Engineering and Systems Development", "Software Systems and Applications", and "Foundational and Trigger Technologies".

The papers included in this book contribute to the understanding of relevant trends of current research on software technologies, including

- Model-driven software engineering approaches for cyber-physical systems and Internet of Things (IoT) systems;
- Artificial intelligence applications for optimization and coordination of complex software systems;
- Code refactoring methods for software energy consumption and software architecture recovery;
- Frameworks and methodologies for context-aware reconfigurable software applications and socio-technical systems; and
- Software engineering tools for automated software engineering and software evaluation.

We would like to thank all the authors for their contributions and also the reviewers who have helped in ensuring the quality of this publication.

July 2021

Hans-Georg Fill
Marten van Sinderen
Leszek Maciaszek

Organization

Conference Chair

Leszek Maciaszek   Wroclaw University of Economics and Business, Poland, and Macquarie University, Australia

Program Co-chairs

Hans-Georg Fill   University of Fribourg, Switzerland
Marten van Sinderen   University of Twente, The Netherlands

Program Committee

Vincent Aranega	University of Lille, France
Pasquale Ardimento	University of Bari, Italy
Marco Autili	University of L'Aquila, Italy
Soumyadip Bandyopadhyay	BITS Pilani, K K Birla Goa Campus, India and Hasso Plattner Institute, Germany
Davide Basile	ISTI CNR, Italy
Yann Ben Maissa	INPT, Morocco
Kwabeno Ebo Bennin	Wageningen University and Research, The Netherlands
Jorge Bernardino	Polytechnic Institute of Coimbra, Portugal
Marco Bernardo	University of Urbino, Italy
Dominique Blouin	Telecom Paris, France
Dominik Bork	TU Wien, Austria
Thomas Buchmann	University of Bayreuth, Germany
Fergal Caffery	Dundalk Institute of Technology, Ireland
Alejandro Calderón	University of Cádiz, Spain
Ana Castillo	Universidad de Alcalá, Spain
Anis Charfi	Carnegie Mellon University, Qatar
Estrela Cruz	Instituto Politécnico de Viana do Castelo, Portugal
Lidia López Cuesta	Universitat Politècnica de Catalunya, Spain
João Cunha	Polytechnic Institute of Coimbra, Portugal
Sergiu Dascalu	University of Nevada, Reno, USA
Cléver Ricardo de Farias	University of São Paulo, Brazil
Steven Demurjian	University of Connecticut, USA
Amleto Di Salle	University of L'Aquila, Italy

Francisco Domínguez Mayo	University of Seville, Spain
Gencer Erdogan	SINTEF, Norway
Morgan Ericsson	Linnaeus University, Sweden
Anne Etien	Université Lille 1, France
Letha Etzkorn	University of Alabama in Huntsville, USA
João Faria	University of Porto, Portugal
Eduardo Fernandez	Florida Atlantic University, USA
Massimo Ficco	University of Campania Luigi Vanvitelli, Italy
Tarik Fissaa	INPT, Morocco
Amit Ganatra	Charotar University of Science and Technology, India
Vinicius Garcia	Federal University of Pernambuco, Brazil
Felix Garcia Clemente	University of Murcia, Spain
Hamza Gharsellaoui	Arab Open University, Saudi Arabia
Paola Giannini	University of Piemonte Orientale, Italy
Christiane Gresse von Wangenheim	Federal University of Santa Catarina, Brazil
Hatim Hafiddi	INPT, Morocco
Stefan Hanenberg	University of Duisburg-Essen, Germany
Jean Hauck	Universidade Federal de Santa Catarina, Brazil
Mercedes Hidalgo-Herrero	Universidad Complutense de Madrid, Spain
Andreas Hinderks	Universidad de Sevilla, Germany
Ralph Hoch	TU Wien, Austria
Andreas Holzinger	Medical University of Graz, Austria
Jang-Eui Hong	Chungbuk National University, South Korea
Miloslav Hub	University of Pardubice, Czech Republic
Thomas Hupperich	University of Münster, Germany
Zbigniew Huzar	Wroclaw University of Science and Technology, Poland
Ivan Ivanov	SUNY Empire State College, USA
Clemente Izurieta	Montana State University, USA
Slinger Jansen	Utrecht University, The Netherlands
Judit Jasz	University of Szeged, Hungary
Bharat Jayaraman	State University of New York at Buffalo, USA
Andres Jimenez Ramirez	University of Seville, Spain
Hermann Kaindl	TU Wien, Austria
Carlos Kavka	ESTECO SpA, Italy
Dean Kelley	Minnesota State University, USA
Takashi Kobayashi	Tokyo Institute of Technology, Japan
Jun Kong	North Dakota State University, USA
Herbert Kuchen	University of Muenster, Germany
Rob Kusters	Open Universiteit Nederland, The Netherlands

Johannes Sametinger	Johannes Kepler University Linz, Austria
Maria-Isabel Sanchez-Segura	Carlos III University of Madrid, Spain
Nickolas Sapidis	University of Western Macedonia, Greece
Istvan Siket	Hungarian Academy of Science, Research Group on Artificial Intelligence, Hungary
Harvey Siy	University of Nebraska at Omaha, USA
Kari Smolander	Aalto University, Finland
Ketil Stolen	SINTEF, Norway
Hiroki Suguri	Miyagi University, Japan
Rosa Sukamto	Universitas Pendidikan Indonesia, Indonesia
Francesco Tiezzi	University of Camerino, Italy
Claudine Toffolon	Université du Maine, France
Porfirio Tramontana	University Federico II of Naples, Italy
Michael Vassilakopoulos	University of Thessaly, Greece
Roberto Verdecchia	Vrije Universiteit Amsterdam, The Netherlands
László Vidács	University of Szeged, Hungary
Tony Wasserman	Carnegie Mellon University, Silicon Valley, USA
Dietmar Winkler	Vienna University of Technology, Austria
Michalis Xenos	University of Patras, Greece
Jinhui Yao	Xerox Research, USA
Murat Yilmaz	Gazi University, Turkey

Additional Reviewers

Peter Alexander	RWTH Aachen University, Germany
Selin Aydin	RWTH Aachen University, Germany
Jorge Barreiros	Polytechnic Institute of Coimbra, Portugal
Jaganmohan Chandrasekaran	University of Texas at Arlington, USA
Róisín Loughran	Dundalk Institute of Technology, Ireland
Mateus Mendes	Polytechnic Institute of Coimbra, Portugal
Breno Menezes	University of Münster, Germany
Rakshit Mittal	Telecom Paris, France
Hana Mkaouar	Telecom Paris, France
Christian Plewnia	RWTH Aachen University, Germany
Gilbert Regan	Dundalk Institute of Technology, Ireland
Alex Sabau	RWTH Aachen University, Germany
Nils Wild	RWTH Aachen University, Germany
Hendrik Winkelmann	University of Münster, Germany

Invited Speakers

Jan Recker	University of Hamburg, Germany
Philippe Cudré-Mauroux	University of Fribourg, Switzerland
Johann Eder	Alpen-Adria Universität Klagenfurt, Austria
Douglas Schmidt	Vanderbilt University, USA

Contents

Linked Data as Medium for Stigmergy-based Optimization and Coordination

Torsten Spieldenner[1,2]([✉]) [iD] and Melvin Chelli[1] [iD]

[1] German Research Center for Artificial Intelligence (DFKI),
Saarland Informatics Campus D3 2, 66123 Saarbrücken, Germany
{torsten.spieldenner,melvin.chelli}@dfki.de
[2] Saarbrücken Graduate School of Computer Science,
Campus E1 3, 66123 Saarbrücken, Germany

Abstract. Optimization through coordination of processes in complex systems is a classic challenge in AI research. A specific class of algorithms takes for this inspiration from biology. Such bio-inspired algorithms achieve coordination and optimization by transferring, for example, concepts of communication in insect swarms to typical planner problems in the AI domain. Among those bio-inspired algorithms, an often used concept is the concept of stigmergy. In a stigmergic system, actions carried out by members of the swarm (or, in AI domains, by single agents), leave traces in the environment that subsequently work as incentive for following agents. While there is a noticeable uptake of stigmergy as coordination mechanism in AI, we see the common understanding of one core element of stigmergic systems still lacking: The notion of the shared digital stigmergic medium, in which agents carry out their actions, and in which traces left by these actions manifest. Given that the medium is in literature considered the element "that underlies the true power of stigmergy", we believe that a well-defined, properly modelled, and technically sound digital medium is essential for correct, understandable, and transferable stigmergic algorithms. We therefore suggest the use of read-write Linked Data as underlying medium for decentralized stigmergic systems. We first derive a set of core requirements that we see crucial for stigmergic digital media from relevant literature. We then discuss read-write Linked Data as suitable choice by showing that it fulfills given the requirements. We conclude with two practical application examples from the domains of optimization and coordination respectively.

Keywords: Linked data · Resource Description Framework · Stigmergy · Nature-inspired algorithm · Digital medium · Optimization · Coordination

1 Introduction

The problem of coordination of agents, tasks, resources, and more, is an ever popular and challenging topic in Artificial Intelligence (AI) research. The need for coordination by this arises in most various domains [1, 8, 12, 24, 36]. The desired effect that is sought

This work has been supported by the German Federal Ministry for Education and Research (BMBF) as part of the MOSAIK project (grant no. 01IS18070-C).

H.-G. Fill et al. (Eds.): ICSOFT 2021, CCIS 1622, pp. 1–23, 2022.
https://doi.org/10.1007/978-3-031-11513-4_1

by coordinating a system is thereby most often optimization, under the assumption that a perfectly coordinated system behaves optimal with respect to utilization of resources, or time it takes for processes implemented in the system to finish.

A specific trend in research seeks inspiration in biology, and tries to transfer concepts from nature to AI systems [5,9,39]. A biological concept that has gained specific attention as basis for nature-inspired algorithms is the concept of *stigmergy* [22], the core concept by which, for example, insect swarms achieve coordination among their members. In a stigmergic system, an action carried out by an individual member of the swarm leaves an observable *trace* within the environment. These traces constitute an incentive for other swarm members to carry out specific actions, leading to an influence-reaction cycle that ultimately leads to the achievement of a common goal by coordinated behavior. In AI, stigmergy-based algorithms have been found a promising approach for more flexible, fault-tolerant, and scalable coordination of complex systems in various domains [13,23,26,33,35].

Stigmergic systems discussed in literature, however, are often very specific to the considered use-case, and focus on models of agents and their behavior in the system, or are very implementation-specific with respect to the discussed system. This makes it hard to identify core concepts in the different algorithms, and transfer them to different use-cases and domains. It is in particular noticeable, that while focusing on specific algorithms and their implementations, existing work marginalizes or ignores the importance of a proper *medium.*

The medium in a stigmergic system is the element in which agents dwell, perform their actions, that is shaped by agents and where agents ultimately leave traces as byproduct of their actions. This gives the medium a central role within the overall system, which is why the medium is in literature also considered the *"the mediating function that underlies the true power of stigmergy"* [21].

Gaining understanding of the concept of the medium is particularly interesting in the world of AI optimization and coordination, where the medium has no tangible physical manifestation, but where agents operate entirely in an environment that is completely digital, while having only abstract correspondences to real world entities. We see a great benefit in a consise common understanding of a digital stigmergic medium for stigmergy-based algorithms, and AI research in general: A well-defined medium as core concept of a stigmergic AI system would support clearer and better explainable designs and algorithms, and increase transferability of published solutions. This medium should be provided by employing widely accepted open standards to be independent of specific use-cases, domains, or technologies that implement the algorithm. It should be based on a well-defined, thoroughly formalized and established foundation to allow for soundly defined, general, transferable solutions.

Such a set of standardized and well-defined tools comes from the world of the *Semantic Web* [4]. Based on the notion of *Linked Data* [6] and typically modeled in terms of the *Resource Description Framework* *(RDF)* [28][1], the Semantic Web is commonly promoted as a generic integration layer for applications from various domains.

Unnoticed by many, one digital stigmergic medium built on concepts of Web and Semantic Web is accessed by billions of users on a daily basis: the Internet is widely

[1] RDF 1.1 Primer document (Jan. 2021): https://www.w3.org/TR/rdf11-primer/.

relies on stigmergic concepts by the way content is provided and selected to presented to individual users [16]. That given, one may expect that a machine readable and writable Linked Data layer (*read-write Linked Data*) in the Semantic Web may as well provide a widely standardized, established, domain-independent interactive medium for stigmergy-based coordination [14, 34].

To this end, this paper makes the following contributions:

- We derive from relevant literature a *set of requirements towards digital media to serve as proper stigmergic medium.*
- We *establish read-write Linked Data as suitable medium* for stigmergic systems.
- We demonstrate the application of read-write Linked Data as stigmergic medium in two scenarios: An *optimization* scenario from an abstract planner domain, and a multi-agent *coordination* scenario from the domain of cyber-physical production.

The remainder of the paper is structured as follows: We review relevant related literature in Sect. 2. In Sect. 3, we recapture core concepts of Linked Data architectures, as well as stigmergic systems. In Sect. 4, we derive requirements towards digital stigmergic media and discuss Linked Data as suitable choice. We demonstrate the application of Linked Data as stigmergic medium in Sects. 5 and 6: Sect. 5 demonstrates how to employ stigmergy in Linked Data to solve the optimization challenge of the Minimize Number of Open Stacks Problem (MOSP) [20]. In Sect. 6, we demonstrate how to achieve multi agent coordination in a cyber-physical production setting. We conclude our work and provide an outlook upon future challenges in Sect. 7.

This paper is an extended version of the paper *"Linked Data as Stigmergic Medium for Decentralized Coordination"* as presented at the 16th International Conference on Software Technologies (ICSOFT 2021) [38]. The original paper was extended with the application demonstration of Linked Data as stigmergic medium in Sect. 5, including all demonstrations of environment and agent models, experiments, and evaluation.

2 Related Work

Stigmergic systems have been thoroughly described and analyzed [14, 22], and also been discussed with respect to applicability in Web-based environments [15, 34].

Stigmergic agent systems vary from conventional agents in that they communicate indirectly via a shared medium/data space. This is also termed in some literature as a *generative communication paradigm* [11, 19]. Some implementations of this paradigm are realized in *Linda*, based on Tuple Spaces [19].

Applications of stigmergy in various domains for coordination can be found in literature, including robotics [23, 26, 31] and cyber-physical manufacturing [12, 36]. Inspiration from the concepts of evaporation and replenishment of pheromones in the ant world have led researchers to explore ways of managing the dynamic requirements of telecommunication networks [7]. It has also been shown that the data aggregated from vehicles plying in a city can be used to predict traffic hot-spots and thus plan optimal routes for navigation [1, 24].

Ant inspired optimization techniques have been a focus of research since the early 1990 s, and various variations have been developed ever since [17, 22]. Bio-inspired algorithms like stigmergy have shown to achieve good performance in decentralized decision making tasks [23]. They also perform well in situations where agents need to recruit peers and coordinate with them for task accomplishment [26]. High dimensional numerical optimization has also been approached using stigmergy (using the Differential Ant-stigmergy Algorithm, DASA) [25]. A distributed variant of the *Hungarian Method* for solving the Linear Sum Assignment Problem (LSAP) was shown by [10], where multiple agents cooperate to find an optimal solution to LSAP without sharing memory, or a central command structure. The field of Multi-Agent Systems (MAS) has also seen a growing interest in stigmergic concepts in recent years [12,13,35,41].

Among the bio-inspired works that have been discussed in this section, the concept of the stigmergic *medium* is not given particular emphasis as described by [22]. The fundamental idea behind the medium being a *shared environment* where agents can sense its state, leave traces or act on it, has not been significantly explored. Some works discussed above, like the one from the domain of traffic planning, completely overlook the medium and rely on direct agent-to-agent communication instead.

The observation that the environment (or medium) is not fully taken advantage of in the context of stigmergy has already been observed in [35]. The need for a common understanding of the environment, as well as the difficulty to map concepts from the real-world to concepts seen in nature to best leverage these algorithms has also been highlighted in [8,40]. In this paper, we discuss and present with appropriate examples, that read-write Linked Data layer is a suitable general stigmergic medium for said purposes.

3   Background

3.1   Resource-oriented Architectures

A Resource Oriented Architecture (ROA) is built around the notion of a *Resource* as common representation for any kind of virtual or real-world entities [18,30]. A resource is typically characterized by a name (identifier), its representation and links between resource representations [30]. Fielding [18] defines a representation as a sequence of bytes and metadata describing those bytes. A resource may have multiple representations, which means they can provide the same content but in different serializations. Detailed considerations of ROA can be found in [18].

3.2   Linked Data Systems

Linked Data[2] is a way to share and structure information using links. Linked Data implements an ROA, and it is built on the *Hypermedia as the Engine of Application State* (HATEOAS) and HyperText Transfer Protocol (HTTP) principles. By this, Linked Data enables software applications and user-agents to discover necessary information to perceive and understand data, explore ways of interacting with resources etc., by following links provided by a server [18]. *Semantic annotations* describe different data

---

[2] https://www.w3.org/standards/semanticweb/data.

fields to data consumers which leads to a uniform understanding of data among different applications.

The *Resource Description Framework (RDF)* is used to model these semantic descriptions [28], (see also footnote [1]). *Statements* about *resources* can be formulated using RDF in terms of *triples* that follow a *subject-predicate-object* structure. The *subject* denotes a resource, the *predicate* is a qualitative aspect of said resources and/or describes the relationship between a *subject* and an *object*. A set of RDF triples constitutes a labeled *graph*, where the subject and object form nodes, connected by a directed edge (from subject to object) that is labeled via the predicate.

3.3 Stigmergic Media

Heylighen concisely summarizes research in the field of stigmergy-based self-organization in [22]. Our discussions of stigmergy is exclusively based on the findings of this paper. However, we would like to emphasize that though the work by Heylighen in [22] covers reseach over several decades, we will also point out work carried out by many different researchers who have a differing view on the stigmergic concept.

Heylighen derives from his findings his own definition of stigmergy as an:

*"indirect, mediated mechanism of **coordination** between **actions**, in which the **trace** of an action left on a **medium** stimulates the performance of a subsequent action"* [22, p. 5].

The core compoents of stigmergy as described in [22] are defined as follows. A causal process that produces a change in the world is the *action*. The part of the world that undergoes changes because of the action, whose state can be sensed by other agents to incite further actions, is the *medium*. The perceivable change in the medium due to the action, which can trigger subsequent actions is the *trace*.

A trace that stimulates agents to perform a specific action, i.e. *affords* the action, is called *Affordance*. Affordances typically encode *condition-action* rules, which causes an agent to perform a action on the fulfilment of a certain condition. Traces that prevents the agents from performing actions are called *Disturbances*.

Heylighen further identifies different variations of stigmergy, depending how the agents interact with the medium (pp. 19–27).

Among them, are *individual* and *collective stigmergy*, depending on whether the medium is worked on by either a single or a team of agents. Another criteria for classifying variations in stigmergy, is if the agents perceive the mere existence of features in the medium (*qualitative stigmergy*) or also take into account the quantities of those features (*quantitative stigmergy*). Another variation is based on if agents react to the direct results of their work in the environment (*sematectonic stigmergy*) or to markers deliberately left by other agents (*marker-based stigmergy*). In addition, a variation also exists depending on if traces left by agents in the medium persist unless they are actively removed (*persistent stigmergy*) or if they dissipate and vanish over time (*transient stigmergy*). Finally, we can also differentiate based on the scope of the traces in the medium, i.e. if they are observable by every agent in the medium (*Broadcast*), or only to specific agents (*Narrowcast*)

For a very thorough elaboration on the various aspects that we covered here in a very shortened manner, we refer the reader to the original paper [22].

4   Linked Data as Digital Stigmergic Medium

In nature, the notions of *agent* and *medium* are determined by nature itself: Ants "agents" are attracted by pheromone traces which are left by other ants and lead towards lucrative sources of food. Here, the ground is the medium over which the agents navigate, and which carries the traces that lead the ant agents to their goal. Termites use clay as medium: not only do they form the medium to build their nest, but the perceived shape of the clay – the progress in construction so far – steers the subsequent actions of the termites. Bees use the air as medium to guide their fellow bees to food sources by dance patterns.

In optimization and coordination scenarios, *"agents"* are usually considered to be software AI user-agents. These AI agents perceive and interact with *digital representation* of the to-be-coordinated concepts, which may correspond to real-world physical artifacts (e.g. physical production machines or robots in manufacturing scenarios, cars and traffic lights in traffic). This distinction between digital and real world is common in agent-based coordination algorithms [15]. The digital representation is also referred to as *Agent Space*, whereas the physical space is referred to as *Artifact Space* [8].

4.1   Requirements for (Digital) Stigmergic Media

From the notions and variations of stigmergic systems in the Sect. 3.3, we derive the following requirements that a digital medium should fulfill to be suited for use in stigmergy-based algorithms:

R1 *(Representation:)* The medium must be capable of *representing* entities of the coordination or optimization domain. The representation capabilities must moreover not only be limited to represent individual entities, but also relations between entitites. The medium thus serves as *Agent Space*. If artifacts in Artifact Space are target of coordination or optimization, the medium must provide a *representation* of the physical entity in the Agent Space. Moreover, *access* to the physical entity must be provided from within the medium, e.g. for agents to switch a real-world traffic light, or start a production process on a production machine via the respective entity representation in the Agent Space.

R2 *(Accessibility:)* The medium must be *accessible* to the agent. This means, an agent must be able to enter the medium, access representations of entities, and perform actions on them. Furthermore, the agent must be able to navigate through the medium to the point where an action is to be performed.

R3 *(Observability:)* The medium must be *observable* (readable) for the agent to perceive and identify conditions of condition-action rules in the medium. For this, the agent needs to be able to at least observe the *existence of effects* (for qualitative stigmergy). The medium should further provide:

R3.1 (Interpretability) of observed effects in the medium in the context of the optimization or coordination domain, so that an agent can correctly set the observed effects into relation with each other.

R3.2 (Quantities): The medium must be able to express *quantities* for coordination by *quantitative* stigmergic effects.

R4 *(Consistency:)* For *collective stigmergy*, the information delivered by the medium must be consistent to different agents at the same point in time. In particular after changes induced by agents as results of their actions, other agents must observe the changed state as actual state of the medium.

R5 *(Malleability:)* Agents must be able to *form* and *change* elements in the medium as result of their action. This covers both interaction with existing entities and changing their state via their representation in the medium, as wells adding new entities, or removing entities from the medium (comparable to leaving pheromone markers, or dissipating markers over time). Such changes should be inflicted to the medium in a controlled manner, leading us to the requirement of *Stability*:

R5.1 *Stability*: It must be possible to perform changes to any entity within the medium *without inflicting unwanted side-effects* to resources outside the scope of a performed action. "Unwanted" is in this case not to be confused with changes that an agent "unintentionally" left as a trace, but to be understood as an effect that changes the state of an entity beyond what was intended by the algorithm.

R6 *(Scopes:)* The medium must be able to limit visibility of entities and effects in terms of scopes to allow *Narrowcast* of stigmergic effects.

4.2 Linked Data as Stigmergic Medium

We in the following show that the above requirements are fulfilled by read-write Linked Data as digital stigmergic medium.

Representation: is covered by the notion of representation space of resources (see Sects. 3.1 and 3.2): Read-write Linked Data being built around resource oriented architectures provides both the tools and best practices of how to represent both real-world and virtual entities in terms of addressable resources. Physical artifacts can be accessed from Linked Data media by having callable HTTP endpoints represented as resources within the medium.

Accessibility: is achieved by building Linked Data around HATEOAS principles. Agents can interact with resources and via HTTP requests. All information about how to interact with a resource is provided by the server that manages the resource. Furthermore, Linked Data defines query interfaces as a common interaction method with Linked Data graphs. Graph query engines like SPARQL[3] allow agents to identify relevant resources as a result of the queries. The capability to explore Linked Data graphs autonomously is provided by links between related resources, which agents can follow to identify relevant related resources. For following links via HTTP operations, it is not necessary to host the medium on a single physical server instance to ensure accessibility: Linked Data principles state that the resolution of URIs is transparent to clients, and agents are not required to make assumptions where the actual data is hosted. When it comes to agent-medium interaction via queries, SPARQL supports the integration of data from different distributed endpoints via federated queries using the SERVICE keyword.[4]

---

[3] W3C SPARQL 1.1 Query Language Recommendation (Apr. 2021): https://www.w3.org/TR/sparql11-query/.

[4] SPARQL Federated Queries: (Apr.2021): https://www.w3.org/TR/sparql11-federated-query/.

Observability: "Existence" of an effect can be encoded in Linked Data by the existence of a respective triple pattern in the Linked Data graph. By this, the existence of an effect as precondition for an action can be verified by matching expected triple patterns against the Linked Data graph via SPARQL queries. The statements encoded by triples are moreover *semantically interpretable* by software agents, as commonly established for Linked Data.

Quantities can be expressed in Linked Data graphs in two ways: either, by explicitly stating a quantity by a numerical value and a fitting data type in a literal node, or by the number of triples rendered to a respective resource. The latter approach is more suitable to determine quantities of the same effect appearing multiple times within the medium (for example, number of markers left on a resource within the medium).

Consistency: is achieved by the notion of state and representation of resources in Linked Data architectures, as outlined in Sects. 3.1 and 3.2. The Linked Data server hosting a resource is in control of providing access to resources, as well as its contents. By the communication between clients and server being stateless (by following REST and HATEOAS principles), the state of the resource as communicated by the server towards clients is independent of the particular client that requests the resource, and by this, consistent among all clients, resp. agents.

Malleability: is a direct result of write-capabilites of read-write Linked Data. Agents may request to change the state of a resource by HTTP PUT/POST/DELETE requests. Agents may moreover employ SPARQL UPDATE requests with INSERT and DELETE statements to modify Linked Data graphs that describe a resource in the medium. The WHERE body of SPARQL UPDATE queries allows to take into account preconditions that need to be fulfilled when performing the update.

Stability during updates is ensured by unambiguous identification of relevant resources via IRIs. By Linked Data design principles, operations on resources do not have side-effects on other resources, and by this, will not inflict undesired changes to resources other than those that the action was performed on. Stability on RDF graph level during write operations is ensured by that adding triple statements to a resource does not change existence or expressiveness of triples already present: by adding triples, statements about a resource may only become more specific, but never eliminate statements that were present before new triples were added.

Scope: can be expressed in read-write Linked Data implicitly by specific triple statements on resources. While all information is still available to every agent without limitation, individual agents may filter for specific resources, based on these resources, and by this scope their perception of the medium w.r.t. certain effects. Scope can moreover be provided by using mechanics of Linked Data datasets and named graphs.[5] Different scopes, i.e. named graphs, are then accessed by agents for example by using FROM and FROM NAMED clauses in the respective SPARQL queries.

By finding all requirements **R1–R6** fulfilled by and materialized via concepts of read-write Linked Data, we derive that read-write Linked Data is without limitations a suitable generic digital medium for stigmergy-based coordination.

---

[5] https://www.w3.org/TR/rdf-sparql-query/#rdfDataset.

5   Optimization: Minimize Open Stacks Example

In the following, we present how to employ stigmergy in a Linked Data medium to solve an abstract scheduling problem, the planner domain of the *Minimize Number of Open Stacks* problem *(MOSP)*. We will model the problem domain in terms of a Linked Data representation, and define three different agent types with increasing complexity of stigmergic principles applied for evaluation. The approach will finally be evaluated by comparing the performance with respect to the commonly employed metric, number of open product stacks created, against the verified optimal solutions as published in [3].

5.1   The Minimize Number of Open Stacks Problem

The Minimize Number of Open Stacks Problem (*MOSP*) is a common scheduling problem to evaluate planner tools, and was one of the planner domains in the Constraint Modelling Challenge 2005[6] and International Planner Competition 5 [20]. The problem is known to be NP hard [29].

This problem assumes a fictional factory that is capable of producing products of different kinds. For items of same kind, it can produce batches of arbitrary size. However, there can always only be one product kind produced at the same time. Initially, the factory receives a number of orders that demand for one or more kinds of products. Whenever the factory produced a kind of product that was requested by one of the orders, a *stack* is opened for the respective order. Subsequent items for this order are added to the stack until all items requested by the order have been added to the stack, which is when the stack of the order will be removed. The goal is now to find an order in which the factory produces batches of product kinds, such that the number of open stacks is minimal.

5.2   Medium Model

We model the scenario in the Linked Data medium as follows: We employ the RDF namespaces `stig:` for elements from the domain of stigmergic principles and effects (i.e., markers and traces), classes from the schema.org Ontology[7] with namespace `schema:` to refer to elements specific to order processes (e.g. orders and products), and `mosp:` as namespace to refer to instances within the minimize open stacks problem. A class of orderable products can then be described by triples of the form (`mosp:RedBox a schema:Product`).

We employ the notion of situated tropistic agents as we described in [37], i.e., agents reside on (virtual) locations (or *"topoi"*), and react based only on perception of their direct surroundings. As discussed in the original publication, this model relates closely to stigmergic principles in nature, and is a very suitable choice to model stigmergic media in Linked Data.

---

[6] http://www.dcs.st-and.ac.uk/ipg/challenge/.
[7] https://schema.org.

In the presented case, we for this describe orders as instance of `schema:Order`, as well as a stigmergic *topos*, i.e., a resource in the Linked Data medium that can be visited and inspected by a tropistic stigmergic agent. Orders that share at least one type of product are perceived as *adjacent* by the agent (see also Listing 1.1). Adjacency implies both that an agent can *perceive* state of the adjacent resource, and move from a resource to an adjacent one as result of its perception.

Listing 1.1. Example of two orders in the minimize open stacks domain that share one common product.

```
1  mosp:order_1  a        schema:Order , stig:Topos ;
2       st:adjacentTo    mosp:order_2 ;
3       schema:orderedItem  mosp:RedBox , mosp:PurpleBox .
4
5  mosp:order_2  a        schema:Order , stig:Topos ;
6       st:adjacentTo    mosp:order_1 ;
7       schema:orderedItem  mosp:BlueBox , mosp:PurpleBox .
```

Open stacks for orders are encoded as triples (`<urn>` a mosp:Stack), with `<urn>` a unique resource identifier that was randomly created when the stack was opened, the respective order linked to it via a relation `mosp:forOrder`, and contained products linked to it via the `schema:orderedItem` relation (see also Listing 1.2).

Listing 1.2. Example of two orders in the minimize open stacks domain that share one common product.

```
1  <urn:>  a        mosp:Stack ;
2       mosp:forOrder   mosp:order_1 ;
3       schema:orderedItem  mosp:PurpleBox .
```

5.3   Agent Models

The presented problem can be solved by a single agent. The general algorithm works as follows: The agent is situated on a `schema:Order` resource o as indicated by a triple `mosp:agentstig:locatedAt <Order>`, where `<Order>` is an order as described above. From here, the agent will perform the following steps:

1. Pick from order o any *product* p with (`<o> schema:orderedItem <p>`); (`<p> a schema:Product`) that is not yet part of any `mosp:Stack`, i.e., any type of product that has not yet been produced.
2. For each `schema:Order` $< o_i >$ that requires this product as indicated by a triple (`<o_i> schema:orderedItem <p>`), add p to the respective stack s_i: `<s_i >` a mosp:Stack ; mosp:forOrder `<o_i>` ; schema:orderedItem `<p>`.
3. For every order that is completed, i.e., for o, s with (`<s> a mosp:Stack ; mosp:forOrder <o>`), $\forall p_k$: (`<o> schema:orderedProduct < p_k >`) $\Rightarrow$ (`<s> schema:orderedProduct < p_k >`), *remove* the stack s, the order o, and their corresponding triples.

4. If there is no order o left, **terminate**. Otherwise, move to another order o and **restart** from **1**.

The number of open stacks is counted before step 3, i.e., before finished stacks are closed.

We will show how the above behavior can be optimized by influencing the agent in its choice of the subsequent order in step 4. We use stigmergic markers to support the agent in preferring certain orders over others, such that the number of open stacks remains minimal. The approach can thus be classified as a hybrid *marker-based* and *sematectonic* stigmergic system (by the agent reacting both to markers, and results of its own work: the types of products already produced), in an *individual stigmergic system*, as there is only one agent that is steered by the results of its own action. For comparison, we have created three different agent behaviours with increasing selectiveness of subsequent orders as follows:

Random Selection: In the simplest case, the agent selects the next order randomly among those that are labeled as `stig:adjacentTo`, i.e., the agent selects any open order that shares at least one kind of product, but neglecting whether the order has already a stack open. The selection of orders in Step 4 of the algorithm works as follows:

4.1 If the order that the agent was situated at was removed in step 3, i.e. there is *no triple* (`mosp:Agent stig:locatedAt <o>`), choose any order o at random.

4.2 Otherwise, select an *adjacent* o_a with `<o> stig:adjacentTo <o_a>`.

4.3 **Restart** from **1**.

Favoring Orders with Stacks: A simple heuristic is to favor orders for which a stack is already open. Producing for an order with an already open stack eliminates the risk that a new stack is created for this specific order. In order to identify orders with open stacks, the agent *marks* in step 2 of the algorithm every order for which it already created a product:

2.1 For each `schema:Order` o_i for which a product was created, create a marker as indicated by the triple (`<o_i> stig:carries [ a stig:Marker ]`).

When moving to another order after step 3, the agent favors orders that carry the *highest amount of markers*, i.e., for which it already produced the most products:

4.1 If the order that the agent was situated at was removed in step 3, i.e. there is *no triple* (`mosp:Agent stig:locatedAt <o>`), choose any order o as order with the highest amount of markers: $o = \underset{count(<m>)}{argmax}(o)(<o> \text{stig:carries } <m>)$

4.2 Otherwise, select an *adjacent* o_a with `<o> stig:adjacentTo <o_a>` and $o_a = \underset{count(<m>)}{argmax}(o_a)(<o_a> \text{stig:carries } <m>)$.

4.3 **Restart** from **1**.

Favoring almost Completed Orders: The efficiency of the previous heuristic can be further improved if among those orders with already open stacks, the agent prefers those that are close to being finished. Preferring almost closed orders increases the probability that the agent will pick an order of which the stack can be closed in the next step, while reducing the risk of an agent choosing a product kind that opens several new stacks from an order with many open products. To identify respective orders, the agent leaves a marker as follows:

2.1 For each `schema:Order` o_i for which a product was created, create a marker as indicated by the triple `<`o_i`> stig:carries [ a stig:Marker ; stig:level ?lvl] .`

`?lvl` refers to the concentration level of the marker, and is equal to the number of remaining products in the stack.

In step 4, when selecting an order to continue with, the agent chooses as follows:

4.1 If the order that the agent was situated at was removed in step 3, i.e. there is *no triple* (`mosp:Agent stig:locatedAt <o>`) , choose any order o as order with the *lowest concentration* of markers: $o = argmin(o)(<o>$ `stig:carries [ a stig:Marker ;   stig:level` $\sum(?lvl)$ `?lvl])`

4.2 Otherwise, select an *adjacent* o_a with `<o> stig:adjacentTo<`o_a`>`, and o_a carrying the lowest concentration of markers, as given in 4.1.

4.3 **Restart** from **1.**

5.4 Evaluation

Implementation of Stigmergic Principles. The presented algorithm implements a single agent. This agent reacts to both markers that were deliberately left on resources, and to results of its work in the environment by checking which kinds of products have already been produced in step 1 of the algorithm. By this, the presented algorithm implements *individual stigmergy* in a *marker-based* and *sematectonic* stigmergic system. The agent does neither maintain memory, nor does it plan or anticipate any future steps, but reacts solely on current observations of its current environment.

Table 1. Dimensions of orders and products per problem domain.

	Miller	NWRS 1	NWRS 2	NWRS 3	NWRS 4	NWRS 5	NWRS 6	NWRS 7	NWRS 8
Orders	20	10	10	15	15	20	20	25	25
Products	40	20	20	25	25	30	30	60	60

Empirical Results. We evaluate above agent models by having them solve 9 instances of MOSP as given in the Constraint Programming Challenge 2005. The problems have increasing complexity. Table 1 lists the numbers of orders and different product types per problem.

The sequence that an agent chooses in a single execution of a particular problem is non-deterministic. Typically, in one step, the agent will face several equally attractive resources as next candidates for a visit in step 4, in which case it will choose one at random. As the agent does not plan ahead, while being equally attractive at the instant, the choice of particular paths may have adverse effects later in the execution. We have therefore executed the experiment for each test instance 10 times. Figure 1 shows the best solution found by the agent out of 10 runs. Figure 2 shows the arithmetic average over the stack sizes as found by a particular agent type over all runs. Both figures also include the proven optimal solution as given in [3].

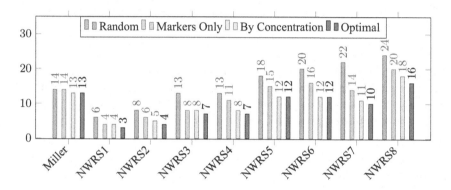

Fig. 1. Minimal stack size found by the different agent models over 10 runs compared to the verified optimal solution.

The experiments show that with increasingly expressive markers, the results of the algorithm improve for all problems, up to very noticeable improvements in the more difficult problem instances NWRS 5 to NWRS 8.

In the simpler examples, even the random walk provides results close to the optimal solution. In these examples, orders have only few products in common, and by this share only few connections with other orders. This leaves only few choices to all of the agents which order to visit next, and reliably guides all types of agents over a close to optimal path.

In the more complex examples with larger and denser orders, in which orders share many products with many other orders, the random agent is more likely to pick a suboptimal path. However, with taking more information about its surrounding into account, the quality of the solution improves significantly, up to the most complex agent finding the close to optimal, or even optimal, solution in all cases.

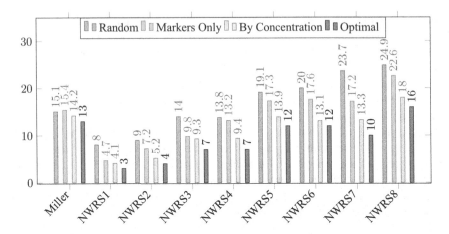

Fig. 2. Arithmetic average of stack sizes out of 10 solutions found by the different agent models compared to the verified optimal solution.

These experiments show that with a sufficiently elaborate interpretation of, and interaction with the environment, stigmergic agents are able to find good quality solutions to complex optimization problems without the need to keep memory, plan ahead, or know the optimization goal at all, as are known benefits of stigmergic systems [22, pp. 13–14].

5.5 Implementation

The above agents were entirely implemented in terms of SPARQL queries that encode the different actions that agents can take. The respective queries are published on GitHub, alongside with the application domain model, and a Postman collection that allows to execute the SPARQL queries against any triple store of choice: https://github.com/dfki-asr/stigmergy-mosp

For evaluation, we used an Apache Fuseki standalone installation.

6   Coordination: Make-to-Order Production

We now show how to employ a read-write Linked Data layer as stigmergic medium for coordination by an application example from the domain of digital manufacturing. The chosen scenario is loosely based on the use case presented in [36]: A (simulated) factory receives orders for simple IoT modules on a "batch size 1" production line as commonly envisioned in Industry 4.0 [27,32]. Received orders trigger the production of the respective customized IoT module, using machines which provide the capabilities to perform manufacturing steps necessary for particular steps during the production process. These steps may include for example the provisioning of plastic casts for casings, soldering electric circuits, or fixing the final model (see Fig. 3).

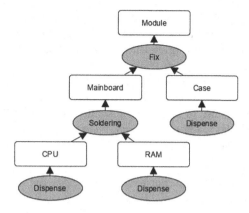

Fig. 3. Process of IoT module production used as example.

Finding and executing the necessary sequence of production steps is done by AI agents. The need for coordination arises as machines are shared between simultaneously executed orders.

The presented coordination algorithm aims at finding a suitable workload distribution among machines for different agents executing different orders, with the goal to complete each order in the shortest possible time.

6.1   Domain Model

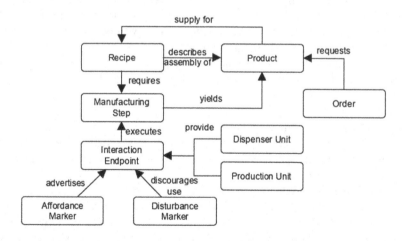

Fig. 4. Domain model of the chosen application example.

The domain model of the application scenario is shown in Fig. 4: An *order* encodes a request for production of a certain product. *Recipes* describe the assembly of a product, and specify other products that are required as supply, as well as which manufacturing step is necessary to assemble these supply products to a higher level product. The required manufacturing steps are provided by machines on the shop floor. Machines offer HTTP endpoints by which their respective production program can be executed, a common assumption for units in automated production [8,36]. These endpoints are offered to user agents via the Linked Data medium. The use of a certain interaction endpoint, and by this, the use of a specific machine on the shop floor, is encouraged or discouraged by stigmergic *affordance- and disturbance markers* on the interaction endpoint in the Linked Data medium.

Listing 1.3. Example of a production recipe using schema and steps vocabularies.

```
1  recipes:main-module rdf:type schema:HowTo ;
2     schema:about mainboard:product ;
3     schema:step steps:solder ;
4     schema:supply [
5       rdf:type schema:HowToSupply ;
6       schema:item cpu:product ] ,
7     [ rdf:type schema:HowToSupply ;
8       schema:item ram:product ] .
```

Within the RDF description of a recipe in the Linked Data medium, the `schema:about` predicate specifies the artifact that results from executing the respective recipe. The required supply from which the product is created is indicated by the `schema:supply` predicate, whereas the production step that needs to be performed to combine the specified supplies to the resulting product is given via the `schema:step` predicate (see Listing 1.3). `schema:` thereby denotes the namespace of the schema.org ontology[8]. We assume a set of supply materials to be provided to the factory without the need for specific production. These supply materials will be provided by dispenser units, and do not require any additional supplies.

Finished products that are available as supplies for subsequent production steps are described in terms of an RDF class, e.g. `<#product>`, `rdf:type`, `cpu:product`.

(Callable) execution endpoint of shopfloor units are provided as `td:InteractionPattern` in a set of triples that is referenced via `td:providesInteractionPattern`. The Interaction Pattern further specifies the step carried out by the respective unit (see also Listing 1.4).

Units that dispense products describe the product that they provide via a triple `<#unit>`, `schema:yield`, `<#productClass>`, with `<#productClass>` referring to the RDF class of the produced product. Dispenser units can dispense more than one class of products. Machines that assemble products from supplied products provide information about the offered production step via a triple `<#unit>,schema:step, steps:<type>`. An example of a simple soldering unit is shown in Listing 1.4.

---

[8] https://schema.org/.

Agents may perform the production step that is offered by a machine and its respective Interaction Pattern by resolving the URI that is provided by the respective Interaction Pattern resource. This URI is identified by the property path `td:isAccessibleThrough/td:href`, with `td:` denoting the namespace of the Web Thing Description ontology[9].

Listing 1.4. Example of a simple description of a workstation that performs a soldering step. The soldering action is executed by calling the respective referenced URI.

```
1  sol:station-1 a td:Thing ;
2    td:thingName "Soldering Station 1"^^xsd:string ;
3    td:providesInteractionPattern sol:soldering .
4
5  sol:soldering a td:InteractionPattern ;
6    td:interactionName "solder"^^xsd:string ;
7    schema:step steps:solder ;
8    td:isAccessibleThrough [
9      td:href <http://10.2.100.17/solder/>
10   ] .
```

Affordances and Disturbances.

Listing 1.5. Example of an affordance marker resource that advertises a `steps:soldering` interaction as relevant for the current order

```
1  <urn:uuid:a526>
2      a stigmergy:marker lef ;
3      stigmergy:marked   sol:soldering ;
4      stigmergy:scope    order:module ;
5      schema:supply   cpu:product,
6                      ram:product ;
7      schema:yield   mm:product .
```

We call a resource that advertises the use of a specific Interaction Pattern endpoint to some executing agent an *Affordance*. In our stigmergic system, we model affordances as *markers* that are left on a `td:InteractionPattern` within the Linked Data medium.

Listing 1.5 provides an example of such a marker: The RDF description of the marker resource specifies which Interaction Pattern it marked (via `stigmergy:marked`), which order will be progressed by executing the respective Interaction Pattern (via `stigmergy:scope`), whether or not the respective step needs particular supplies to be present to be executed (`schema:supply`), and finally, which product will be the result of calling the respective Interaction Pattern resource (`schema:yield`). Multiple Interaction Patterns can be advertised by the same marker. If more than one interaction pattern is marked, it is up to an executing agent to choose which of the endpoints to call.

---

[9] https://www.w3.org/2019/wot/td.

The decision which of the advertised endpoints to choose is further influenced by *disturbance* markers. These markers will discourage agents from visiting a marked resource. If an affordance marker links to several resource endpoints, an executing agent will decide for an endpoint that is the least influenced by disturbance markers. The algorithm will be furthered detailed out in Sect. 6.2.

6.2   Algorithm and Agent Models

The stigmergic algorithm to coordinate a production process within a Linked Data medium as described in the previous section is implemented in two steps by two classes of agents: *marker* agents and *builder* agents.

Marker agents traverse graphs in the Linked Data medium and generate *production markers* as affordances on resources that describe machines in the Artifact space. An example of a production marker is shown in Listing 1.5. These production markers attract builder agents to the respective advertised endpoints. Builder agents execute advertised production endpoints as soon as the production requirements (supplies) are met.

Marker Agents. A marker agent's goal is to identify all *suitable* production units that will be involved in the process of producing a particular order. The agent maintains a list "unvisited" that contains nodes it would like to visit, but has not yet. To lay out markers on every relevant resource, the agent will traverse recipe resources and leave markers in the Linked Data medium as follows:

1. Check for any *order* resources that does not yet carry a *handled* mark. Find the resource that represents the class of the ordered product by following the link given via the schema:orderedItem property. Add this resource to unvisited. Mark the order as *handled*.
2. From a resource r in unvisited, find a respective recipe blueprint b that contains a triple (b, schema:about, r), i.e., the recipe for the respective product.
3. *Visit all interaction patterns i* matching the schema:step given by b; if the step is steps:dispense, find the respective interaction patterns of dispenser units that schema:yield r.
4. Leave a *mark* on each visited i (for both production and dispenser, cf. Listing 1.5).
5. For each resource s in schema:supplies of b, add s to unvisited. If no schema:supply is specified, or the link points to an empty set (rdf:nil), do nothing. Remove the current resource r from unvisited.
6. If unvisited is empty, **terminate**; else, **go to 2.**

The mark that the agent leaves in Step 4. is of the format given in Listing 1.5. It provides information about the scope in terms of the order for which it was placed if the marker should only be visible for a specific group of agents (*Narrowcast*), and moreover specifies the required supplies s for this step. By the presented algorithm, a marker agent is solely driven by the structure of the knowledge graphs about products and recipes as provided by the Linked Data medium. Each subsequent step is solely decided by the state of the currently visited resource. Its behavior can by this be classified as a *sematectonic stigmergic* agent.

Builder Agents. Builder agents are attracted to markers left by marker agents and call the respective `InteractionPattern` endpoints. A Builder agent proceeds as follows:

1. Find markers m left by marker agents. If the builder agent is bound to a specific scope (i.e. fulfilling a particular order), it will only follow markers in its scope (i.e., with a matching $(m, \texttt{stig:scope}, order)$ triple present.
2. For each m, check, e.g. via a fitting SPARQL query, if for each *supply* s specified by the marker via $(m, \texttt{schema:supply}, s)$, there exists a product p that is a product of class s, as encoded by a triple $(p, \texttt{rdf:type}, s)$.
3. For each marker m for which supplies are fulfilled, visit the Interaction Pattern resource i that is marked via $(m, \texttt{stig:marked}, i)$ and that carries the *least amount of disturbance markers*, Execute the action endpoint that is identified via `td:isAccessibleThrough/td:href`.
4. Leave a disturbance marker on the interaction pattern resource, and remove the affordance marker.

6.3   Evaluation

Implementation of Stigmergic Principles. In the presented algorithm, several agents with different competences (marker and builder agents) jointly solve the given problem. Agents react to both markers left by other agents, and traces that occur as byproduct of work: Builder agents are attracted by markers left by both marker agents (affordance markers), and other builder agents (disturbance markers), and their reaction is further influenced by the existence of supply products as result of previous production steps.

The presented algorithm can thus be classified as *collective stigmergy* in a stigmergic system with *marker-based* and *sematectonic* elements.

We will now further analyse the emergence of benefits of stigmergic systems (see also [22, pp.13–14]) by the use of Linked Data as stigmergic medium for the presented algorithm:

Agents in the presented algorithm do not maintain long-term memory, but only react and follow links based on observation of their immediate environment, resp. the semantic information that describes the resources that they currently inspect. The condition-action-rules by which agents react to resources are generic, and do not include situation-specific decisions that would explicitly model a given goal. By this, agents do *not plan or anticipate*, nor do they maintain any notion of higher objective or goal.

Agents do not require to keep memory as all necessary information to execute the algorithm is written to and provided by the resources in the medium. So is information to establish *communication between agents*. The need for direct communication is eliminated by modelling interaction through following markers left by other agents. Agents are moreover not *aware* of each other. They only interact with the Linked Data medium, in which the agents themselves are not, and do not need to be, represented. This also implies that agents *do not need to be simultaneously present*.

The correct *sequence* of steps arises from the a production marker describing preconditions that need to be fulfilled before executing the endpoint that carries the marker. There is no requirement to encode the sequence of steps explicitly in the model of the markers in terms of explicitly stating an order sequence in which markers should be visited by agents.

Non-necessity for commitment is achieved by having no explicit assignment of tasks to agents. Agents decide autonomously and spontaneously which resource to visit solely from the state of *resources in the medium*. Any agent can react to any marker at any point of time, and by this decide to continue a production task according to the agents' competence from any arbitrary step.

Finally, there is *no centralized coordination or control* authority that agents need to consult, or by which they are controlled. Coordination arises solely from resource states and markers left in the medium.

Correctness of the Algorithm. The algorithm models the process of handling one order, with the ordered product defining the expected result of running the algorithm. Marker agents start their program from the resource that describes the ordered product, and recurse into following links to resources describing the production of required results. By this, it is ensured that over the total production process, all needed supplies will be available eventually. It can easily be shown that the marker agent's algorithm will terminate as soon as all dispenser units that provide dispensable supplies (leaf nodes in the graph in Fig. 3) are assigned with a marker. Builder agents will execute their algorithm until the last production marker is consumed. Consuming a production marker and executing the respective Interaction Endpoint will always lead to producing a product that is required to achieve the set production goal, either in terms of required supplies, or eventually, with more and more supplies met, the ordered final product.

For several orders executed in parallel, production units will be marked with independent markers for each order. By having separate markers per order, and having builder agents removing the marker they followed after executing the production step, it is ensured that for every order, every production step is executed exactly once. The concept may be extended for products to require more than one instance of a supply product. In this case, a marker agent would leave a marker per required instance of a supply.

The opportunity for coordination arises in Step 3. of the builder agent algorithm: For every production step, markers are left on every machine that provides the necessary step to carry out the respective production step as specified by the recipe. Builder agents that follow the marker trace choose independently which of the marked interaction endpoints they actually execute. This decision is based on the number of disturbance markers left on the resource. The more agents visit and execute the same endpoint, the more disturbance markers are left on the machine, and agents will be more likely to divert to less busy machines to complete their order.

The algorithm at this point ignores transport of products on the shop floor. A more sophisticated heuristic may take into account also transport times between machines between the different steps.

6.4 Implementation

We implemented the example using the Unity 3D game engine to simulate the factory, a Fuseki triple store to host the read-write Linked Data medium, and the AJAN agent platform[10][11] [2] to implement the behaviors of both marker and builder agents. All related resources will be published on GitHub: https://github.com/dfki-asr/stigmergy-demo

7   Conclusion and Future Work

In this paper, we have thoroughly analyzed read-write Linked Data as a digital medium for stigmergy-based optimization and coordination mechanisms. This analysis was based on common general characteristics of stigmergic systems in literature. We have identified direct correspondences between these characteristics, and central features of Linked Data systems. By this, we showed that read-write Linked Data provides a suitable digital medium for stigmergy-based coordination algorithms.

We demonstrated the effectiveness of Linked Data as stigmergic medium by demonstrating the application of it in two practical use-cases: One from the domain of planning, and one from the domain of multi-agent coordination in a cyber-physical manufacturing scenario for customized digital production. The experiments from the planner domain showed that stigmergic Linked Data systems are in principle capable of solving planning problems. The more information the agent is able to derive from the environment and markers left during the process, the higher the quality of the solution, up to solution qualities as found by classic planner approaches. We plan to strengthen Linked Data as medium for stigmergy-based optimization by applying the concepts of stigmergy to a variety of additional planner domains. The example from the coordination domain demonstrated that by proper employment of Linked Data as stigmergic medium, coordination arises in a self-organized fashion.

The given examples are intended to be conceptual examples of how these and similar problems may be tackled using Linked Data as underlying medium. We plan to apply the approach to additional planner problems and application domains to show generality.

Central features of stigmergic systems are robustness and resilience towards disturbance in the optimization domain during execution. Experiments that demonstrate these features for the presented Linked Data medium are currently carried out, and are planned to be published as future work.

References

1. Alfeo, A.L., Cimino, M.G., Egidi, S., Lepri, B., Vaglini, G.: A stigmergy-based analysis of city hotspots to discover trends and anomalies in urban transportation usage. IEEE Trans. Intell. Transp. Syst. **19**(7), 2258–2267 (2018). https://doi.org/10.1109/TITS.2018.2817558
2. Antakli, A., et al.: Optimized coordination and simulation for industrial human robot collaborations. In: Bozzon, A., Domínguez Mayo, F.J., Filipe, J. (eds.) WEBIST 2019. LNBIP, vol. 399, pp. 44–68. Springer, Cham (2020). https://doi.org/10.1007/978-3-030-61750-9_3
3. de la Banda, M.G., Stuckey, P.J.: Dynamic programming to minimize the maximum number of open stacks. INFORMS J. Comput. **19**(4), 607–617 (2007)

---

[10] https://github.com/aantakli/AJAN-service.
[11] https://github.com/aantakli/AJAN-editor.

4. Berners-Lee, T., Hendler, J., Lassila, O., et al.: The semantic web. Sci. Am. **284**(5), 28–37 (2001)
5. Binitha, S., Sathya, S.S.: A survey of bio inspired optimization algorithms. Int. J. Soft Comput. Eng. (IJSCE) **2**(2), 137–151 (2012). http://citeseerx.ist.psu.edu/viewdoc/download?doi=10.1.1.458.811&rep=rep1&type=pdf
6. Bizer, C., Heath, T., Idehen, K., Berners-Lee, T.: Linked data on the web (ldow2008). In: Proceedings of the 17th International Conference on World Wide Web, pp. 1265–1266 (2008)
7. Bonabeau, E., Henaux, F., Guérin, S., Snyers, D., Kuntz, P., Theraulaz, G.: Routing in telecommunications networks with ant-like agents. Lect. Notes Comput. Sci. (including subseries Lect. Notes Artif. Intell. Lect. Notes Bioinform.) **1437**(1), 60–71 (1998). https://doi.org/10.1007/bfb0053944
8. Charpenay, V., et al.: Mosaik: a formal model for self-organizing manufacturing systems. IEEE Pervasive Comput. **20**(1), 9–18 (2020)
9. Chiong, R.: Nature-Inspired Algorithms for Optimisation, vol. 193. Springer, Berlin (2009). https://doi.org/10.1007/978-3-642-00267-0
10. Chopra, S., Notarstefano, G., Rice, M., Egerstedt, M.: A distributed version of the Hungarian method for multirobot assignment. IEEE Trans. Robot. **33**(4), 932–947 (2017). https://doi.org/10.1109/TRO.2017.2693377
11. Ciancarini, P., Gorrieri, R., Zavattaro, G.: Towards a calculus for generative communication. In: Najm, E., Stefani, J.-B. (eds.) Formal Methods for Open Object-based Distributed Systems. IAICT, pp. 283–297. Springer, Boston (1997). https://doi.org/10.1007/978-0-387-35082-0_21
12. Cicirello, V.A., Smith, S.F.: Wasp-like agents for distributed factory coordination. Auton. Agent. Multi-Agent Syst. **8**(3), 237–266 (2004). https://doi.org/10.1023/B:AGNT.0000018807.12771.60
13. De Nicola, R., Di Stefano, L., Inverso, O.: Multi-agent systems with virtual stigmergy. Sci. Comput. Program. **187**, 102345 (2020). https://doi.org/10.1016/j.scico.2019.102345
14. Dipple, A., Raymond, K., Docherty, M.: Stigmergy within web modelling languages : positive feedback mechanisms. eprints.qut.edu.au (2013)
15. Dipple, A., Raymond, K., Docherty, M.: General theory of stigmergy: modelling stigma semantics. Elsevier (2014). https://doi.org/10.1016/j.cogsys.2014.02.002
16. Dipple, A.C.: Standing on the shoulders of ants: stigmergy in the web. In: Proceedings of the 20th international conference companion on World Wide Web, pp. 355–360 (2011)
17. Dorigo, M., Blum, C.: Ant colony optimization theory: a survey. Theoret. Comput. Sci. **344**(2–3), 243–278 (2005)
18. Fielding, R.T., Taylor, R.N.: Architectural styles and the design of network-based software architectures, vol. 7. University of California, Irvine Irvine (2000)
19. Gelernter, D.: Generative communication in linda. ACM Trans. Program. Lang. Syst. (TOPLAS) **7**(1), 80–112 (1985)
20. Gerevini, A.E., Haslum, P., Long, D., Saetti, A., Dimopoulos, Y.: Deterministic planning in the fifth international planning competition: PDDL3 and experimental evaluation of the planners. Artif. Intell. **173**, 619–668 (2009). https://doi.org/10.1016/j.artint.2008.10.012
21. Heylighen, F.: Mediator evolution: a general scenario for the origin of dynamical hierarchies. Worldviews Sci. Us. (Singapore: World Sci.) **44**, 45–48 (2006)
22. Heylighen, F.: Stigmergy as a universal coordination mechanism: components, varieties and applications. Human Stigmergy: Theoretical Developments and New Applications; Springer, New York (2015)
23. Jevtić, A., Gutierrez, Á., Andina, D., Jamshidi, M.: Distributed bees algorithm for task allocation in swarm of robots. IEEE Syst. J. **6**(2), 296–304 (2012). https://doi.org/10.1109/JSYST.2011.2167820

24. Kanamori, R., Takahashi, J., Ito, T.: Evaluation of traffic management strategies with antic-ipatory stigmergy. J. Inf. Process. **22**(2), 228–234 (2014). https://doi.org/10.2197/ipsjjip.22.228

25. Korošec, P., Šilc, J., Filipič, B.: The differential ant-stigmergy algorithm. Inf. Sci. (2012). https://doi.org/10.1016/j.ins.2010.05.002

26. Krieger, M.J., Billeter, J.B., Keller, L.: Ant-like task allocation and recruitment in cooperative robots. Nature **406**(6799), 992–995 (2000). https://doi.org/10.1038/35023164

27. Lasi, H., Fettke, P., Kemper, H.-G., Feld, T., Hoffmann, M.: Industry 4.0. Bus. Inf. Syst. Eng. **6**(4), 239–242 (2014). https://doi.org/10.1007/s12599-014-0334-4

28. Lassila, O., Swick, R.R., et al.: Resource description framework (RDF) model and syntax specification (1998)

29. Linhares, A., Yanasse, H.H.: Connections between cutting-pattern sequencing, vlsi design, and flexible machines. Comput. Oper. Res. **29**(12), 1759–1772 (2002)

30. Lucchi, R., Millot, M., Elfers, C.: Resource oriented architecture and rest. European Communities, Assessment of impact and advantages on INSPIRE, Ispra (2008)

31. Matarić, M.J., Sukhatme, G.S., Østergaard, E.H.: Multi-robot task allocation in uncertain environments. Autonom. Robot. **14**(2–3), 255–263 (2003)

32. Mrugalska, B., Wyrwicka, M.K.: Towards lean production in industry 4.0. Procedia Eng. **182**, 466–473 (2017)

33. Nguyen, A.A.: Scalable, decentralized multi-agent reinforcement learning methods inspired by stigmergy and ant colonies, pp. 1–50 (2021). http://arxiv.org/abs/2105.03546

34. Privat, G.: Phenotropic and stigmergic webs: the new reach of networks. Univ. Access Inf. Soc. **11**(3), 323–335 (2012). https://doi.org/10.1007/s10209-011-0240-1

35. Ricci, A., Omicini, A., Viroli, M., Gardelli, L., Oliva, E.: Cognitive stigmergy: towards a framework based on agents and artifacts. In: Weyns, D., Parunak, H.V.D., Michel, F. (eds.) E4MAS 2006. LNCS (LNAI), vol. 4389, pp. 124–140. Springer, Heidelberg (2007). https://doi.org/10.1007/978-3-540-71103-2_7

36. Schraudner, D., Charpenay, V.: An http/rdf-based agent infrastructure for manufacturing using stigmergy (01), 197–202 (2020). https://doi.org/10.1007/978-3-030-62327-2_34

37. Schubotz, R., Chelli, M., Spieldenner, T.: stigld: stigmergic coordination of linked data agents. In: Pan, L., Cui, Z., Cai, J., Li, L. (eds.) Bio-Inspired Computing: Theories and Applications. BIC-TA 2021. Communications in Computer and Information Science, vol. 1566, pp. 174–190. Springer, Singapore. https://doi.org/10.1007/978-981-19-1253-5_13

38. Spieldenner., T., Chelli., M.: Linked data as stigmergic medium for decentralized coordination. In: Proceedings of the 16th International Conference on Software Technologies - ICSOFT, pp. 347–357. INSTICC, SciTePress (2021). https://doi.org/10.5220/0010518003470357

39. Tzanetos, A., Fister, I., Jr., Dounias, G.: A comprehensive database of nature-inspired algorithms. Data Brief **31**, 105792 (2020)

40. Valckenaers, P., Hadeli, Germain, B.S., Verstraete, P., Van Brussel, H.: Mas coordination and control based on stigmergy. Comput. Ind. **58**(7), 621–629 (2007). https://doi.org/10.1016/j.compind.2007.05.003

41. Yu, X., Cheng, T.: Research on a stigmergy-driven & MAS-based method of modeling intelligent system, pp. 1042–1047 (2020). https://doi.org/10.1109/cisp-bmei51763.2020.9263567

Object Parsing Expressions for Unplanned, Unmodified, and Incremental Grammar Reuse

Stefan Sobernig$^{(\boxtimes)}$

Institute for Information Systems and New Media,
WU Vienna, Welthandelsplatz 1, 1020 Vienna, Austria
stefan.sobernig@wu.ac.at

Abstract. Developing families of software languages requires, among others, composable grammar definitions. Object Parsing-Expression Grammars (OPEGs) serve as such grammars that can be composed without preplanning and in an unmodified manner, either via grammar unions or via fine-grained grammar transformations. In addition, OPEGs help avoid typical pitfalls (*abstraction mismatches*) of using intermediate parse representations (e.g., parse trees) when parsing to object graphs. The paper documents the design and implementation of OPEGs on top of a packrat parser as well as advanced features of OPEGs (e.g., handling multi-value properties, non-positional parsing). An OPEG implementation is available as part of DjDSL, a development system for domain-specific languages (DSLs).

Keywords: Parsing expression · Object grammar · Language-product line · Language family · Grammar reuse · Grammar composition · Grammar transformation · Domain-specific language · DSL

1 Introduction

Language-product line engineering [15, 18, 20, 23, 30] shift emphasis from developing and analysing a single software language to developing and to analysing a language family. Known language families are expression languages [35] and state-machine modelling languages [5, 36]. Shared goals are to minimise preplanning effort as well as, at the same time, to reuse development artefacts and language tooling when creating and maintaining a language family in an unmodified manner.

Within a language family, as an offspring, a given language is defined via composing language-definition artefacts such as definitions of abstract and concrete syntaxes, context conditions, behaviour, and test cases. This composition must be tackled at different levels of language definition and language processing (abstract syntax, context conditions, behaviour implementation; [31]).

Reusing existing syntax definitions without preplanning and without modification is the key objective. This way, tracking any modification in the source definitions comes for free; there is no need to propagate changes explicitly. The resulting grammar is ideally formed by referencing the source grammars, rather than cloning them. There are

© Springer Nature Switzerland AG 2022
H.-G. Fill et al. (Eds.): ICSOFT 2021, CCIS 1622, pp. 24–40, 2022.
https://doi.org/10.1007/978-3-031-11513-4_2

two barriers to syntax definitions becoming reusable without preplanning and without modification: parsing ambiguity and mapping ambiguity [4, 31].

Parsing ambiguity is defined as the (typically, unwanted) property of a syntax definition causing a corresponding parsing procedure (parser, interpreter) to produce no parse at all; or more than one parse, all valid under a given definition. This ambiguity can arise as an unwanted consequence of a composition: Two unambiguous grammars may enter a composition and turn into an ambiguous composed grammar [7, 33].

Mapping ambiguity is the (unwanted) property of a syntax definition leading to constructing higher-level parse representations (abstract syntax graphs, ASG) from one initial valid lower-level parse that are not fit for a given task (e.g., analysing the abstract-syntax structure). This ambiguity can arise from *abstraction mismatches* when mapping a concrete syntax to an object-oriented language model as the abstract syntax [17] (e.g., representing non-terminals as classes). Ambiguous parsing then adds to an ambiguous mapping, with alternative valid parses not mapping to one and the same abstract-syntax structure.

This paper extends [31] by reporting on critical design and implementation decisions on Object Parsing-Expression Grammars (OPEGs) which address both parsing and mapping ambiguity. The fine-grained grammar transformations introduced first in [31] include rule extractions with and without symbol rewriting, transitive symbol rewriting as well as rule removals (see Sect. 4). Adding to [31], this extended paper elaborates on the challenge of mapping ambiguity (abstraction mismatches, Sect. 2.2) and additional details of object parsing expressions (multi-valued properties in Sect. 3.2, non-positional parsing in Sect. 3.3). Section 4.1 adds a discussion on the necessary composition operations. Furthermore, the design and the proof-of-concept implementation as an extended packrat parser are documented in Sect. 5.

The implementation, the running examples as well as the code listings are available from a supplemental Web site.[1]

2 Background

2.1 Parsing Expressions

A parsing expression defines a pattern to match (recognise) and, if matched, to consume a specified fragment of input. A *Parsing-Expression Grammar* (PEG; [10]) is defined as a 4-tuple $G = (N, T, R, e_S)$. N denotes the finite set of non-terminals, T is the finite set of terminals, R is the finite set of rules, and e_S is the start expression. Each rule $r \in R$ is a pair (A, e) typically written as a maplet $A \leftarrow e$, with $A \in N$ and e being (another) parsing expression. For a comprehensive introduction to parsing expressions, please refer to [31].

A characteristic operator of parsing expressions is the *choice* operator for defining alternate sub-expressions. The *alternate* sub-expressions are tried in their definition order. The first one to succeed wins, the others are discarded. The choice operator gives rise to important difficulties when composing parsing expressions such as language hiding (see Sect. 6).

---

[1] https://github.com/mrcalvin/djdsl.

2.2 Parsing to Objects: Abstraction Mismatches

Syntax-driven developer tools for software languages and their different ("parsing") pipelines for processing program text produce and, subsequently, operate on different representations of the processed input: *parse representations*. Parse representations abstract from the concrete-syntax structure to render a program text or script more eligible to run tooling operations on them. Parse representations in their role as abstractions can be qualified along different dimensions, for example, their purpose for tooling, their characteristics as data structures, and selected (including non-functional) quality attributes.

Tooling operations on parse representations include analysis operations, code generation, visualisation, debugging, and syntax rendering. Each of these operations can be further divided into sub-activities (e.g., syntax rendering can result in a pretty-printed string or an editable projection). Along this dimension, parse representations are commonly grouped into parse trees and abstract-syntax trees (AST; [25], Chap. 4). As data structures, parse representations can be devised as trees, graphs with/ without direction, graphs with/ without cycles, as well as COMPOSITE [12] structures with homogeneous vs. heterogeneous elements [25].

An important objective is to avoid introducing abstraction mismatches when processing a character-based input into a parse representation [17]. An *abstraction mismatch* ([37]; Chap. 3) of a given parse representation denotes a misfit of a chosen parse abstraction given a modelling or processing operation on a program or script (e.g., for some analysis operation, code generation, visualisation, debugging, and syntax rendering). Commonly applied representation choices are non-terminals as object-classes, (unnamed, nested) rule sub-clauses as subclass hierarchies, or factoring out shared sub-clauses as subclasses. Generally speaking, mismatches result from ill-choosing inheritance-based, decomposition-based, or mixed encodings of parsing structures in terms of object graphs [2, 17].

A misfit is then observed in terms of violations of three quality attributes of the chosen representation for this operation ([25]; Sect. 4.2):

- *Density* (a.k.a. compactness): Does the parse representation contain elements unnecessary for a given operation?
- *Meaningfulness* (a.k.a. robustness): Is the parse representation robust to changes of the concrete-syntax definition or of the syntax processor?
- *Convenience* (a.k.a. traversability): Can the parse representation be efficiently and conveniently walked for a given operation?

The presence of an abstraction mismatch requires some compensation action. Compensations include additional transformation steps on an ASG or providing additional safety belts (e.g., abstract-syntax constraints for disambiguation). The extended parsing expressions introduced in Sect. 3 help avoid abstraction mismatches.

3 Advanced Object Parsing Expressions

Object-Parsing Expression Grammars (OPEGs) contain *extended* parsing expressions to process the consumed syntactic structure into an object graph. The basic object-parsing expressions include instantiation generators for object generation (including alternates) and assignment generators. They have been introduced in [31] and are briefly summarised in Sect. 3.1. They become enriched by handling multi-valued properties (collections; see Sect. 3.2) and non-positional parsing of object properties (see Sect. 3.3).

As in [31], these advanced object parsing expressions are presented by referring to the running example of modelling the state machine driving "Miss Grant's Controller" (see Listing 1), for the sake of allowing cross-reading.

```
2    start idle

3

4    state idle
5        on doorClosed go active

6

7    state active
8        on lightOn go waitingForDrawer
9        on drawerOpened go
                waitingForLight

10

11   state waitingForDrawer
12       on drawerOpened go unlockedPanel

13

14   state unlockedPanel
15       go idle on panelClosed

16

17   state waitingForLight
```

Listing 1. Miss Grant is told to maintain a secret compartment in her bedroom. This compartment requires a particular sequence of actions from her side to become unlocked for her to open. The corresponding state-machine models the modal behaviour of the software-based compartment controller, reacting to Miss Grant's input actions (see [11], Section 1.1.1). This is reproduced from [31] to allow for cross-reading.

3.1 Basics

Instantiation Generators: compute one or several instantiations of object-classes when their rule is applied, based on the matched input. Listing 2 shows a grammar excerpt with two rules E and ON, with WS handling and discarding whitespace characters. Rule E consumes trigger-event definitions for state machine transitions of the form **on** doorClosed (line 5, Listing 1). It features the rule element Event enclosed by single grave accents (` ... `) as an instantiation generator. Upon matching input, the generator will instantiate an object-class Event.

Instantiation generators fully integrate with alternate sub-expressions and the semantics of ordered choices, that is, each alternate sub-expression can contain a different instantiation generator. The instantiation generators can point to the same or different object-classes. Listing 3 demonstrates how two alternative writing styles for transitions (i.e., on-go vs. go-on) could be defined as alternates.

```
   E     ←  `Event`  ON NAME ;
  NAME   ←  name:<alnum>+;
   ON    ←  WS 'on' WS;
```

Listing 2. An excerpt from an Object Parsing-Expression Grammar (OPEG), showing three parsing rules in EBNF-like notation. The first rule exemplifies the use of an instantiation-generator expression.

Assignment Generators: complement an instantiation generator to mark recognised and consumed values from the processed input as values to become assigned to the properties of objects created by an instantiation generator. Listing 2 shows the example of an assignment generator for a property name. The so-generated assignment binds any value returned from applying the parsing expression <alnum>+, that is, a string of at least one alphanumerical character.

```
  T  ←
       `Transition`  trigger:E GO target:<
          alnum>+ /
       `Transition`  GO target:<alnum>+
          trigger:E;
```

Listing 3. Alternate sub-expression using instantiation generators; taken from [31].

Assignment generators allow objects to become related in two ways: (1) When an assignment generator refers to a bare parsing expression, the result computed by this parsing expression will become assigned directly. (2) Assignment generators can be used to relate objects independently from the parse. This is required because an abstract-syntax graph typically involves some form of *circular initialisation* [28]. This refers to associations (references) established between objects beyond those induced by the parse, i.e., at different times of a parse. Circularity requires, to be fully resolved, that all objects to enter circular relationships have been fully initialised before. This is achieved by query generators (see [31] for the details).

3.2   Multi-valued Properties

Parsing expressions can contain repetition operators for consuming zero-or-more ($e*$) and one-or-more ($e+$) occurrences of input matched by the operand expression. At the level of the abstract-syntax graph, these collections of consumed matches naturally map to multi-valued object properties (collections). Object parsing expressions allow for defining multi-valued assignments, across multiple definition levels of assignment generators, to bind value collections to multi-valued properties of objects.

```
  M  ←  `StateMachine`  START start:<alnum>+
        states:S+ ;
  S  ←  `State`  STATE name:<alnum>+ transitions:T*
        ;
```

Listing 4.

Listing 4 contains the two top-level parsing rules for the small state-machine language. The RHS of rule M contains an assignment generator states with its parsing expression S+ that will bind one or more instantiations of the State class. This defined by the corresponding rule for the S non-terminal (see line 2 of the same listing). The parsing expression of rule S itself collects zero or more instantiations of the Transition class returned by the T rule (see Listing 3).

In accordance with standard normalisation rules for the two repetition operators, their desugared forms using multiple occurrences of the same-named assignment operator or using right-recursive refactorings are supported to the same effect.

Key to appreciate this idea is that the repeated occurrences of an assignment generator in the (intermediate) parse tree are muxed into single, multi-valued assignment calls; and not repeated single-valued ones. The latter would effectively redefine the object state, rather than setting a multi-valued property once.

```
    M    ← `StateMachine` START start:<alnum>+ states:S
         states:S* ;
    S    ← `State` STATE name:<alnum>+ TRANS? ;
TRANS    ← transitions:T TRANS*;
```

Listing 5.

3.3 Non-positional Parsing

Parsing rules and their decomposition into alternates and non-terminals are orthogonal to the placement of instantiation and assignment generators. Parsing rules can be freely re-structured. For example, a refactoring can introduce or factor out sub-expressions into new non-terminals and it can remove non-terminals. The aims are to best organise the syntax definition and to improve ill-defined grammars (e.g., left recursion in parsing grammars), however, *without* affecting the object graph to be generated. Relocating assignment generators into separate rules also has the benefit of reusing syntax and assignment fragments for different instantiation generators (e.g., name or identifier patterns).

Consider the rule defining non-terminal E of Listing 2 (line 1) and the subordinate rule NAME (line 2). The first contains the instantiation generator, the second features the assignment generator.

The result of two separate expressions will be exactly the same as using a single parsing expression featuring both generators. That is, an instance of class Event of name doorClosed. This is despite the fact that the structure of the parse tree differs. Relocating assignment generators into separate rules also has the benefit of reusing syntax and assignment fragments for different instantiation generators (and the language-model concepts). For instance, name or identifier patterns can so be defined in one rule and shared by different language-model elements. This is possible even in the case that the elements are not in a reuse relationship in their language model.

4   Composing Parsing Expressions

A grammar composition relates a receiving parsing grammar and one or more composed parsing grammars, yielding a resulting parsing grammar. The fundamental unit of composition are parsing rules [31]. Composition operations on the rules include overriding, combination, and restriction (see Sect. 4.1). In OPEGs, they are realised by so-called merges and transforms (see Sect. 4.2). This way, a developer can realise non-trivial syntax-level compositions such as syntax unification (see Sect. 4.3).

4.1   On Composition Operations

There are three basic operation types for composing production and parsing grammars: overriding, combination, and restriction (see also [16]).

Overriding: yields a resulting definition in which rules, non-terminals, or alternates of the receiving grammars *entirely replace* rules, non-terminals, or alternates of the composed grammar. This leaves the resulting grammar without access to the overridden rules. Formally, overriding is realised as a *union with override* operation between the receiving and the composed rules sets ([29], Sect. 5). This union operation does not qualify non-terminals at the LHS (or, RHS for that matter) for their origin (i.e., receiving or composed grammars), but considers just the unqualified non-terminal names. In case of same-named non-terminals between matching pairs of rules, the rule of the receiving grammar is carried over into the resulting grammar. The composed grammar's rule is effectively lost. *union with override* is the default composition operation, e.g., in ANTLR (grammar imports; [26], pp. 257) and Ensō [33].

Combination: differs from pure overriding by preserving and by linking the potentially overridden (composed) rules or rule elements with the overriding (receiving) ones. For example, the two RHS of a matching pair of receiving and composed rules are combined *as alternates* to each other in a combined rule in the resulting grammar. Hence, this is sometimes referred to as (simple) *union with override/ combine.* Special care must be given to combinations when the alternation is non-commutative as in parsing expressions (ordered choices; see Sect. 4.2).

Restriction: refers to the receiving grammar being able to selectively mark composed rules or their rule elements for not entering the resulting grammar. Restrictions can be implemented in different manners, assuming the following composition procedure: (1) A (disjoint) union of the rules from the receiving and from the composed grammars is formed, (2) overriding and combination operations are performed, and (3) any *useless* rules (non-terminals) are removed to form the resulting grammar.

Against this background, the following variants of restriction can be realised:

- *Renaming*: As part of step (2), a dedicated renaming of a non-terminal by the receiving grammar can be used to render the non-terminal unreachable in the resulting definition. This effectively removes the entire corresponding rule from the resulting definition in step (3). SDF allows for this renaming [34].

– *Filtering*: As a new step (4), after having computed the resulting grammar, filters may be applied to suppress rules or rule elements based on filtering conditions. Filtering conditions can range from exact matching of rule-element labels (alternates in *Rats!*) to matching rule patterns (applied to RHS in Art [16]).

Object Parsing-Expression Grammars (OPEGs) support overriding, combination, and restriction (via filtering) in accordance with requirements of parsing grammars. In Sect. 4.2, concrete composition operations for OPEGs are introduced. This also highlights specifics to PEGs (as opposed to production grammars).

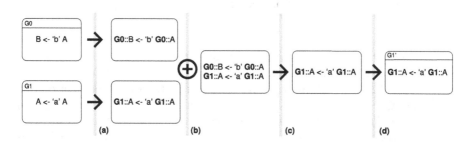

Fig. 1. A procedural overview of creating a *resulting* grammar including transforms in four steps (a–d): (a) **narrow**: non-terminals in the input rules-sets are turned into qualified symbols; (b) **compose**: the (disjoint) union of the input rules-sets is formed; (c) **modify**: the transformation operations (e.g., append, removal) are performed; (d) **clean**: cleaning operations on unrealisable and unreachable non-terminals are performed. Taken from [31].

4.2 Merges and Transforms

Two or more OPEGs can enter a *merges* relationship. Figure 1 defines a merge relationship between two grammars: G1 acts as the receiving, G0 as the composed one. The merges relationship does *not* directly determine which kind of composition operation is to be performed between receiving and composed grammars. For this, the receiving grammar can also define grammar *transforms* to implement different composition operations. These include simple union with override in the absence of transforms, as well as different variants of extraction and of restriction in the presence of transforms.

The composition behaviour in presence of transformations is implemented on the procedure illustrated in an informal manner in Fig. 1 (steps a–d; [31]).

In step (c), the actual transforms are applied. An overview of the available operators is presented in Table 1. As an example, an extract w/o rewrite ($\Leftarrow$, (1) in Table 1) selects the RHS expression of the referenced rule (e.g., G0::A) and introduces it into the receiving rules set. Introduction refers to either creating a new rule G1::A with the extracted RHS or appending the selected RHS as an additional alternate to an existing rule. For a comprehensive presentation of transforms, please see [31].

The generators for instantiations, assignments, and queries become combined, extracted, and removed with the surrounding parsing expressions or sub-expressions

Table 1. Overview of OPEG transforms; taken from [31].

	Op	Type	Description	Example
1	$\Leftarrow$	Binary	Extract w/o rewrite	A $\Leftarrow$ G0::A
2	$\Leftrightarrow$	Binary	Extract w/ rewrite	A $\Leftrightarrow$ G0::A
3	$\overset{*}{\Leftrightarrow}$	Binary	Transitive extract w/rw	A $\overset{*}{\Leftrightarrow}$ G0::A
4	$\Rightarrow$	Unary	Remove	G0::B $\Rightarrow$
5	$\leftarrow$	Binary	Op. 1 w/o generators	A $\leftarrow$ G0::A
6	$\leftrightarrow$	Binary	Op. 2 w/o generators	A $\leftrightarrow$ G0::A
	None	N/A	Union with override	G1 merges set G0

(alternates) according to the stipulated behaviour of the first four transforms (1–4 in Table 1). To reuse parsing (sub-)expressions without their generators (e.g., to attach matches to an alternative generator), there are two transform operators that operate on the plain expressions, effectively excluding the generators (see operators 5 and 6 in Table 1). An (**5**) extract w/o rewrite w/o generators operator ($\leftarrow$) selects the RHS expression of the referenced rule (e.g., G0::A), omitting any generators, and introduces it into the receiving rules set (see also operator 1). An (**6**) extract w/ rewrite w/o generators operator ($\leftrightarrow$) performs the extraction/ introduction and patches the namespace prefixes (see also operator 2), again, omitting any generators.

OPEG merges and transforms support developers in realising the entire range of the syntax-level language compositions [8] including syntax extension, extension composition, extension unification, and restriction [31]. Section 4.3 exemplifies syntax unification.

```
state active
    on lightOn go waitingForDrawer
    on drawerOpened go
        waitingForLight
        [ counter > 3 ]
```

Listing 7. One guarded transition for Miss Grant's Controller; taken from [31].

4.3   Application (ex.): Syntax Unification

Consider two separately developed languages. These are a Boolean and comparison expression language (BCEL) and a state-machine-definition language (SMDL), with the later capable of modelling "Miss Grant's Controller". The BCEL is a candidate of a functional kernel language [35] to become unified with SMDL to implement *guarded transitions*. This is known as an example of language unification [31].

A guarded transition is a transition that is annotated by a guard expression and whose firing is controlled by the prior evaluation of the attached guard expression. If the guard is evaluated to true at that time, the transition is enabled, otherwise, it is disabled and will not fire. Listing 7 shows two transitions, one with and the other without a guard expression.

A unification is marked by two or more composed grammars being merged by a receiving (unifying) grammar. The running example requires the developer to define a receiving grammar that merges the BCEL's grammar and the SMDL grammar. Guard expressions are attached to the rules responsible for `Transition` instantiations, namely by "injecting" an assignment generator to associate guard expressions with transitions. This leaves the two source grammars untouched. Please refer to [31] for the details. OPEGs with transforms allow for the unanticipated, the unmodified, and the controlled reuse of two independently developed syntaxes to form a unified syntax.

5 Design and Implementation

5.1 Packrat Parsing

A Parsing-Expression Grammar (PEG) acts both as a specification of a software language and the specification of a top-down parser for that language [21]. The PEG operators (e.g., choice) and the resulting PEG properties (unambiguity, unlimited look-ahead, limited backtracking) allow for a linear-time implementation of a corresponding parser. This parsing style has been referred to as *packrat parsing*. This extends without restrictions to OPEG-based parsers and interpreters.

A packrat parse can be modelled as top-down, left-right walk of a recognition table ([14], Sect. 15.7.2). Implementation-wise, a packrat parser is a recursive-descent parser that avoids repeated calls to its parsing procedures for already visited input positions and memoizes (caches, "hoards") intermediate parsing results. Cached results are the matches for given input positions. As the size of the former dimension can be considered fixed (number of non-terminals and the input length) and the cached matches are of constant size (position and range), parsers settle at a linear time complexity.

When considered in combination, the characteristics of PEGs, as well as their operator types and behaviours yield important properties of a PEG and its corresponding parser:

A PEG (PEG-based parser) is inherently *unambiguous* in that a recognition program derived from it will produce one parse or parsing result. This is a consequence of the ordered choice and the greediness of expressions when consuming input. While this property makes them unsuitable for natural-language processing, it fits the requirements of defining syntaxes of software languages (e.g., general-purpose and domain-specific ones) and to derive efficient as well as practical parser implementations.

A PEG (PEG-based parser) has unlimited look-ahead. This results from the availability of not- and and-predicates and from the operators' greediness. This is also beneficial to avoid certain types of ambiguity (e.g., longest-match ambiguity).

A PEG (PEG-based parser) limits the rolling-back from unsuccessful (failing) alternates when attempted in top-down, depth-first visits through nested expressions with alternates. The use of ordered choice, as well as the unlimited look-ahead, result in this limited *backtracking*.

Apart from handicraft parsers for a given PEG, PEG-based frameworks have devised different implementation techniques, incl. grammar interpreters and generators for stack-based packrat parsers. The latter accept a PEG as input and generate a

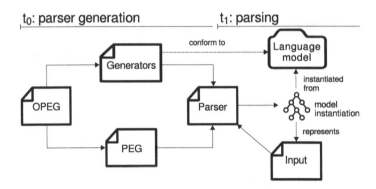

Fig. 2. Overview of the processing pipelines in djdsl::opeg: (a) parser generation and (b) parsing.

derived parser against a VIRTUAL MACHINE [1, 19, 22]. This is also the case the OPEG implementation accompanying this paper. This is also the case for the for the *parsing tools* (PT) component reused by the proof-of-concept implementation. The VIRTUAL MACHINE for packrat parsers is called PARAM and offers different programming interfaces. These include an object-oriented one that allows for the generative and compositional reuse of stack-based parsing methods (see also Sect. 5).

5.2   DjDSL

The OPEG implementation of DjDSL, the proof-of-concept, is realised as an extension to the Tcl package PT (for "Parsing Tools") that forms part of the Tcl Library (tcllib). The extension is itself organised as a Tcl package: djdsl::opeg. The required package pt provides, among others, an NX-based parsing runtime shared by all generated parsers. In this approach, a PEG or an OPEG is not associated with a specific recursive-descent parser [27] or a grammar interpreter [6]. Rather, a grammar, first, is processed to produce a parser program made up of parsing instructions. Parsing instructions deal with character testing, input handling, status as well as error handling. Second, a VIRTUAL MACHINE [1] executes the parsing instructions of a parser program that, in turn, changes the machine's state. The machine's state (in a simplified form) is implemented by a number of stacks for managing the current input position, backtracking positions etc. In addition, the machine's state contains stores for non-terminal and terminal caches. In pt, this stack-based virtual parsing machine is called PARAM for "PAckRAt Machine". The NX implementation of the PARAM realises the grammar-specific and the basic parsing instructions as methods. With this, the PARAM be refined via NX composition techniques (e.g., mixins).

The proof-of-concept implementation extends the parser generator and the PARAM to support *object parsing expressions* as introduced in Sect. 4. This is achieved without modifying the underlying NX PARAM implementation, nor the implementation of pt. To produce a PARAM parsing program from an OPEG (see *parser generation* in Fig. 2), the OPEG is rewritten to break apart generators and parsing expressions. This is the responsibility of the djdsl::opeg::Rewriter component (see Fig. 3) which acts as a post-processor on a parsed OPEG. The results are a collection of generators (instantiation and assignment) and an ordinary PEG. The latter is the used by the pt parser generator to create a Parser class. This parser is associated with the collection of generators and instruments the virtual parsing machine to indirect selected instruction calls (e.g., when executing choices) to enact the respective generators. For this purpose, the generated Parser class inherits from djdsl::opeg::Engine (see also Fig. 3). When clients present input to the generated Parser (see *parsing* in Fig. 2), a parse is created that carries embedded annotations about enacted generators. The parse is then consumed in a bottom-up pass to create a language-model instantiation. The actual instantiation is managed by indirection to a ModelFactory (see Fig. 3).

Clients defining an OPEG and requesting a parse based on some input interact with three components of djdsl::opeg: djdsl::opeg::Grammar, djdsl:: opeg::Engine, and djdsl::opeg::ModelFactory (see Fig. 3).

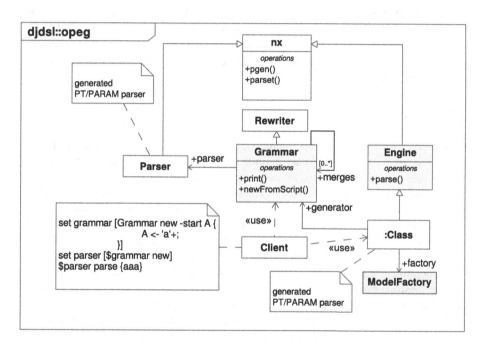

Fig. 3. Structural overview of infrastructure for object parsing-expression grammars (OPEG).

Grammar. The class djdsl::opeg::Grammar is used by clients to define an OPEG. Grammar definition can be achieved by submitting a collection of parsing rules (via new), a complete OPEG script (newFromScript), or by pointing to a grammar file (newFromFile). From this Grammar instantiation, the generation of a parser can then be requested. In addition, Grammar instantiations can be related to each other via the merges attribute. This relationship between Grammar instantiations lays the foundation for the grammar-composition techniques presented in Sect. 4. Besides, Grammar provides for utilities to inspect on an OPEG (e.g., rules set) and the resulting parses (e.g., a pretty printer).

Engine. The class djdsl::opeg::Engine defines and implements the basic interface of all generated PARAM parsers. Most importantly, it offers different methods to submit input text to parsing. Whatever the parsing facility used by a client, the type of result value is determined by a ModelFactory. Internally, the Engine class is also responsible for instrumenting the PARAM to set instantiation and assignment generators in motion.

ModelFactory. When instantiation generators are dispatched, this is achieved by indirection via a djdsl::opeg::ModelFactory. This allows for plugging-in a different STRATEGY [12] of assembling a language-model instantiation, or a custom postprocessor. A client can pick from a set of predefined subclasses of ModelFactory (e.g., one for DjDSL's language models, one for plain NX classes) or define a custom subclass or factory object. In absence of a specific ModelFactory, the default is to employ a generic TEMPLATE METHOD indirection [32]: Non-terminal matches are turned into pre-formatted calls to deferred method implementations, to be provided by the client developer.

6   Discussion

Preplanning: Anticipated versus Unanticipated Composition.   Preplanning means anticipating future uses of a syntax definition. Preplanning effort can be reduced by adopting adequate techniques that allow a language developer to leave the existing definitional assets unmodified. Indicators of unmodified reuse are repeatedly stated in challenges and tasks raised for the series of Language-Workbench Competitions [9].

Unmodified reuse is particularly relevant for syntax definitions such as parser definitions and grammars. Consider the example of syntax migrations. In *concrete-syntax migration*, a requirement might emerge that a purely syntactic change to a textual notation is committed (e.g., renaming of a keyword) that leaves the produced parse representation (abstract syntax) untouched. In the reverse case, an *abstract-syntax migration*, source text should be carried over unmodified on an evolved abstract syntax (e.g., an abstract-syntax entity is split in two related entities). OPEGs do not require any preplanning for such syntax migrations.

Language Hiding.   Language hiding is caused by a (greedy) alternate of a choice expression preventing any later alternate from being applied to inputs that it could otherwise match [10,27]. This is the flip side of the otherwise beneficial property of PEGs precluding ambiguity under composition. Language hiding has implications for composition operations as introduced in Sect. 4.2, in that alternates become automatically (combination) or selectively added (extraction with and without insertion position). OPEGs take precautionary counter-measures to avoid unintended language hiding: For example, alternates introduced by DSL extensions are prepended to those of the receiving grammar. This follows from the assumption that, in extensions, the aim is to capture longer prefixes. Beyond that point, fine-grained control during composition by the developer are supported (e.g., explicit alternate positioning).

7   Related Work

Object-Parsing Expression Grammars (OPEGs) are inspired by object (production) grammars [33], and their take on realising *composable* and *modular* grammars. The relationship between object grammars and grammar reuse in language-product line development [8], however, has first been elaborated on in [30,31]. As for domain-specific languages (DSLs), Fowler gives a short excursus on the grammar-based composition for DSLs [11, Sect. 31.2]. This is discussed mainly regarding the trade-off between succinctness and (extended) expressiveness in the design of a single DSL. Rather than bloating the language model and syntax of a single DSL, composing a derived one from language-model fragments is proposed (i.e., syntax extension).

Early approaches addressed selected limitations of grammar composition as perceived at the time, such as lexer conflicts or closed grammar definitions. A first contribution to opening up grammar definitions included *syntax modules* of the series of Syntax Definition Formalisms (SDF, SDF2, SDF3; [34]). SDF also resolved known composability issue by operating on scannerless and generalised parsing (i.e., scannerless GLR).

The grammar-inclusion mechanism by TXL [3] allowed a developer to scatter rule definitions over different files, rooted under one start symbol. In addition, TXL provided for a `refine` to replace or add a new alternate to a given rule.

Of practical importance are grammar imports by ANTLR ([26], pp. 257) ANTLR applies a union-with-override technique, with particularities regarding different types of definition artefacts. As ANTLR serves as the parsing infrastructure for several language development systems such as Xtext [2], MontiCore [17], MetaDepth [24], grammar imports have seen uptake.

Rats! [13] set the ground for basic compositions of Parsing-Expression Grammars (PEGs). These are realised for rules and alternates using dedicated transformations (add, delete, append). In addition, *Rats!* was the first to document practical barriers to composing PEG-based syntax definitions (e.g., due to ordered choices).

8   Concluding Remarks

Object Parsing-Expression Grammars (OPEGs) define a concrete syntax *and* the mapping to an object-oriented primary abstract syntax (language model). This is further facilitated by allowing for parsing input directly to multi-valued object properties (collections) and by parsing to object properties in a non-positional manner. This way, abstraction mismatches of parse representations (e.g., decomposition mismatches) are avoided. In addition, OPEGs are composable via different composition techniques, ranging from simple grammar unions and to fine-grained grammar transformations. This way, the advanced grammar compositions relevant for realising language-product lines become possible: extensions, unification, extension composition, and derivative grammars (see also [31]). OPEGs are shown to be implementable on top of a pack-rat parser (commonly used to implement parsers for parsing grammars). OPEGs are available as an integral part of the language-development system DjDSL.

References

1. Avgeriou, P., Zdun, U.: Architectural patterns revisited: A pattern language. In: Proceedings of 10th European Conference on Pattern Languages of Programs (EuroPlop 2005), pp. 1–39. Irsee, Germany, July 2005
2. Bettini, L.: Implementing Domain-Specific Languages with Xtext and Xtend. 2nd edn. Packt Publishing, Birmingham (2013)
3. Cordy, J.R.: The TXL source transformation language. Sci. Comput. Program. **61**(3), 190–210 (2006). https://doi.org/10.1016/j.scico.2006.04.002
4. Degueule, T.: Composition and Interoperability for External Domain-Specific Language Engineering. Theses, Université de Rennes 1, [UR1], December 2016. https://hal.inria.fr/tel-01427009
5. Degueule, T., Combemale, B., Blouin, A., Barais, O., Jézéquel, J.M.: Melange: a meta-language for modular and reusable development of dslsa meta-language for modular and reusable development of DSLs. In: Proceedings of 2015 ACM SIGPLAN International Conference on Software Language Engineering (SLE 2015), pp. 25–36. ACM (2015). https://doi.org/10.1145/2814251.2814252
6. Dejanović, I., Milosavljević, G., Vaderna, R.: Arpeggio: a flexible peg parser for python. Knowl.-Based Syst. **95**, 71–74 (2016). https://doi.org/10.1016/j.knosys.2015.12.004
7. Diekmann, L., Tratt, L.: Eco: a language composition editor. In: Combemale, B., Pearce, D.J., Barais, O., Vinju, J.J. (eds.) SLE 2014. LNCS, vol. 8706, pp. 82–101. Springer, Cham (2014). https://doi.org/10.1007/978-3-319-11245-9_5
8. Erdweg, S., Giarrusso, P.G., Rendel, T.: Language composition untangled. In: Proceedings of Twelfth Workshop on Language Descriptions, Tools, and Applications (LDTA 2012), pp. 7:1–7:8. ACM (2012). https://doi.org/10.1145/2427048.2427055
9. Erdweg, S., et al.: Evaluating and comparing language workbenches: Existing results and benchmarks for the future. Comput. Lang. Syst. Struct. **44**(Part A), 24–47 (2015). https://doi.org/10.1016/j.cl.2015.08.007
10. Ford, B.: Parsing expression grammars: a recognition-based syntactic foundation. In: Proceedings of 31st ACM SIGPLAN-SIGACT Symposium on Principles of Programming Languages (POPL2004), pp. 111–122. ACM (2004). https://doi.org/10.1145/964001.964011
11. Fowler, M.: Domain Specific Languages. 1st edn. Addison-Wesley, Boston (2010)
12. Gamma, E., Helm, R., Johnson, R.E., Vlissides, J.: Design Patterns - Elements of Reusable Object-Oriented Software. Addison Wesley Professional Computing Series, Addison-Wesley, Boston, October 1995
13. Grimm, R.: Better extensibility through modular syntax. In: Proceedings of 27th ACM SIGPLAN Conference on Programming Language Design and Implementation (PLDI 2006), pp. 38–51. ACM (2006). https://doi.org/10.1145/1133981.1133987
14. Grune, D., Jacobs, C.J.H.: Parsing Techniques. MCS, Springer, New York (2008). https://doi.org/10.1007/978-0-387-68954-8
15. Jézéquel, J.-M., Méndez-Acuña, D., Degueule, T., Combemale, B., Barais, O.: When systems engineering meets software language engineering. In: Boulanger, F., Krob, D., Morel, G., Roussel, J.-C. (eds.) Complex Systems Design & Management, pp. 1–13. Springer, Cham (2015). https://doi.org/10.1007/978-3-319-11617-4_1

16. Johnstone, A., Scott, E., van den Brand, M.: Modular grammar specification. Sci. Comput. Program. **87**, 23–43 (2014). https://doi.org/10.1016/j.scico.2013.09.012
17. Krahn, H., Rumpe, B., Völkel, S.: Monticore: a framework for compositional development of domain specific languages. Int. J. Softw. Tools. Technol. Transfer **12**(5), 353–372 (2010). https://doi.org/10.1007/s10009-010-0142-1
18. Kühn, T., Cazzola, W., Olivares, D.M.: Choosy and picky: configuration of language product lines. In: Proceedings of 19th International Conference on Software Product Line (SPLC 2015), pp. 71–80. ACM (2015). https://doi.org/10.1145/2791060.2791092
19. Kuramitsu, K.: Nez: Practical open grammar language. In: Proceedings of 2016 ACM International Symposium on New Ideas, New Paradigms, and Reflections on Programming and Software (Onward! 2016), pp. 29–42. ACM (2016). https://doi.org/10.1145/2986012.2986019
20. Liebig, J., Daniel, R., Apel, S.: Feature-oriented language families: a case study. In: Proceedings of 7th International Workshop on Variability Modelling of Software-intensive Systems (VaMoS 2013), pp. 11:1–11:8. ACM (2013). https://doi.org/10.1145/2430502.2430518
21. Mascarenhas, F., Medeiros, S., Ierusalimschy, R.: On the relation between context-free grammars and parsing expression grammars. Sci. Comput. Program. **89**, 235–250 (2014). https://doi.org/10.1016/j.scico.2014.01.012
22. Medeiros, S., Ierusalimschy, R.: A parsing machine for PEGs. In: Proceedings of 2008 Symposium on Dynamic Languages (DLS 2008), pp. 2:1–2:12. ACM (2008). https://doi.org/10.1145/1408681.1408683
23. Méndez-Acuña, D., Galindo, J.A., Degueule, T., Combemale, B., Baudry, B.: Leveraging software product lines engineering in the development of external DSLs: a systematic literature review. Comput. Lang. Syst. Struct. **46**, 206–235 (2016). https://doi.org/10.1016/j.cl.2016.09.004
24. Meyers, B., Cicchetti, A., Guerra, E., de Lara, J.: Composing textual modelling languages in practice. In: Proceedings of 6th International Workshop on Multi-Paradigm Modeling (MPM 2012), pp. 31–36. ACM (2012). https://doi.org/10.1145/2508443.2508449
25. Parr, T.: Language Implementation Patterns: Create Your Own Domain-Specific and General Programming Languages. 1st edn. Pragmatic Bookshelf, Raleigh (2009)
26. Parr, T.: The Definitive ANTLR 4 Reference. 2nd edn. Pragmatic Bookshelf, Raleigh (2013)
27. Redziejowski, R.R.: Some aspects of parsing expression grammar. Fundamenta Informaticae **85**(1–4), 441–454 (2008)
28. Servetto, M., Mackay, J., Potanin, A., Noble, J.: The billion-dollar fix. In: Castagna, G. (ed.) ECOOP 2013. LNCS, vol. 7920, pp. 205–229. Springer, Heidelberg (2013). https://doi.org/10.1007/978-3-642-39038-8_9
29. Simons, A.J.H.: The theory of classification, part 9: Inheritance and self reference. J. Object Technol. **2**(6), 25–34 (2003)
30. Sobernig, S.: Variable Domain-specific Software Languages with DjDSL. Springer (2020). https://doi.org/10.1007/978-3-030-42152-6
31. Sobernig, S.: Object parsing grammars with composition. In: Proceedings of 16th International Conference on Software Technologies (ICSOFT'2021), pp. 373–385. SCITEPRESS (2021). https://doi.org/10.5220/0010558303730385
32. Sobernig, S., Zdun, U.: Inversion-of-control layer. In: Proceedings of 15th Annual European Conference on Pattern Languages of Programming (EuroPLoP 2010), ACM (2010). https://doi.org/10.1145/2328909.2328935
33. van der Storm, T., Cook, W.R., Loh, A.: The design and implementation of object grammars. Sci. Comput. Program. **96**, 460–487 (2014). https://doi.org/10.1016/j.scico.2014.02.023
34. Visser, E.: Syntax Definition for Language Prototyping. Ph.D. thesis, University of Amsterdam (1997). http://eelcovisser.org/wiki/thesis

35. Voelter, M.: The design, evolution, and use of KernelF. In: Rensink, A., Sánchez Cuadrado, J. (eds.) ICMT 2018. LNCS, vol. 10888, pp. 3–55. Springer, Cham (2018). https://doi.org/10.1007/978-3-319-93317-7_1
36. Wille, D., Schulze, S., Schaefer, I.: Variability mining of state charts. In: Proceedings of 7th International Workshop on Feature-Oriented Software Development (FOSD 2016), pp. 63–73. ACM (2016). https://doi.org/10.1145/3001867.3001875
37. Zdun, U.: Language Support for Dynamic and Evolving Software Architectures. Doctoral thesis, University of Essen, January 2002

A Methodology for Organizational Data Science Towards Evidence-based Process Improvement

Andrea Delgado[✉], Daniel Calegari, Adriana Marotta, Laura González, and Libertad Tansini

Instituto de Computación, Facultad de Ingeniería, Universidad de la República, 11300 Montevideo, Uruguay
{adelgado,dcalegar,amarotta,lauragon,libertad}@fing.edu.uy

Abstract. Organizational data science projects provide organizations with evidence-based business intelligence to improve their business processes (BPs). They require methodological guidance and tool support to deal with the complexity of the socio-technical system that supports the organization's daily operations. This system is usually composed of distributed infrastructures integrating heterogeneous technologies enacting BPs and connecting devices, people, and data. Obtaining knowledge from this context is challenging since it requires a unified view capturing all the pieces of data consistently for applying both process mining and data mining techniques to get a complete understanding of the BPs execution. We have presented the PRICED framework in previous works, which defines a general strategy for performing data science projects. In this paper, we propose a methodology with phases, disciplines, activities, roles, and artifacts, providing guidance and support to navigate from getting the execution data, through its integration and quality assessment, to mining and analyzing it to find improvement opportunities.

Keywords: Process mining · Data mining · Data science · Methodology · Organizational improvement · Business intelligence

1 Introduction

Business Processes (BPs) are at the center of organizations' daily operation, supported by a combination of traditional information systems (IS) and Process-Aware Information Systems (PAIS) [17] usually managing structured and unstructured data. The complexity of this socio-technical system composed of distributed infrastructures with heterogeneous technologies enacting business processes, connecting devices, people, and data, adds many challenges for organizations. Obtaining valuable information and knowledge from this context is challenging. It requires a unified view capturing all the pieces of data consistently for applying both process mining [1] and data mining [32] techniques to get a complete understanding of the business process execution.

Supported by project "Minería de procesos y datos para la mejora de procesos en las organizaciones" funded by Comisión Sectorial de Investigación Científica, Universidad de la República, Uruguay.

© Springer Nature Switzerland AG 2022
H.-G. Fill et al. (Eds.): ICSOFT 2021, CCIS 1622, pp. 41–66, 2022.
https://doi.org/10.1007/978-3-031-11513-4_3

Organizational data science projects provide organizations with evidence-based business intelligence to improve their business processes. Data science [1,23] emerged as an interdisciplinary discipline responding to the problem of management, analysis, and discovery of information in large volumes of data. Data science projects require methodological guidance and tool support to deal with the complexity of such socio-technical systems. There are methodologies guiding both kind of projects, e.g., PM^2 [18] for process mining, and CRISP-DM [31], and SEMMA [29] for data mining. However, they consider them separate initiatives due to a compartmentalized vision of the process and organizational data. Process data is usually managed within a Business Process Management Systems (BPMS) [9]. In contrast, organizational data is stored in distributed heterogeneous databases, not wholly linked to the BPMS.

In [15] we proposed the PRICED framework (for Process and Data sCience for oRganIzational improvEment) guiding organizational data science projects to find improvement opportunities within an organization. It involves methodologies, techniques, and tools to provide organizations with key elements to analyze their processes and organizational data in an integrated manner. It considers three main aspects: integrating process and organizational data into a unified view [8] for applying process and data mining techniques over the same data set [2,12], corresponding data quality assessment [4], and evaluating compliance requirements for business processes [19]. In [14], we introduced a concrete methodology defining phases, disciplines, activities, roles, and artifacts to provide guidance and support for concrete projects. The methodology covers the extraction of systems execution data and its integration and quality assessment to evaluate the results of mining and analysis techniques to find improvement opportunities. We also provide an example of the application of the methodology as proof of concept, and in [12] we applied it in the context of E-government.

In this paper, we provide a substantially extended and thoroughly revised version of [14]. We extend the work mentioned above by providing:

1. a description of two models that are part of the conceptual dimension that supports the methodology: the Business Process and Organizational Data Quality Model (BPODQM) [4], and the Business Process Compliance Requirements Model (BPCRM) [19] (Sect. 3);
2. a detailed description on how process and data mining techniques can be applied, from the integration of process and organizational data to its combined application based on developed tools (Sect. 3);
3. an extension of the application of the methodology presented, including the integrated process and data mining analysis and evaluation view, and a new example with focus on compliance requirements evaluation (Sect. 4).

The rest of the paper is structured as follows. In Sect. 2 we introduce the methodology by presenting its static and dynamic views. In Sect. 3 we provide a deeper description of the conceptual, technical, and tool dimensions supporting the methodology. In Sect. 4 we describe examples of application. In Sect. 5 we present methodological approaches related to our proposal. Finally, in Sect. 6 we provide conclusions and an outline of future work.

2   Methodological Dimension of the PRICED Framework

In [14, 15] we introduced the methodological dimension of the PRICED framework, composed of a static and a dynamic view. The **static view** defines the different elements involved within the methodology, i.e., phases, disciplines, activities, roles, and artifacts. It helps to understand *what* needs to be done (artifacts), *how* it should be done (activities), and by *whom* (roles and responsibilities). The **dynamic view** describes a lifecycle guiding the efforts from getting the execution data to mining and evaluating the results to find improvement opportunities. In other words, it defines *when* the activities that must be performed. In what follows, we present both views, as done in [14].

2.1   Static View

Figure 1 summarizes the static view that is presented in detail next. It shows the disciplines and their activities, and, for each activity, the roles involved and the input and output artifacts used and generated by the activity, respectively.

Integrated Process and Data Mining and analysis Methodology: Static view

Disciplines & Activities		Roles	Input	Output
Process & Data Extraction and Integration	PDE1 – Select business processes	Business Analyst, Business Manager, Data Scientist	Business needs	BP & data m/a document
	PDE2 – Define mining/analysis goals	Business Analyst, BP Responsible, Data Scientist	Business needs	BP & data m/a document*
	PDE3 – Identify process and data sources	Business Analyst, BP Responsible, Data Scientist	BP & data m/a document	BP & data m/a document*
	PDE4 – ETL process and organizational data	Data Scientist	BP & data m/a document	ETL description, Metamodel
	PDE5 – Integrate process and organizational data	Data Scientist	Metamodel	Integ. dsc, integ. Metamodel
Process & Data Quality	PDQ1 – Specify Data Quality Model	Business Analyst, BP Responsible, Data Scientist	BP & data quality Model	BP & data quality document
	PDQ2 – Evaluate quality characteristics	Business Analyst, BP Responsible, Data Scientist	Metamodel, Ext. event log, BP & data quality doc.	BP & data quality document*
	PDQ3 – Improve quality characteristics	Data Scientist	BP & data quality doc., BP & data quality Model	BP & data quality document*
Process & Data Preparation	PDP1 – Build extended event log	Data Scientist	Integrated Metamodel	Extended event log
	PDP2 – Build integrated Data Warehouse	Data Scientist	Integrated Metamodel	Data Warehouse
	PDP3 – Filter event log and data	Data Scientist	Extended event log	Extended event log*
Process & Data Mining and Analysis	PDMA1 – Select mining/analysis approach	Data Scientist	BP & data m/a document, m/a approaches catalog	BP & data m/a document*
	PDMA2 – Select mining/analysis tools	Data Scientist	BP & data m/a document, m/a tools catalog	BP & data m/a document*
	PDMA3 – Execute mining/analysis approach	Data Scientist	Ext. event log, DW, BP & data m/a document	BP & data m/a document*
	PDMA4 – Evaluate mining/analysis results	Business Analyst, BP Responsible, Data Scientist	BP & data m/a document	BP & data m/a document*
Process & Data Compliance	PDC1 – Identify compliance requirements	Business Analyst, BP Responsible, Data Scientist	BP compliance reqs. Model	BP compliance reqs. document
	PDC2 – Evaluate compliance requirements	Business Analyst, BP Responsible, Data Scientist	BP & data m/a document	BP compliance reqs. document*

* in an output artifact indicates the document was updated in the execution of the corresponding Activity

Fig. 1. Summary of the static view of the methodology (from [14]).

Disciplines and Activities. Disciplines are usually used for grouping related activities regarding the topic they deal with, e.g., data quality assessment. We define five disciplines to tackle the different issues, with associated activities to guide the work to be carried out.

Process and Data Extraction and Integration (PDE). This discipline groups activities that deal with the identification, definition of goals, and extraction of process and organizational data from associated sources and its integration within a unified metamodel [11].

PDE1 - Select Business Processes. To identify and select business processes from the organization that will be the object of mining efforts to identify improvement opportunities. To define the mining/analysis effort goals, including the selection of execution measures when applicable.

PDE2 - Define Mining/Analysis Goals. To define the purposes of the mining/analysis efforts for the selected business processes and integrated process and organizational data, such as the need to know process variants that behave differently regarding the data they manage, the process model that better explains the process data, participants and roles involved in types of traces or managing specific types of data, among others. Also, execution measures such as duration of traces and/or activities and/or compliance requirements such as message interaction order in choreographies or tasks execution patterns between different process participants in collaborative processes can be defined/selected.

PDE3 - Identify Process and Data Sources. To identify the sources of process and organizational data that must be integrated to serve as the mining effort's input. It includes evaluating and analyzing the availability of elements needed to access and obtain data from the corresponding sources (i.e., BPMS process engine, organizational databases with their history logs).

PDE4 - ETL Process and Organizational Data. To carry out the ETL process to extract process data from the BPMS process engine and heterogeneous organizational databases and corresponding history logs to the metamodel, we have defined [11]. The metamodel includes four quadrants: process definition, process instances (i.e., cases), data definition, and data instances.

PDE5 - Integrate Process and Organizational Data. To execute matching algorithms over the data loaded in the metamodel, find and define relationships between process instance variables (in the process instances quadrant) and organizational data attributes (in the process instances quadrant). Several options can be used to discover these relationships. We implemented a basic algorithm [11] based on values and timestamps.

Process and Data Quality (PDQ). This discipline groups activities that deal with the selection, evaluation, and improvement (cleaning) of quality characteristics of the integrated data (i.e., integrated metamodel and generated extended log). In [6] the authors identify four main categories for quality issues in event logs: missing data, incorrect data, inaccurate data, and irrelevant data. We have defined a Business Process, and Organizational Data Quality Model (BPODQM) [4] in which specific dimensions, factors, and metrics for the integrated data from process and organizational databases are provided (c.f. Sect. 3). It is based on previous quality models we have defined for other contexts [10, 34], and on [35].

PDQ1 - Specify Data Quality Model. To instantiate the BPODQM, select which quality characteristics will be evaluated over which data and how the evaluation is done. A quality model defines which quality dimensions and factors are considered, which data they apply and how they are measured. The dimensions, factors, and metrics defined in BPODQM are specific to the context of process logs and associated organizational data, but not necessarily all these elements must be present in every particular case. Also, the selected metrics may be adapted to the particular needs and available tools for processing data.

PDQ2 - Evaluate Quality Characteristics. To evaluate the selected quality characteristics over the integrated process and organizational data, detecting quality problems that should be resolved before the mining/analysis effort. To do this, the specified data quality model metrics are measured over the extended event log (or the integrated metamodel). Results are obtained for each one that gives insight regarding the quality of the dataset.

PDQ3 - Improve Quality Characteristics. To take the necessary corrective actions to eliminate the detected quality problems, cleaning the event log and associated organizational data. It can include removing data, i.e., unwanted outliers, duplicates, null values, correcting data according to a specific domain of possible values, etc.

Process and Data Preparation (PDP). This discipline group activities dealing with the preparation of the integrated data to be used as input for the mining/analysis effort. It includes taking data to the format that will allow mining (i.e., extended event log) or performing the analysis (i.e., data warehouse). We have defined two extensions to the event log format for i) including corresponding organizational data in events; ii) including participants in events and messages exchanged for collaborative processes and including data regarding message interaction participants for choreographies.

PDP1 - Build Extended Event Logs. To automatically generate the extended log from the integrated metamodel as input for the mining/analysis effort. It includes gathering all integrated process and organizational data for each corresponding event when it applies, the involved participants in collaborations and messages exchanged, and messages interactions in choreographies. We have defined two extensions for the eXtensible Event Stream (XES) [24] following the definitions of the standard (c.f. Sect. 3).

PDP2 - Build Integrated Data Warehouse. To generate the integrated data warehouse from the integrated metamodel, be used as input for the analysis effort. We defined dimensions directly related to the metamodel quadrants, i.e., process-definition, process-instance, data-definition, and data-instance, adding a user dimension, a time dimension, and an entity relations dimension to capture entities references. It is based solely on the relationships between process and organizational data that we previously discovered in the metamodel using matching algorithms. The fact table relates the dimensions mentioned before. We include process duration and element duration to analyze execution times for both process and elements, and we also included the value of attributes. The data warehouse allows crossing processes and organizational data to provide an integrated view of the BPs execution.

PDP3 - Filter Event Log and Data. To filter the extended event log to be able to perform additional perspective mining over the data, e.g., to partition the log in process variants with similar behavior based on control flow or on the type of organizational data they manage, or by applying compliance rules, or selecting cases based on duration, among others.

Process and Data Mining and Analysis (PDMA). This discipline groups activities that select, execute, and evaluate approaches and tools for the mining/analysis effort. We also provide a catalog of existing techniques and algorithms of process and data mining approaches and existing tools implementing them, and new definitions and tools to support integrated analysis. It helps organizations use the methodology to find all the information and guidance they need in one place, to carry out the mining/analysis effort, easing its adoption.

PDMA1 - Select Mining/Analysis Approach. To select the mining and/or analysis approach to apply to the data, i.e., discovering process models (based on algorithms such as inductive miner, heuristic miner, or BPMN miner, among others), conformance and/or enhancement of process models for process mining approaches, and/or descriptive (clustering, decision trees, association rules) or predictive (classification, regression) for data mining approaches, crossing data from the business process perspective with the organizational data perspective (c.f. Sect. 3). Also, compliance requirements and execution measures can be selected as the desired approach to applying to the data. We provide a catalog of existing techniques and algorithms with a summary and corresponding links for each one.

PDMA2 - Select Mining/Analysis Tools. To select the mining tool to be used corresponding to the chosen approach since different tools and/or plug-ins implement different algorithms. Also, for analysis, the tool depends on the approach selected, i.e., the data warehouse can be used to cross-process and organizational data, or the execution measures can be evaluated in a specific tool. We provide a catalog of tools and the support they provide.

PDMA3 - Execute Mining/Analysis Approach. To carry out the selected mining/analysis approaches in the selected tools over the integrated data, including execution measures analysis and compliance requirements evaluation. It includes dealing with data input issues and tool execution problems, i.e., significant execution times, that would need to return to previous activities to correct the data's problems or change the approach or tool selected.

PDMA4 - Evaluate Mining/Analysis Results. To evaluate the results of the mining/analysis effort from different perspectives, including the answers to goals and information needs to be defined by the business area, and more technical elements such as the correctness of results (i.e., measures such as fitness or recall, precision, overfitting, and underfitting), assessing of statistical significance, and other elements to evaluate the technical soundness of the results obtained. The business evaluation of mining/analysis results will lead to valuable information and knowledge on the organization's actual execution of business processes, identifying improvements opportunities to be carried out to generate a new version of the process.

Process and Data Compliance (PDC). This discipline groups activities that deal with the identification and evaluation, business process compliance requirements. We have defined a Business Process Compliance Requirements Model (BPCRM) [20] in which specific dimensions, factors and controls for collaborative BPs are defined (c.f. Sect. 3). It is mainly based on the compliance perspectives proposed in [27] as well as on the pattern vision presented in [30].

PDC1 - Identify Compliance Requirements. To instantiate the BPCRM to select specific dimensions, factors, and corresponding controls to evaluate compliance requirements for the process selected for the mining/analysis effort. It includes collaborative and choreography processes, which are the focus of the compliance model. The BPCRM, as the BPODQM quality model, defines specific dimensions, factors, and controls to evaluate compliance requirements over collaborative BPS. The compliance requirements modeling language [19] is used for specifying process compliance requirements over the process to be evaluated.

PDC2 - Evaluate Compliance Requirements. To evaluate the results of the compliance requirements specified over the process within the extended event log, including process and organizational data, to analyze violations in traces that do not comply with the requirements specified. We define a post mortem compliance evaluation over the extended event logs from BPs execution. Compliance requirements evaluation will get valuable information and knowledge on the actual execution of BPs, focusing on collaborations and choreographies, detecting violations to norms and business rules that should be corrected in a new version of the process.

Roles and Artifacts. There are four roles within the methodology. The *Business Manager* supervises and leads a company's operations and employees. Since it is interested in improving business processes, it selects the business processes that will be analyzed. From there, the *BP Responsible* (also known as Process Owner) is in charge since it is responsible for managing such process from end-to-end. In this context, it participates in providing domain information and requirements, e.g., providing access to data sources, defining analysis goals, and also on the evaluation activities of the methodology. The *Business Analyst* also participates in the same activities as the BP Responsible, bridging the gaps between IT and the business. Finally, the *Data Scientist* represents the more technical role responsible for making value out of data, from getting and integrating the source information to analyzing it.

Concerning the artifacts, the primary artifacts of the methodology are the integrated metamodel that integrates process and organizational data, the extended event log and the data warehouse used for the analysis, and the data quality and compliance requirements models that are refined for each specific process. Also, there are other documents describing business needs, business process and data mining and analysis, and tools catalog, among others.

2.2 Dynamic View

Figure 2 presents a summary of the dynamic view of the methodology, showing for each phase and corresponding sub-phase, the activities that are performed, and their order, i.e., previous activities. The dynamic view is composed of three iterative phases: *Enactment*, *Data*, and *Mining/Analysis*. The Enactment phase corresponds to the actual execution of processes from which data is registered. The Data phase involves the inception, extraction, integration, preparation, and cleaning of data. Finally, the Mining/Analysis phase considers the selection and execution of the mining/analysis approaches and the evaluation of their results.

We also integrated an existing Improvement phase from the Business Process Continuous Improvement Process (BPCIP, [16]) methodology to carry out the improvement

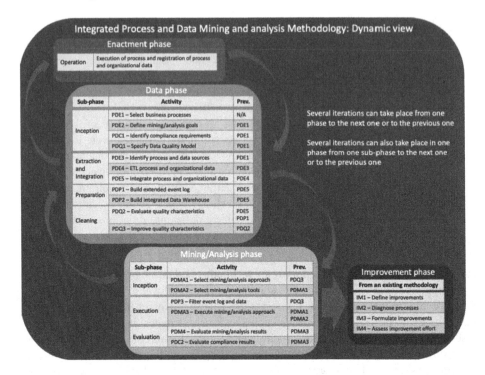

Fig. 2. Summary of the dynamic view of the methodology (from [14]).

effort over the selected processes. This phase consists of defining the specific improvements that are going to be integrated into the improvement phase of the BP lifecycle,
a diagnosis of the maturity of the BP process involved to assess the appropriateness of
such improvement, a refinement of the improvements that need to be done, and the final
assessment of such improvement effort.

3   PRICED Dimensions Supporting the Methodology

The conceptual dimension of the PRICED framework defines concepts for process
and data mining, data quality, and process compliance that support the methodological dimension presented in the last section. Also, the methodology requires the definition of technical and tool dimensions, techniques, algorithms, and tools for its concrete
application.

In what follows, we firstly present the general approach for process and organizational data integration, including the extensions for event logs we have defined to
deal with integrated process and organizational data and collaborative BPs. Then, we
present two main concepts of the conceptual dimension: the Business Process and Organizational Data Quality Model (BPODQM) [4], and the Business Process Compliance
Requirements Model (BPCRM) [19], which allow us to select quality characteristics
and compliance requirements to be evaluated over the extended event logs. Finally, we

describe the approach for integrated process and data mining techniques over the integrated data.

3.1 Process and Data Integration Approach

During the Data phase of the methodology, we extract process and organizational data and integrate it into a unified view. Data is structured based on a generic metamodel called Business Process and Organizational Data Integrated Metamodel (BPODIM), and an algorithm matches process and organizational data exploiting their data values, and timestamps [8].

As shown in Fig. 3, we envision a general mechanism to extract data from heterogeneous databases at two levels: i) the process level, from different BPMS and corresponding process engines databases (i.e., Activiti BPMS with PostgreSQL, Bonita BPMS with MySQL, etc.); ii) organizational data level, from different and heterogeneous databases (relational or NoSQL, i.e., PostgreSQL, MySQL, MongoDB, Cassandra, Neo4j, etc.). We are currently defining this ETL process. It is based on extending a previous definition of a Generic API for BPMS [13] and a new Generic API for databases (SQL/NoSQL) [22, 26], allowing us to decouple the ETL process from a specific implementation of the sources.

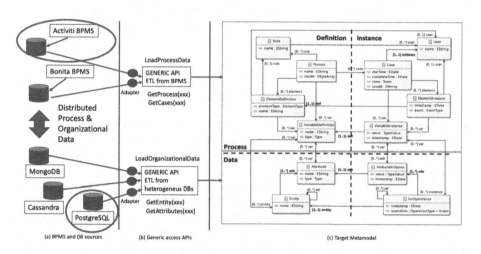

Fig. 3. ETL for process and organizational data (from [14]).

Once the data is integrated within a database whose schema is based on the BPODIM metamodel, it is prepared to be used within the mining/analysis phase. For this, we build a generic data warehouse [2] and extended event logs based on the eXtensible Event Stream (XES) standard [24]. An XES log represents events grouped in traces (cases) for a given process. They are used as input for applying integrated process and data mining techniques, as is described in Sect. 3.4. XES provides an extension mechanism for defining new attributes to events, e.g., organizational, representing roles, and time, representing timestamps. We have defined two extensions to deal with organizational data and collaborative BPs, not just process orchestrations as usual.

The Organizational Data extension [4] defines string attributes representing organizational data associated with each event. For each event, we describe the list of variables and entities, which contains a list of the attributes related to the event. Variables correspond to process variables handled by an event, i.e., an activity within the BPMS execution (top-right quadrant of the BPODIM metamodel). Entities, and their corresponding attributes, correspond to the organizational data registered in the organizational database. They are linked to the variables through the matching algorithm (bottom-left and right quadrants). For each element in the list, we register its value and its type. In the case of attributes that matched a specific variable, we register a reference to such variable. The Collaborative BPs extension [20] define string attributes to identify the participants associated with the events, in two scenarios: the owner of the event within a collaboration between two or more participants and the sender/receiver for message elements, and within a choreography which is focused on the interchange of messages, only the sender/receiver for message elements. We also represent the type of element in both extensions, e.g., user task, service task, send or receive message task, etc.

We automatize all the processes from the data extraction to the generation of the extended event logs and data warehouse, following a model-driven approach. In particular, we have defined a chain of model transformations that takes the information within the database registering the metamodel information and generating a model conforming to the BPODIM metamodel, and then an Acceleo model-to-text transformation for generating the XES file.

3.2   Business Process and Organizational Data Quality Model

As said before, we defined the BPODQM data quality model to manage data quality issues in log data, first evaluating and then cleaning. It is based on previous quality models we have defined for other contexts [10,34], and on [35]. This model comprises all the quality aspects that should be considered, how these aspects should be measured, and the elements of the log data corresponding to process events and the organizational databases, over which the quality aspects apply. These quality aspects are organized in quality dimensions, which in turn are composed of quality factors. One or more metrics are defined for each quality factor, which specifies how the factor is measured. Each metric is defined for a certain data granularity, which is the data unit whose quality will be measured and to which the quality measures will be associated.

Considering the log data, whose quality should be measured, and its format, specific granularities are defined as follows: **attribute value**, which is the particular value of an attribute, **attribute**, which refers to the set of values corresponding to the same key, **event**, which involves all data included in an event data, and **log**, which is used for metrics that refer to the whole log.

The data quality dimensions and factors included in BPODQM are presented in the following. A more detailed description of the metrics can be found in [4].:

- *Accuracy* dimension, which is related to the correctness of the data with respect to a referential value. The quality factors that compose this dimension are *syntactic accuracy*, *semantic accuracy* and *precision*.
- *Consistency* dimension, which addresses the problem of consistency between data. The quality factors corresponding to this dimension are *domain consistency*, *inter-element consistency* and *intra-element consistency*, the first one representing consistency of a data value concerning a particular domain, and the second and third ones representing consistency between two data values of the same data element, and two data values of different elements, respectively.
- *Completeness* dimension, which refers to the absence of data that should be present. Two factors are defined for this dimension: *coverage* and *density*. The first one explores what portion of the real-world entities are represented in the data. The second one focuses on how many data values that should be present are not, for example, appearing as NULL values.
- *Uniqueness* dimension, which addresses the problem of duplicate data. The quality factors considered in this dimension are *duplication free* and *contradiction free*, each one evaluating if the data is not duplicated and, in the case, it is duplicated, if it has no contradictions, respectively.
- *Freshness* dimension, which is related to the consistency of the log data timestamps.
- *Credibility* dimension, which is composed of two factors: *provenance* and *trustworthiness*. The first one refers to the credibility of the responsible of the log data and the event origin, and the reproducibility of a log, and the second one is related to the believability of data.
- *Security* dimension, which is composed by three factors: *user permissions*, *encrypted data*, and *anonymity*, each one addressing the problems of user rights, data encryption and data anonymization, respectively.

We have developed a ProM plug-in that uses the extended event log with integrated process and organizational data as input to support the automated evaluation of event log data quality with the BPODQM (Sect. 4).

3.3   Business Process Compliance Requirements Model

The Bussiness Process Compliance Requirements Model (BPCRM) aims to provide a library of built-in compliance elements in order to facilitate the specification and validation of compliance requirements over collaborative BPs The model comprises a set of more than seventy predefined compliance controls, which are organized in five dimensions and twenty-one factors. These elements are mainly based on the compliance persepectives proposed in [27] as well as on the pattern vision presented in [30].

The set of generic compliance controls apply to both the collaboration and choreography views of collaborative BPs. In addition, they can be instantiated over a concrete process in order to specify particular compliance requirements, and used as input to evaluate violations with process mining. Therefore, the proposed model constitutes a catalogue of compliance controls (patterns), which can be used for two purposes: the specification of compliance requirements and the validation of compliance rules.

Next, the compliance dimensions and factors that conform the BPCRM and examples of compliance factors for each dimension are presented. For a complete description of the model and its components refer to [20].

- *Control Flow* dimension deals with compliance aspects related to the occurrence and order of tasks as well as their flow [28]. This dimension has eleven controls which are organized into five factors: Tasks, Sequence Flow, Parallel Flow, Exclusive Flow and Alternative Flow. For example, one of the compliance controls within this dimension enables the specification of requirements such as *"if activity A is not present, then activity B must not be present"*.
- *Interaction* dimension deals with compliance aspects related to message exchanges between participants as well as their flow [28]. This dimension has eleven controls which are organized into two factors: Send/Receive Messages and Message Flow. For example, one of the compliance controls within this dimension enables the specification of requirements such as *"if message M is exchanged, then message N must not be exchanged, and vice versa"*.
- *Time* dimension deals with compliance aspects related to points in time as well as time intervals and conditions [28]. This dimension has twelve controls which are organized into three factors: Point in Time, Interval and Duration. For example, one of the compliance controls within this dimension enables the specification of requirements such as *"if activity A occurs then activity B must occur within interval I"*.
- *Resources* dimension deals with compliance aspects related to the resources used in processes as well as their relations [28]. This dimension comprises controls which are organized into seven factors: Roles, Staff Members, Groups, Organizational Units, Participants, Resource Relations, and Performer Relations. For example, one of the compliance controls within this dimension enables the specification of requirements such as *"if activity A is performed by user U and activity B is performed by user V, then U and V are assigned to organizational unit O"*.
- *Data* dimension deals with compliance aspects related to data elements used in processes as well as their relations and flows [28]. This dimension has twenty controls which are organized into four factors: Data Objects, Data Containers, Data Relations and Data Flow. For example, one of the compliance controls within this dimension enables the specification of requirements such as *"data object DO written by activity A must be contained in message M"*.

We have developed a ProM plug-in that uses the extended event log for collaborative BPs as input, to support the automated evaluation of compliance requirements over the event log data with the BPCRM (Sect. 4).

3.4   Integrated Process and Data Mining Approach

The integrated process and data mining approach we have defined operates over the Organizational Data extension for the event logs. Organizational data is included in the corresponding event as described above. We apply data mining techniques over organizational data from the events to view the process traces that manipulated such data.

We use process mining techniques over process data to discover traces with different behavior and relate it to the data they manage.

For example, in the Loan request process from a bank, clients can submit their request, including identification data and the requested amount. The process registers these data in an external organizational database where loan requests are maintained, apart from the process data. Traditionally data is analyzed without linking it to the process, and the process is analyzed without connecting it to the data it managed. For example, with data mining, patterns regarding the loan request data can be discovered, relating different attributes, but not with the process execution that managed the data.

With our integrated approach, apart from grouping traces regarding control flow behavior (i.e., process variants), we can group them by values of the organizational data. For example, regarding the result of the loan request: was it approved or rejected? Who managed the approval? or the ranks of the amount requested. Then we can analyze each group of traces to find common elements that could have led to one or the other outcome using the control flow behavior, i.e., discovering the process for each group. Without including organizational data in the event log, this type of analysis is not possible. Also, we can analyze each process variant based on the behavior it groups, i.e., which activities are executed and in what order, and analyze the organizational data related to this specific type of path over the process to discover common data elements that are related with the variant.

We have developed a ProM plug-in that uses the extended event log with integrated process and organizational data as input and implements the integrated process and data mining approach. It provides the most common data mining techniques for analysis: decision trees, clustering, and association rules, as well as the process mining techniques that are already provided in the framework (Sect. 4).

4 Applications of the Methodology

This section presents two examples of applying the methodology on actual BPs regarding our university and e-Government processes from the Uruguayan digital services. The "Students Mobility" BP, has been introduced in [11] and corresponds to the application for students' scholarships to take courses at other universities. The "Passport request" BP has been introduced in [19] and corresponds to the collaborative BP for requesting a passport by a citizen. In the first case, we present a step-by-step application of the methodology showing the integrated process and organizational data approach, data matching, quality evaluation, process mining tools, and data warehouse for analysis, but with no compliance requirements evaluation. In the second case, we focus on the compliance evaluation approach, showing the use of the compliance requirements specification, execution, and evaluation.

4.1 Students Mobility BP with Organizational Data Extension

The simplified BPMN 2.0 process depicted in Fig. 4a begins when a new mobility call is defined and the period for receiving student's applications is opened. Students present their applications with the required documentation within the Registration Office. After

15 days, the period is closed, and all submitted applications go through an assessment to see if they comply with the call. Those complying go through an evaluation panel evaluation, where applications are ranked and scholarships are assigned. Finally, the School board approves the assignments, notifies applicants about the results, and asks the selected ones to sign a contract for the scholarship and get paid.

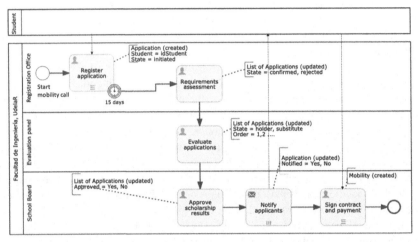

(a) Students Mobility business process (from [11])

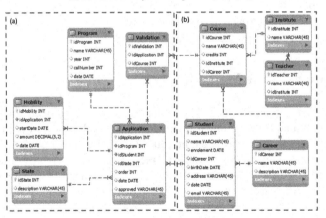

(b) Extended data model for the Students Mobility business process

Fig. 4. Students mobility proof of concept (from [14]).

The data model shown in Fig. 4b presents an excerpt of the organizational data model extended from [11]. In the left side (a), there are specific tables to support the "Students mobility" process, i.e., the mobility Program, Application (with reference to the Student) and Validation (with reference to Course) tables, as well as the Mobility table to register the scholarships that were assigned. The State table registers the states that the application goes through the process control flow. In the right side (b), there are tables containing organization's master data, i.e., `Student` that apply to the call, their `Career` and `Course` to validate the courses selected which are associated to an `Institute` and with a `Teacher` responsible of it.

This process was implemented and executed in Activiti 6.0 BPMS[1] community edition using a PostgreSQL[2] database for the organizational data. We applied process and data mining techniques using Disco[3] and ProM[4], and built a data warehouse using Pentaho Platform[5].

Execution of the Methodology. Since the methodology covers any mining/analysis effort, some activities may not apply to specific scenarios. In this case, we describe the activities we performed for each phase defined in Sect. 2.

Enactment Phase. The Enactment Phase does not have any concrete activity within the methodology. It consists of the organization's actual operation, where processes are executed, and process and organizational data are registered in their corresponding databases. In Fig. 4, comments in the "Student Mobility" show when an activity access the data model to insert, query or modify data, e.g., within the "Register Application" task, the `Application` table is accessed to create a new application for a specific student with `State` "Initiated".

Data Phase. The Data Phase is essential for the mining/analysis efforts since the final outputs of this phase are the integrated process and organizational data, improved, cleaned, and with a minimum quality level to be used as a valuable input for the Mining/Analysis Phase.

Inception In this sub-phase, we define the basis for the mining/analysis efforts.

PDE1 - Select Business Processes. We select the "Student mobility" process already introduced.
PDE2 - Define Mining/Analysis Goals. Business people (e.g., the process owner) define several business questions about the domain with a mixed perspective of data and processes, such as:
  - Which organizational data were managed by cases that took the longest to execute?
  - Which organizational data are involved in cases where no successful results were obtained?
  - Which cases in the successful path are related to specific organizational data?

---

[1] https://www.activiti.org/.

[2] https://www.postgresql.org/.

[3] https://fluxicon.com/disco/.

[4] https://www.promtools.org/.

[5] https://www.hitachivantara.com/en-us/products/data-management-analytics/pentaho-platform.html.

- Which users are involved in the cases that took the longest to execute or the ones that correspond to the successful path?
- Are there paths defined in the process model that are never executed in the actual operation?

PDC1 - Identify Compliance Requirements. We did not perform this activity since there were no compliance requirements defined for the process.

PDQ1 - Specify Data Quality Model. We selected basic quality characteristics from the BPODQM model, to be checked over the integrated data:

- Dimension: *Accuracy*, Factor: *Syntactic accuracy*, Metric: *Format*
- Dimension: *Completeness*, Factor: *Density*, Metric: *Not null*
- Dimension: *Uniqueness*, Factor: *Duplication-free*, Metrics: *Duplicate attribute/event*

Extraction and Integration. In the Extraction and Integration sub-phase, we perform activities for extracting and loading process and organizational data into the metamodel and integrating data by finding the corresponding relationships between events (i.e., activities) and organizational data that they handled.

PDE3 - Identify Process and Data Sources. With the information of the "Students mobility" process technical infrastructure, we identify the BPMS process engine database and the organizational database and corresponding access data (i.e., machine and SID) and permits. As it is common practice in the configuration of databases, it should have been configured to allow historical logging, which we use to get all organizational data related to the process execution under evaluation in the defined period.

PDE4 - ETL process and Organizational Data. In Fig. 3, we describe the process for performing this activity. We used two databases in this proof of concept (within the ellipsis on the figure's left side): the Activiti BPMS engine database and a relational PostgreSQL database for the organizational data. We also implemented the metamodel in a PostgreSQL database.

PDE5 - Integrate process and organizational data. After the process and organizational data are loaded into the metamodel, we executed the matching algorithm to find the relations between the metamodel's process-instance and data-instance quadrants. Our basic data matching algorithm is based on discovering matches between variables (from the process-instance quadrant) and attributes instances (from the data-instance quadrant) by searching similar values within a configurable period near the start and complete events timestamps. The initial definitions for integrating data can be seen in [11].

Preparation. In this sub-phase, we focus on putting the data in a suitable format to use as input for the mining/analysis effort.

PDP1 - Build Extended Event Logs. We automated this activity with a model-to-text transformation from the integrated metamodel to the extended event log, including the organizational data related to each process event.

PDP2 - Build Integrated Data Warehouse. We defined a generic data warehouse that has no domain-specific elements regarding the process or organization involved. We also automated the loading process from the integrated metamodel. The data warehouse has a star schema representing the four metamodel quadrants as dimensions and others such as users and time. We also define several measures regarding duration and values in the fact table.

Cleaning. In this sub-phase, we performed the following activities.

PDQ2 - Evaluate Quality Characteristics. We checked some of the primary factors selected, such as date format, not null for timestamps, not null, and no duplicates for event names. To do so, we used the ProM plug-in we have developed that automatically analyzes the extended event log with integrated data evaluating quality issues as defined in the BPOQM model. In Fig. 5 we present an example of the results of the analysis for Dimension Accuracy, Factor Syntactic accuracy, and Metric Format applied to date.

PDQ3 - Improve Quality Characteristics. As it can be seen in Fig. 5 we found some inconsistencies in the date format for timestamps that were corrected, no nulls were found, and some duplicates on event names were corrected based on domain information.

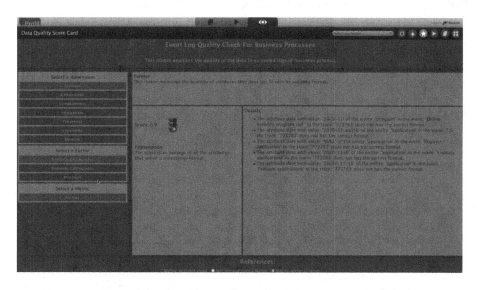

Fig. 5. ProM quality plug-in for extended event logs with integrated data.

Mining/Analysis Phase. The Mining/Analysis Phase is the core of the mining/analysis effort, where an integrated view of process and data mining is applied. Approaches and tools are selected, and the integrated data is analyzed to discover valuable information on process execution and improvement opportunities.

Inception. In this sub-phase, we select approaches and tools for the mining/analysis effort.

PDMA1 - Select Mining/Analysis Approach. As an analysis approach, we used the data warehouse to answer some of the questions included in the mining/analysis effort goals. We also use process and data mining approaches over the extended event log to provide another view of the integrated data. In addition, we also used our approach for integrated process and data mining over process and organizational integrated data.

PDMA2 - Select Mining/Analysis Tools. We selected the Pentaho platform to implement the data warehouse and the mining tools Disco and ProM to analyze the extended log, including our ProM plugin for integrated process and data mining for the extended log. The same data was loaded in every tool, i.e., integrated process and organizational data from the metamodel. However, as the analysis focus is different, it allows us to analyze data from different perspectives, providing a complete view on process execution.

Execution. In this sub-phase, we inspected and filtered the extended event log and data and executed the mining/analysis activities.

PDP3 - Filter Event Log and Data. We inspected the extended event log to analyze the process cases, the organizational data that was integrated with their data, and different process variants. Figure 6 shows Disco the frequency of selected elements in the extended event log: a) entities and b) corresponding attributes from the organizational data; and c) associated process variables. In Fig. 6 a), it can be seen that organizational tables: `Application`, `Program`, and `Validation` are present in the extended event log, which were defined in the data model presented in Fig. 4b.

PDMA3 - Execute Mining/Analysis Approach. Regarding process mining, we used the extended event log we generated as input to discover the process model in Disco and with the BPMN miner plug-in in ProM, to analyze the execution against the defined model. Figure 6 d) shows the model discovered in ProM, and Fig. 6 e) shows the model discovered in Disco. Activities do not completely correspond to the model presented in 4a. We also worked with the data warehouse, crossing data from different dimensions to answer the questions defined, e.g., which courses and from which careers have been involved in cases that took more than 15 days to complete? (in the example, 15 days equals 200.000 milliseconds). We filtered data by the relation validation-course, which defines the courses included in the applications with the case id and the corresponding attributes. As rows, we included attributes from dimensions "Entityrelation", "ProcessInstance", "DataDefinition" and "DataInstance". We selected the "Process duration" measure and filtered it by duration over 200.000 milliseconds. Figure 7 shows the results in Pentaho.

Regarding the integrated process and data mining approach that is implemented in our ProM plug-in, we analyzed the extended event log based on organizational data to know the cases that were associated with these data, for example, cases that have scholarships approved and rejected, cases that manage different ranks of amounts for scholarships, teachers that were involved in evaluating the scholarships, etc. We can then analyze the resulting cases to see whether there is a different or specific behavior associated with the organizational data. In Fig. 8 we present an example of the results for clustering cases based on approved and rejected scholarships. It can be seen that when selecting one case in the cluster on the left panel, on the main panel, the path of the case over the process model is highlighted.

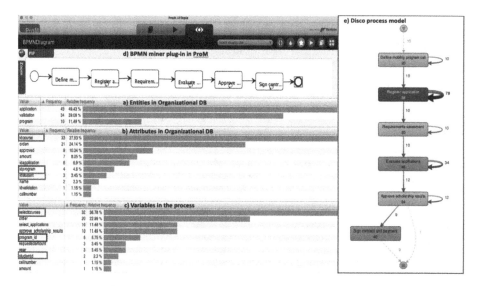

Fig. 6. Extended event log analysis: a) entities; b) attributes; c) process variables; d) ProM model; and e) Disco model.

Evaluation. In this sub-phase, we perform the activities to evaluate mining/analysis results obtained using the selected tools.

PDMA4 - Evaluate Mining/Analysis Results. Regarding the process models discovered by ProM and Disco, although this process is elementary, several issues were detected. For instance, the activity "Notify applicants" was absent in both models, pointing to an implementation problem. Concerning the data warehouse and the example question, a career with id 80 presented the most cases with process duration over the defined limit, leading to an analysis of the type of courses that students select, which can cause the delays. The integrated analysis over the extended log also gave us insight into the execution of the process and the relation with organizational data, particularly for the approved and rejected results for scholarships.

PDC2 - Evaluate Compliance Results. We omitted this activity since there were no compliance requirements defined for this particular process.

Improvements regarding issues discovered were not performed since new iterations over the data need to be done to obtain a deeper analysis of the results.

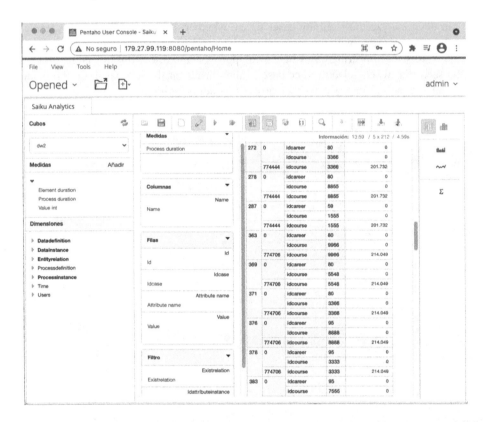

Fig. 7. Data warehouse result for courses and careers involved in cases that took more than 15 days to complete.

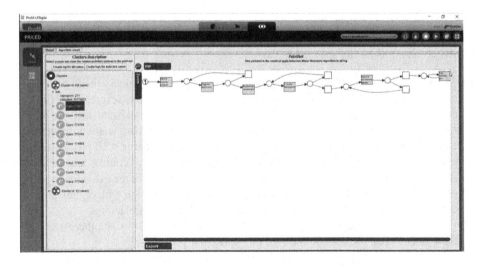

Fig. 8. ProM plug-in for integrated process and data mining over integrated data.

4.2   Passport Request BP with Collaborative Extension

The Passport request BP allows a citizen to request a passport interacting with several e-Government organizations. In the first place, the e-Government National Agency (AGESIC) receives the request and interacts with the National Identification Agency (DNIC) to schedule a meeting for issuing the passport. The DNIC interacts with the National Police office (DNPT) to check the Judicial record's background of the citizen. If there is none, the meeting is carried out, and the passport can be issued or not, depending on the defined criteria. If the citizen has judicial records or the response is not received within 24 h, the meeting is canceled. Figure 9a shows the collaborative BP [20] using BPMN 2.0, and Fig. 9b its choreography [19].

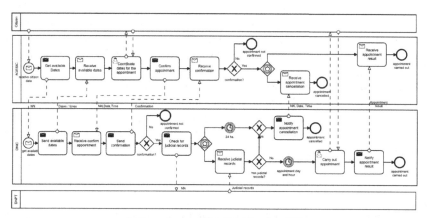

(a) Passport request BP collaboration from [20]

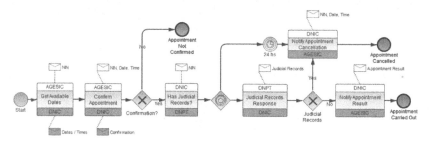

(b) Collaborative Passport request BP choreography view from [19]

Fig. 9. Passport request proof of concept.

Execution of the Methodology. In this case, we focus only on the activities we performed for identifying, executing, and evaluating compliance requirements. The rest of the activities for each phase defined in Sect. 2 are the same as in the previous example, i.e., selecting BPs, evaluating data quality, etc.

PDC1 - Identify Compliance Requirements. We selected compliance requirements from the BPCRM model to be evaluated over the choreography:
- Dimension: *Interaction*, Factor: *Send/Receive Messages*, Control: *M coabsent N*
- Dimension: *Interaction*, Factor: *Message flow*, Control: *R between M and N*

The first control *M coabsent N* is instantiated over the choreograpy as: If *Judicial records response* is not exchanged, then *Notify appointment result* must not be exchanged, and the second control *R between M and N* is instantiated as: *Judicial records response* is exchanged between *Has judicial records* and *Notify appointment result*.

PDMA3 - Execute Mining/Analysis Approach. The compliance analysis over the extended collaborative event log is implemented in our ProM plug-in, taking as input the compliance requirements for the process, i.e., the instantiation of controls for the specific messages, tasks, etc., and the extended event log for the collaborative BP (collaboration, choreography). In Fig. 10 we present an example of the results. Non-compliant traces are shown in the summary panel with the number and percentage of trace violations. Different control results for the choreography can be seen in [20].

PDC2 - Evaluate Compliance Results. Several traces presented violations regarding the two selected controls. In the first case, a message appeared in some traces where it should not occur since the first message was not present. In the second case, a message was not exchanged in the correct order. It requires looking deeper into the violating traces to gain insight into the causes.

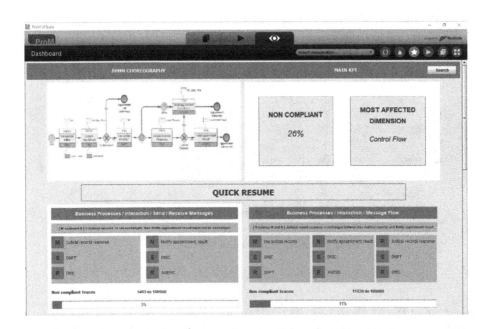

Fig. 10. ProM plug-in for compliance requirements evaluation choreography view.

5 Related Work

CRISP-DM [31], KDD [7], and SEMMA [29] are the most common methodologies for performing classical data-centric analysis. None of them include detailed guidelines on identifying and incorporating data useful to analyze organizations' processes and improve them. CRISP-DM was initially developed in IBM for data mining tasks, and it is used for a wide variety of projects. It consists of a cyclic model with the following defining stages that can be reversed: Business understanding, Data understanding, Data Preparation, Modeling, Evaluation, and Deployment. KDD is a method to guide specialists in extracting patterns and required information from data. It consists of five stages: Selection, Preprocessing, Transformation, Data Mining, and Interpretation/Evaluation. Finally, SEMMA is also a cyclic method that does not focus as heavily on data-specific stages. In this case, a wide range of algorithms or methods are used.

From the business process perspective, in [18], the authors propose PM^2, a methodology to guide the execution of process mining projects with different goal levels. It consists of six stages with their corresponding activities: *planning*, for setting up the project and defining the research questions; *extraction*, for extracting data and process models; *data processing*, for creating appropriate event logs; *mining & analysis*, for applying process mining techniques; *evaluation*, for relating the analysis findings to improvement ideas; and *process improvement & support*, for modifying the actual process execution. This methodology is consistent and complementary with ours. Planning, extraction, and data processing stages are considered within the data phase of our methodology. They also consider enriched event logs with external data, but they neither pay special attention to organizational data nor related problems as quality assessments. Mining & analysis and evaluation stages are also considered within the Mining/Analysis phase, but in this case, they provide deeper information that ours can use. Finally, the process improvement stage is considered by integrating an Improvement phase from the BPCIP methodology [16].

Although there are many data quality proposals on data quality methodologies and frameworks, e.g., [3,33], to the best of our knowledge, none of them are focused on integrated process and organizational data quality management for process mining activities. In our work, we select and adapt the main tasks of existing approaches to our needs, obtaining the three proposed tasks (definition of data quality model, evaluation, and improvement of the quality characteristics).

Various approaches propose activities for business process compliance [21]. The COMPAS project defines a life cycle with four phases (e.g., evaluation) [5]. The C^3 Pro Project describes a design-time methodology for compliance of collaborative workflows [28]. The MaRCo Project defines activities for compliance management [25] (modeling, checking, analysis, enactment). However, they neither consider these activities in the context of an integrated methodology nor leverage process and data mining for compliance control and analysis.

6 Conclusions

We have presented the PRICED methodology to carry out process and data mining and analysis efforts over integrated process data and organizational data. The static view of the methodology includes the definition of disciplines, tasks, roles, and artifacts, and the dynamic view comprises phases and sub-phases to guide the work within the framework. Key elements of our proposal include: (i) a metamodel-based integration of process and organizational data from process engines and distributed organizational DBs; (ii) a quality model for quality assessment over the integrated data; (iii) a compliance requirements model for compliance assessment over collaborative BPs; (iv) extended event logs and a data warehouse to be used for mining/analysis over the integrated data; (v) and integrated process and data mining/analysis approaches over the integrated data to provide a complete view of the organization's actual operation.

Also, we have provided two applications of the methodology. The first one focused on integrated process and organizational data, and the second focused on collaborative BPs. Both applications allowed us to show the utility of the elements defined in the methodology.

We believe it is a valuable tool to guide organizations' mining/analysis efforts towards evidence-based process improvement, with a complete and integrated data view. Nevertheless, we are still improving the whole framework, applying it over more complex processes and heterogeneous organizational data to assess its capabilities. We are also performing further analysis over the integrated data, with different process and data mining approaches.

Acknowledgement. We would like to thank students: Alexis Artus, Andrs Borges, Federico Prez, Francisco Betancor, Fabin Gambetta, Juan Canaparo, Martn Rubio, for their work in the PRICED framework and prototypes.

References

1. van der Aalst, W.M.P.: Process Mining - Data Science in Action, 2nd Edn. Springer, Berlin (2016). https://doi.org/10.1007/978-3-662-49851-4
2. Artus, A., Borges, A., Calegari, D., Delgado, A.: Integrated process data and organizational data analysis for business process improvement. In: Golfarelli, M., Wrembel, R., Kotsis, G., Tjoa, A.M., Khalil, I. (eds.) DaWaK 2021. LNCS, vol. 12925, pp. 207–215. Springer, Cham (2021). https://doi.org/10.1007/978-3-030-86534-4_19
3. Batini, C., Scannapieco, M.: Data and Information Quality. DSA, Springer, Cham (2016). https://doi.org/10.1007/978-3-319-24106-7
4. Betancor, F., Pérez, F., Marotta, A., Delgado, A.: Business process and organizational data quality model (BPODQM) for integrated process and data mining. In: Paiva, A.C.R., Cavalli, A.R., Ventura Martins, P., Pérez-Castillo, R. (eds.) QUATIC 2021. CCIS, vol. 1439, pp. 431–445. Springer, Cham (2021). https://doi.org/10.1007/978-3-030-85347-1_31
5. Birukou, A., D'Andrea, V., Leymann, F., Serafinski, J., Silveira, P., Strauch, S., Tluczek, M.: An integrated solution for runtime compliance governance in SOA. In: Maglio, P.P., Weske, M., Yang, J., Fantinato, M. (eds.) ICSOC 2010. LNCS, vol. 6470, pp. 122–136. Springer, Heidelberg (2010). https://doi.org/10.1007/978-3-642-17358-5_9
6. Bose, R.P.J.C., Mans, R.S., van der Aalst, W.M.P.: Wanna improve process mining results? In: 2013 IEEE Symposium on Computational Intelligence and Data Mining (CIDM), pp. 127–134 (2013)
7. Brachman, R.J., Anand, T.: The process of knowledge discovery in databases. In: Advances in Knowledge Discovery and Data Mining, pp. 37–57. MIT Press, Cambridge (1996)

8. Calegari, D., Delgado, A., Artus, A., Borges, A.: Integration of business process and orga-nizational data for evidence-based business intelligence. CLEI Electron. J. **24**(2), 7:1-7:19 (2021)
9. Chang, J.: Business Process Management Systems: Strategy and Implementation. CRC Press, Boca Raton (2016)
10. Cristalli, E., Serra, F., Marotta, A.: Data quality evaluation in document oriented data stores. In: Woo, C., Lu, J., Li, Z., Ling, T.W., Li, G., Lee, M.L. (eds.) ER 2018. LNCS, vol. 11158, pp. 309–318. Springer, Cham (2018). https://doi.org/10.1007/978-3-030-01391-2_35
11. Delgado, A., Calegari, D.: Towards a unified vision of business process and organizational data. In: XLVI Latin American Computing Conference (CLEI), pp. 108–117. IEEE (2020)
12. Delgado, A., Calegari, D.: Discovery and analysis of e-government business processes with process mining: a case study. In: 55th Hawaii International Conference on System Sciences, (HICSS) (2022)
13. Delgado, A., Calegari D., Arrigoni A.: Towards a generic BPMS user portal definition for the execution of business processes. In: XLII Latin American Computer Conference - Selected Papers, CLEI 2016 Selected Papers, Valparaiso, Chile, 10–14 October 2016, pp. 39–59. Else-vier (2016)
14. Delgado, A., Calegari, D., Marotta, A., González, L., Tansini, L.: A methodology for inte-grated process and data mining and analysis towards evidence-based process improvement. In: Proceedings of the 16th International Conference on Software Technologies (ICSOFT), pp. 426–437. ScitePress (2021)
15. Delgado, A., Marotta, A., González, L., Tansini, L., Calegari, D.: Towards a data science framework integrating process and data mining for organizational improvement. In: 15th International Conference on Software Technologies (ICSOFT), pp. 492–500. ScitePress (2020)
16. Delgado, A., Weber, B., Ruiz, F., de Guzmán, I.G.R., Piattini, M.: An integrated approach based on execution measures for the continuous improvement of business processes realized by services. Inf. Softw. Technol. **56**(2), 134–162 (2014)
17. Dumas, M., van der Aalst, W.M., ter Hofstede, A.H.: Process-Aware Information Systems: Bridging People and Software through Process Technology. Wiley, Hoboken (2005)
18. van Eck, M.L., Lu, X., Leemans, S.J.J., van der Aalst, W.M.P.: PM^2: a process mining project methodology. In: Zdravkovic, J., Kirikova, M., Johannesson, P. (eds.) CAiSE 2015. LNCS, vol. 9097, pp. 297–313. Springer, Cham (2015). https://doi.org/10.1007/978-3-319-19069-3_19
19. González, L., Delgado, A.: Towards compliance requirements modeling and evaluation of e-government inter-organizational collaborative business processes. In: 54th Hawaii Interna-tional Conference on System Sciences, (HICSS), pp. 1–10. ScholarSpace (2021)
20. González, L., Delgado, A.: Compliance requirements model for collaborative business pro-cess and evaluation with process mining. In: XLVII Latin American Computing Conference (CLEI) (2021)
21. Hashmi, M., Governatori, G., Lam, H.P., Wynn, M.T.: Are we done with business process compliance: state of the art and challenges ahead. Knowl. Inf. Syst. **57**(1), 79–133 (2018)
22. Hecht, R., Jablonski, S.: Nosql evaluation: a use case oriented survey. In: 2011 International Conference on Cloud and Service Computing, pp. 336–341 (2011)
23. IEEE: Task Force on Data Science and Advanced Analytics. http://www.dsaa.co/
24. IEEE: IEEE standard for extensible event stream (XES) for achieving interoperability in event logs and event streams. In: IEEE Std 1849–2016, pp. 1–50 (2016)
25. Kharbili, M.E., Ma, Q., Kelsen, P., Pulvermueller, E.: CoReL: policy-based and model-driven regulatory compliance management. In: IEEE 15th International Enterprise Dis-tributed Object Computing Conference, IEEE, August 2011

26. Khasawneh, T.N., AL-Sahlee, M.H., Safia, A.A.: Sql, newsql, and nosql databases: a comparative survey. In: 2020 11th International Conference on Information and Communication Systems (ICICS), pp. 013–021 (2020)
27. Knuplesch, D., Reichert, M.: A visual language for modeling multiple perspectives of business process compliance rules. Softw. Syst. Model. **16**(3), 715–736 (2016). https://doi.org/10.1007/s10270-016-0526-0
28. Knuplesch, D., Reichert, M., Ly, L.T., Kumar, A., Rinderle-Ma, S.: Visual modeling of business process compliance rules with the support of multiple perspectives. In: Ng, W., Storey, V.C., Trujillo, J.C. (eds.) ER 2013. LNCS, vol. 8217, pp. 106–120. Springer, Heidelberg (2013). https://doi.org/10.1007/978-3-642-41924-9_10
29. Mariscal, G., Marbán, O., Fernández, C.: A survey of data mining and knowledge discovery process models and methodologies. Knowl. Eng. Rev. **25**(2), 137–166 (2010)
30. Papazoglou, M.P.: Making business processes compliant to standards and regulations. In: 15th International Enterprise Distributed Object Computing Conference, IEEE, August 2011
31. Shearer, C.: The CRISP-DM model: the new blueprint for data mining. J. Data Warehouse. **5**(4), 13–22 (2000)
32. Sumathi, S., Sivanandam, S.N.: Introduction to Data Mining and its Applications, Studies in Computational Intelligence, vol. 29. Springer, Berlin (2006)
33. Tepandi, J., et al.: The Data Quality Framework for the Estonian Public Sector and Its Evaluation. In: Hameurlain, A., Küng, J., Wagner, R., Sakr, S., Razzak, I., Riyad, A. (eds.) Transactions on Large-Scale Data- and Knowledge-Centered Systems XXXV. Lecture Notes in Computer Science(), vol. 10680, pp. 1–26. Springer, Berlin (2017). https://doi.org/10.1007/978-3-662-56121-8_1
34. Valverde, M.C., Vallespir, D., Marotta, A., Panach, J.I.: Applying a data quality model to experiments in software engineering. In: Indulska, M., Purao, S. (eds.) ER 2014. LNCS, vol. 8823, pp. 168–177. Springer, Cham (2014). https://doi.org/10.1007/978-3-319-12256-4_18
35. Verhulst, R.: Evaluating quality of event data within event logs:an extensible framework. Master's thesis, Eindhoven University of Technology (2016)

Feedback Generation for Automatic User Interface Design Evaluation

Jenny Ruiz[1]([✉]) [iD] and Monique Snoeck[2] [iD]

[1] University of Holguin, 80100 Holguin, Cuba
`jruizp@uho.edu.cu`
[2] KU Leuven, 3000 Leuven, Belgium
`monique.snoeck@kuleuven.be`

Abstract. During the last decades the interest to study User Interfaces (UI) has increased. However, the learning of UI design is a difficult process. To obtain better results, novel UI designers need guidance through this process. Feedback is among the most important factors to improve knowledge and skill acquisition. Nevertheless, the complexity of providing individual feedback is remarkable: it is a time-consuming task and requires a fair amount of expertise. This paper presents the Feedback ENriched user Interface Simulation (FENIkS) as a solution to this problem. FENIkS is a UI design simulation tool, based on model-driven engineering. The students design the UI through different models while automatically receiving feedback on how design principles have been applied through several options. From the models it is possible to generate a working prototype, enriched with feedback that explains the application of design principles. This paper describes the foundations of FENIkS for the automatic UI design evaluation that further allows generating automatic feedback. It explains FENIkS' design: the meta-model and how design options, design principles and types of feedback are used to automatically generate feedback. The perceived usability was positive evaluated. The results of the experimental evaluation demonstrated that FENIkS improves students' understanding of design principles.

Keywords: Automated feedback · User Interface design · Presentation model · Model-driven engineering · User interface generation

1 Introduction

Software applications are highly used in everyday life. The importance of User Interfaces (UI), as the means that allows the interaction between the end user and the application [1], has increased. As a consequence, there is a need to evaluate usability, defined by ISO 9241–11 as the degree to which a system can be used by specified users to achieve specified goals with effectivity, efficiency and satisfaction in a given context of use. Evaluation methods and technology that supports UI design are also required.

The design of UIs is a complex process that ideally results in a usable and useful interactive system. The difficulties are associated to its interdisciplinary nature, the need for designing for several contexts of use and for understanding a wide range of approaches.

© Springer Nature Switzerland AG 2022
H.-G. Fill et al. (Eds.): ICSOFT 2021, CCIS 1622, pp. 67–93, 2022.
https://doi.org/10.1007/978-3-031-11513-4_4

The complexity brings difficulties for the usability evaluation that also requires time, effort and experts. Therefore, any degree of automation brings benefits.

Novel UI designers need guidance through the learning process of UI design including the usability evaluation of the UIs. To improve their design skills, they require a large amount of practice and clues about their efforts. Feedback has proved its value to improve knowledge and skill acquisition [2].

In general, providing individual feedback is a complex and time-consuming task and requires a fair amount of expertise. Providing feedback for UI design is particularly challenging because of its inherent complexity. Giving personal feedback is even more complex and time consuming, especially when a student addresses a difficult exercise. The fact that the student can address a problem through many valid solutions calls for individual feedback. Technology can be used to provide more frequent and immediate feedback [3]. There are a few approaches to support the learning of UI design [4–6], although without providing for automated feedback.

In order to cope with the need for providing feedback for UI design, and, at the same time, automatic usability evaluation, we proposed Feedback ENriched user Interface Simulation (FENIkS). FENIkS is a UI design simulation tool able to automatically provide instant feedback to the students about how they apply UI design principles.

This paper extends previous work [7] by describing the foundations of FENIkS by presenting a Systematic Literature Review (SLR) on automatic usability evaluation to select the most appropriate techniques to build FENIkS. We also present an analysis of UI design principles to make a selection of those used for the automatic usability evaluation and for the generation of feedback. This paper also presents more details about the experimental evaluation. The remainder of this paper is as follows: Sect. 2 examines the related work on automated feedback and UI design teaching support. Section 3 presents the selection of techniques for the automatic usability evaluation. Section 4 describes FENIkS. Section 5 presents the evaluation and Sect. 6 concludes the paper.

2   Related Work

This section analyzes the approaches related to our work from four perspectives: automated feedback generation for learning support, teaching support for UI design, feedback to non-usability experts at design time and pattern-driven approaches.

Automated Feedback for Learning Support. There is a growing body of knowledge on automated feedback. In [8] the authors reviewed 109 papers on automated feedback. While they were able to derive a general framework (TAF-ClaF), generally speaking, the approaches are as diverse as the learning topics that are supported by automated feedback. In terms of the TAF-ClaF dimensions, our aim is to develop expert-driven and task-adaptive automated feedback using both expert-knowledge on UI design best practices and student answers. Students will have access to the feedback on request. The feedback is both corrective and suggestive as the student will receive additional information besides the correctness of their choices.

Teaching Support for UI Design. The authors of [6] propose a hypertext module called UID tutorial. This UID tutorial presents good and bad examples, i.e. UI that are compliant with design principles or not. The author of [5] propose an approach with examples to give recommendations about which media is appropriate for different cases. An example of a game is proposed by [4] to support the teaching of usability engineering life cycle, prototyping and heuristic evaluation. This game shows examples of web interfaces, where the student needs to select which heuristics are applied.

Feedback to Non-usability Experts at Design Time. The authors of [9] propose an approach to elicit usability requirements at early stages of the software development process providing feedback to non-experts. This approach provides the non-usability experts with interface design and usability guidelines through questions that need be asked to the end-user. Usability requirements are obtained from the answers.

Pattern-driven Approaches. Patterns transmit experience about recurrent problems, while making expert knowledge explicit to novices. In [10] there is an approach with examples of abstract UI patterns. It can be seen as a form of feedback that documents problems and the corresponding solutions. OO-Method [11] uses patterns in a presentation model to capture user's preferences, in a similar way to our approach.

The approach presented in this paper differs from prior works in several ways. The approaches that support the generation of automated feedback for learning support are very diverse, and thus not always fit for UI design. Those approaches that support UI design by providing example-based help do not provide feedback related to a real design, something possible in FENIkS. The most significant difference is, therefore that FENIkS allows testing the compliancy of UI design principles in an actual UI that is designed by the student through the specification of domain and presentation models.

3   Techniques for the Automatic UI Design Evaluation

To select the foundations for the automatic UI design evaluation we focus on usability evaluation. Subsection 3.1 presents a SLR on automatic usability evaluation. Subsection 3.2 presents the selection of design principles to be further incorporated in FENIkS.

3.1   Automatic Usability Evaluation

We performed an SLR to determine relevant works in the field of automatic usability UI evaluation, following the guidelines proposed by Kitchenham and Charters [12]. The guidelines propose three phases: planning, conducting and reporting.
Planning the SLR. The main research questions that need to be answered are:

- RQ1: Which general techniques are used in the automatic usability evaluation?
- RQ2: Which usability techniques are used in the automatic evaluation?
- RQ3: What automation level is achieved by the researchers?
- RQ4: What kind of UI are evaluated?

We performed our search on the Scopus database, one of the largest databases of the peer reviewed literature covering all important publishers such as ACM, IEEE, Springer, Elsevier and many more. We identified key words from the research questions. A traditional search was performed that allowed determining the most appropriate search terms. The terms were validated by two experts in the field. The final search string used was: TITLE-ABS-KEY ((automatic) AND usability AND (evaluation OR study OR experiment)) AND (LIMIT-TO (SUBJAREA, "COMP") OR LIMIT-TO (SUBJAREA, "ENGI")). To assess the quality of the query, we checked that the studies we already knew to be relevant (such as [13, 14]) appeared in the results.

Reporting the SLR. The query resulted in a collection of 418 papers dating from 2009 to 2019. The inclusion and exclusion criteria should allow the identification of existing literature reviews on usability evaluation, methods, techniques, tools used for the automatic evaluation of UIs. The inclusion and exclusion criteria were as follows (Table 1):

Table 1. Inclusion and exclusion criteria.

Inclusion criteria	Exclusion criteria
Papers presenting a literature review on usability evaluation	Papers analyzing methods, techniques or tools in an initial development phase
Papers describing a method for usability evaluation	Papers analyzing methods, techniques or tools for the non-automatic usability evaluation
Papers describing a technique for usability evaluation	Proceedings
Papers describing a tool for usability evaluation	Papers presenting works to improve the usability
Unique paper	Duplicated paper

We analyzed the 418 papers: we discarded 373 papers, 45 papers were retained. Table 2 shows the details of the papers discarded according to the exclusion criteria.

Table 2. Number of discarded papers according to the exclusion criteria.

Criteria	Amount
Non-automatic usability evaluation	262
To improve the usability but not for usability evaluation	62
Proceeding	39
Initial development phase	8
Duplicated paper	2
Total	**373**

The SLR was focused on the evolution of usability evaluation. Even when several authors publish many papers about usability, very few focus on automatic evaluation: 262 papers investigate usability evaluation without any level of automation. The average per year of papers investigating non-automatic evaluation is 26.2 papers, while the average for automatic evaluation is 4.09: a maximum of 6 papers in 2009, 2017 and 2018.

In order to answer the research questions we analyzed every paper in detail. The full list of papers and their classification can be found here: https://zenodo.org/record/557 8029.

We analyzed the information to answer RQ1: *Which general techniques are used in the automatic usability evaluation?* Not all 45 papers propose general techniques for automatic usability evaluation. Figure 1 shows the breakdown for the relevant papers. Next, we describe a selection of the approaches to illustrate the used techniques.

A model-based technique is used the most. In [14], the authors propose a tool based on PALADIN models. It defines a common notation to describe the interaction in several multi-modal contexts, comparing usability of the different systems. In [15], the authors propose a solution to monitor the interaction between the users and the systems based on a continuous, real-time usability evaluation. The tool registers the user's activities using Petri nets. Usability deviations are detected assuming a task model previously defined to be compared with the user's activities. In [16], the authors propose the necessary requirement for the usability formalisms in model-based approaches based on specification of structured UI. The authors of [17] propose a predictive usability evaluation with an approach that uses usability metrics. The metrics are the key to predict the usability and can be adapted to task, user and conceptual models.

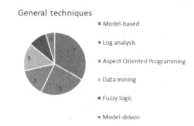

Fig. 1. General techniques used in the automatic usability evaluation.

The authors of [18, 19] use log analysis to make a remote usability evaluation from a daily behavior analysis of the registered users. The tools identify potential usability issues, for example in web applications [18]. The tool proposed by [19] also allows adding new behaviors to be analyzed that were not included in the original set.

In [20] opinion mining is proposed as an automatic technique to evaluate usability. The model obtains knowledge from the user opinions to improve the usability. In [13], there is a methodology to build tools. The authors train a set of classifiers to extract usability problems and compare them with those found with heuristic evaluation.

Aspect oriented programing has been used for usability evaluation. The authors of [21] propose the tool AJMU to evaluate user tasks on desktop applications In [22], the authors describe the development of a tool that can be dynamically configured to capture specific events. This kind of approach helps to the non-programmers in the automatic usability evaluation process without modifying the software.

Fuzzy logic is used by [23, 24]. In [23] there is a combination of automatic usability evaluation with manual evaluation to calculate measures, e.g. the structural complexity of web sites. Using these results the authors propose a fuzzy model to evaluate the usability. In [24] a tool evaluates complex interactive systems based on fuzzy logic.

Model-driven engineering is only used by [25]. The authors propose to reduce the quality fails detected from the evaluation of quality attributes evaluation. This approach uses a requirement meta-model. The approach is focused on the extension of conceptual models used by web engineering methodologies to consider the usability requirements.

Regarding RQ2: *Which usability techniques are used in the automatic evaluation?,* usability guidelines are more used (11), followed by user testing (8), usability metrics (5), heuristics (4), and patterns (4). The next paragraph illustrates the different approaches by means a few selected papers.

A first example of automatic evaluation via guidelines is A4U [26], which analyzes results from usability tests. It allows human evaluation and includes results of semi-automatic guideline-based evaluation. MAUVE evaluates web application usability [27] by specifying and updating guidelines to be validated. In [28] the authors use Web page analyzer and GTMetrix that use guidelines for didactic applications. MenuErgo [29] allows the automatic evaluation of menu bars for graphical UI using guidelines. In [30] there is a tool for the automatic evaluation of interactive web systems. The tool is based on web services using a set of guidelines to evaluate graphic controls. The authors of [31] evaluate the guidelines and make annotations to indicate how they have been applied for web applications for blind users.

The approach proposed by [32] combines the use of guidelines with usability test for automatic evaluation. These authors present an approach that defines strategies of generic tests to evaluate the usability guidelines. To that end, they extend the language PBGT's PARADIGM with test usability patterns. It is possible to build test models from usability tests that can be generated and executed automatically in a web site.

The authors of [28] combine user testing with automated tools for the evaluation of web applications, while in [13] user testing and heuristics are combined with data mining. In [33], the authors propose an automatic evaluation plugin to detect defects related to the quality of mobile user interface. This plugin allows the measurement of several usability metrics to predict the quality of interfaces from the usability perspective.

The automation level was analyzed on every found approach in order to answer RQ3: *What automation level is achieved by the researchers?* In this case, we found that the majority of the analyzed works (40 works) achieve full automation in the evaluation, while only 5 works report semi-automatic usability evaluation.

Finally, the last RQ4: *What kind of UI are evaluated?* was analyzed. The majority of the analyzed works evaluates the usability of UI for web applications (21), followed by UI for mobile (3), desktop (3), devices applications (3) and multi-modal (2). There are less approaches that evaluate usability of multimedia applications, user manual, multi-agent systems, adaptive UI, advance human machine interface, and biometric recognition applications with only one work. Some works propose approaches to evaluate more than one kind of UI. There are 8 works that evaluate UIs in general.

Identified Challenges. There is an evolution in the automatic usability evaluation. Some challenges identified by [34], for example the lack of quantitative data and subjective information, have been tackled by [20]: it uses data mining to extract knowledge from user opinions. Another challenge was the combination of heuristics with automatic usability evaluation. This has been tackled with artificial intelligence by [35].

There are potential uses for automatic usability evaluation that should be further explored such as the simulation of the interaction: there is an initial work in [17]. The use of MDE should be further explored, only used by [25]. This kind of approaches provides several benefits where the creation of models as primary artifacts that allow describing the UI in an abstract way. Then it allows obtaining specific implementations through model transformations, facilitating the interoperability between systems.

Considering the results of previous approaches proposed in the analyzed literature, we propose an approach which combines the techniques most used in the literature for the automatic usability evaluation with model-driven engineering. Model-based is the general technique most used for automatic usability evaluation. In previous work we analyzed how, in UI design, model-based approaches are evolving to model-driven approaches [36]. We propose to integrate a model-driven approach with usability guideline validation, which is the usability technique most used with good results.

In order to build the proposed approach, we identified which usability guidelines could be used in an automatic usability evaluation for a didactic approach. The next subsection identifies first the UI design principles, then the associated guidelines.

3.2 UI Design Principles for the Automatic Usability Evaluation

A proper UI should be designed in a way that satisfies the users' needs, capabilities and limitations [37]. The study of the human interaction with computers has led to the generalization of some design principles that help to design usable UIs. These principles allow guiding the software design, with a positive effect on usability [38].

Due to the fact that UI design principles are high level concepts and beliefs and there is a need for a concrete way to apply them, the authors also used guidelines associated to the principles. As presented in the previous section, the use of guidelines is the most used technique for the automatic usability evaluation. This section analyzes the UI design principles and guidelines to be incorporated in the tool proposed in this paper.

To be able to incorporate design principles in an automatic way by means of MDE transformations it is necessary to select principles that can be translated into testable rules. Training in design involves learning about principles [39], but the wide variety of design principles can make it very difficult for novel designers to understand where their focus should be. Therefore, we focused on a core set of UI design principles.

In previous work [40] we made an analysis of the definition of design principles. We looked for authors that propose UI design principles [41, 42] in the literature to select the most important principles. We found 41 authors of design principles from a set of 475 papers. We extracted 16 authors that are cited at least twice in the set of found papers. We analyzed their three most cited works. This allowed us extracting 257 principles that included variations of the same principle. We unified the variants (principles similar by name, by concept, etc.), and, considering their scientific influence (their citation number in the literature), we derived a set of 36 design principles.

While citation number gives an idea of the impact a work has, there is still a need for evidence of the use of the design principles. Empirical validation plays an important role by providing evidence of the use in reality. The authors of [43] proposed ergonomic criteria (some of them divided into sub-criteria) to define dimensions of usability that can be matched to design principles. Ergonomic criteria can also be helpful for UI teaching purposes. According to [44], Bastien and Scapin's ergonomic criteria have an impact on their use to elicit usability problems, and are objectively applicable by designers, while benefiting the novices more than experts. The proposed criteria were empirically validated for reliability [45] and their effectiveness for UI evaluation [46].

Ergonomic criteria are dimensions of usability that encompass heuristics and principles. As [47] explains, "usability guidelines are often indistinguishable from design principles, but they must be formulated in a way so as to be testable". The level of how trustable a guideline is, is not equal [48]. It can be related to the validation by experimental results to the associated principles or heuristics. We use examples of associated guidelines to the matching between principles, ergonomic criteria and guidelines.

Some of the principles could be directly matched to ergonomic criteria or sub-criteria (11), while others could be matched to guidelines (7) that were presented alongside the ergonomic criteria. Out of the total, 18 could not be matched. Table 3 presents the matching of the principles to the ergonomic criteria in the validation proposed by [43].

Table 3. Design principles with their corresponding ergonomic criteria.

Principle	Ergonomic criteria	Guideline
Offer informative feedback	Guidance: Immediate feedback	
Strive for consistency	Consistency	
Prevent errors	Error management: error protection	
Minimize user's memory load	Workload	
Simple and natural dialog	Compatibility	Dialogues should reflect data structures that correspond to their mental models
Provide good error messages	Error management: quality of error messages	
Allow users to use the keyboard or mouse	Adaptability: user experience	Allow experienced users to by-pass a series of menu selections with equivalent shortcuts
Speak the user's language	Compatibility	Labels, prompts, and guidance messages should be familiar to users and task-oriented

(continued)

Table 3. (*continued*)

Principle	Ergonomic criteria	Guideline
	Significance of codes	
Help and documentation	Guidance: prompting	Provide on-line help, guidance
Make things visible	Guidance: grouping/distinction of items. Grouping/distinction by format	
Actions should be reversible	Explicit control: explicit user action	Provide a cancel option with to erase any changes
Give the user control	Explicit control: user control	
Help users recognize, diagnose, recover from errors	Error management: error correction	
Flexibility and efficiency of use	Adaptability: flexibility	
Structure the user's interface	Guidance: grouping/distinction of items + Grouping/distinction by location	
Allow users to change focus	Explicit control: user control	Users should have the control over the screen pages
Allow users to customize the interface	Adaptability: flexibility	Provide means to control display configuration
		Provide means to change the data entry sequence to respect user preferred sequence
Provide visual cues	Guidance: prompting	

Each guideline should be assigned to one ergonomic criteria. As the abstraction level of the analyzed principles is not always the same, in some cases an ergonomic criterion is matched to more than one principle but at a different level. For the principles matched to an ergonomic criterion, the associated guidelines are considered subsumed by it.

We note that some principles can be incorporated in an MDE tool with a manageable amount of effort while for other principles this would require a lot of effort, for demanding the implementation of difficult techniques. We studied several guidelines per principle and analyzed how many could be implemented. The more guidelines can be implemented, the easier we consider its implementation. Table 4 shows the list of principles and their level of implementation difficulty (Easy: E, Medium: M, Hard: H).

Table 4. Design principles and implementation difficulty.

Design principle	E	M	H
Total:	8	4	6
Prevent errors	X		
Provide good error messages	X		
Allow users to use the keyboard or mouse	X		
Provide visual cues	X		
Offer informative feedback	X		
Strive for consistency	X		
Make things visible	X		
Structure the user's interface	X		
Actions should be reversible		X	
Help users recognize and recover from errors		X	
Allow users to change focus		X	
Help and documentation		X	
Minimize user's memory load			X
Simple and natural dialog			X
Give the user control			X
Speak the user's language			X
Flexibility and efficiency of use			X
Allow users to customize the interface			X

In this first version we implemented feedback for the easiest to implement principles: *Prevent errors, Provide good error messages, Allow users to use the keyboard or mouse, Provide visual cues, Offer informative feedback, Strive for consistency, Make things visible* and *Structure the UI*.

4 FENIkS

FENIkS is an extended version of JMermaid: a tool for teaching conceptual modeling, based on MERODE. MERODE is an MDE method that allows the specification of an enterprise system from a conceptual domain model. The model is platform independent and sufficiently complete for the automatic generation of the system's code from it. The generated prototype is enriched with didactic feedback supporting the learning of conceptual modeling, the effectiveness of which has been proven [49].

JMermaid was extended with FENIkS to support the learning process of UI design including the usability evaluation of the UIs, for novel UI designers. FENIkS focuses on the learning of UI design principles for the functional aspects of graphical UIs. FENIkS incorporates two extra models: the Abstract User Interface (AUI) model (describes the UI in a technology-agnostic way) and the presentation model (captures the characteristics of the UI layout and components and the user preferences [50]). Subsection 4.1 describes the models. Subsection 4.2 presents how the feedback provided by FENIkS was conceived. Subsection 4.3 presents details of the implementation.

4.1 Models

FENIkS is a UI design simulation tool, based on model-driven engineering. This kind of approaches are capable of generating UIs (semi) automatically from models of different abstraction levels. This section presents the models of FENIkS.

Conceptual Domain Model. MERODE uses a conceptual domain model for the definition of the classes of objects in an enterprise. In UI design a domain model describes the classes of objects manipulated by a user while interacting with a system. FENIkS merged those two definitions to improve the generation of a fully functional prototype.

The conceptual model of MERODE is composed of a class diagram, an object event table, and finite state machines that allow capturing the enterprise object behavior. The domain classes including structure (attributes) and behavior (methods) are described by the class diagram. This diagram also describes the associations between the classes. The object event table indicates which business events create, update or delete objects. When an event affects objects of a certain type, this gives –accordingly- rise to create, modify or end methods in the corresponding class. This information is captured in a table associating object types and event types. The life cycle of objects of a given class is specified by the finite state machine. There is a correspondence between the events triggering the transitions in the finite state machine and those that are represented in the object event table [51]. With the supporting tool is possible to model different views of the system. The consistency of the three views is managed: all the specifications that can be derived from one view to other are automatically generated by the tool.

Presentation Model. In UI design a presentation model is used to specify the UI by describing "the constructs that can appear on an end user's display, their layout characteristics, and the visual dependencies among them" [52]. The presentation model has a static part and a dynamic part. The static part describes the design of the UI as a composition of standard widgets like buttons, menu, etc. The dynamic part displays application dependent data that typically changes at run-time.

In some approaches the presentation model is mainly used as abstract or concrete UI model. Others, like OO-Method [11], use the presentation model to capture the user preferences by means of patterns. A presentation model allows personalizing the UI using user preferences. The presentation model of FENIkS is in line with this last definition. FENIkS' presentation model captures code generation options that define how the generated prototype will show the information and how the interaction will be.

With JMermaid it was only possible to generate a default UI composed of a window showing a list of instances of a single domain class, a window to view the details of one object and a default input window to trigger the execution of a business event. FENIkS allows defining the UI of these default services and allows defining extra output services (or reports) to show information the user wants to see. An example of extra output services is combining data from many domain objects.

Windows and input aspects are defined by the presentation meta-model of FENIkS [53]. The additional output services are captured through the meta-object type Report and the associated meta-object types. A Report is composed of a selection of object types that need to be shown and a selection of their attributes and associations.

The definition of the dynamic aspects of the reports requires relevant parts of the MERODE meta-model related to the presentation meta-model. Rather than showing all objects, attributes and association, for each report it can be defined which objects, attributes and associations need to be presented to the user in the report. The presentation model retrieve the required information from the class diagram.

The preferences related to how elements of the UI should be configured are captured by the meta-classes 'Window aspect' and 'Input aspect'. 'Window aspects' capture the preferences related to the static layout of the top level containers of the generated prototype and how the information is displayed. Some examples are: how the pagination will be, if there will be shortcuts for interacting with the system. The preferences for input services are captured by 'Input aspect'. These preferences are related to the way users will input the information into the generated prototype. Examples are what kind of widgets are needed for inputting the information, how the validation of the inputs will be performed (or not) and what kind of error messages will be shown.

Abstract User Interface Model. AUI models are important due to the fact that software applications can be accessed by users from a huge variety of contexts of use [54]. The AUI model defines the UI independent from modality, user interaction or platform. In FENIkS, the AUI model is generated from the presentation and domain models.

The fact that the AUI represents the UI without considering any modality of interaction or platform is important to help designers in understanding the main principles behind the generation of the UI. An AUI for a default UI can be obtained by means of a model to model transformation from the conceptual model of MERODE. Figure 2 shows the process for obtaining the final UI for just one context of use.

To keep the scope of the research manageable this research considers the target platform for which code will be generated as the only dimension of the context of use. The other context aspects not considered have been grayed out in Fig. 2. Future translation for other contexts of use are possible thanks to the use of an AUI model.

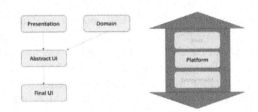

Fig. 2. Models used in FENIkS for one context of use [7].

FENIkS' AUI meta-model is based on the AUI meta-model of the User Interface eXtensible Markup Language (UsiXML), proposed by [54]. FENIkS uses concepts of the

MERODE domain model (for the default output and input services) and the presentation model (for the reports), to generate the AUI model. The AUI meta-model is linked to the relevant concepts of the MERODE meta-model [55].

Capturing the preferences for the UI generation in a single place, the presentation meta-model, allows FENIkS applying the chosen options in a consistent way through the UI. The student mandatorily has to define the Window and Input aspects. For each of these aspects the student can set a number of options. Some of the options are at the abstract level and other are at the concrete level. The abstract level features are used to generate the AUI model. The concrete level features are used to generate the final UI.

4.2 FENIkS Feedback

The UI is designed by setting a number of options in the presentation model. The student receives feedback while setting the options in the presentation model and in the generated prototype. Next we describe the design and implementation of the feedback.

UI Design Principles for Feedback. FENIkS supports UI design based on the set of UI design principles presented in Subsect. 3.2: *Prevent errors, Provide good error messages, Allow users to use the keyboard or mouse, Provide visual cues, Offer informative feedback, Strive for consistency, Make things visible* and *Structure the UI.*

The use of MDE makes possible that certain principles are automatically applied. In FENIkS a number of principles were chosen to be taken care of by the UI designer by choosing the right UI design options: 'to actively observe' principles. Other principles were chosen to be automatically supported: 'observed by default' principles.

FENIkS provides corrective feedback about compliance with these two categories of principles. There are four 'to actively observe' principles, whose compliance is influenced by the designer's choices in the presentation model. Depending on the chosen options, the principles are well applied or violated in the generated prototype. Three additional principles are 'observed by default' in FENIkS. The feedback explains the reasons why they are well applied. Table 5 shows the selected UI design principles and the way they are applied in the generation process.

Table 5. UI design principles applied in the generation process.

Principle	'To actively observe'	'Observed by default'
Prevent errors	X	X
Provide good error messages	X	X
Allow users to use either keyboard or mouse	X	
Provide visual cues	X	X
Offer informative feedback		X
Strive for consistency		X
Make things visible		X
Structure the UI		X

For the principles that need to be actively observed the designer selects the options as defined by Windows and Input aspects. Each principle can have one or many options with correct or incorrect values. If the designer selects a correct value for an option this implies that the generated UI will be compliant with the guidelines of the associated principle. If the designer selects an incorrect value the principle will be violated. For a better understanding, Table 6 shows the principles, options and associated values.

Table 6. Design principles and associated features [7].

Principle	Option	Correct value	Incorrect value
Prevent errors	Validate boolean data	True (Compliant)	False (Not compliant)
	Validate integer data	True (Compliant)	False (Not compliant)
	Validate empty data	True (Compliant)	False (Not compliant)
	Generate components by the attribute data type	True (Components are generated according to attribute data type)	False (All the components are generated as input text boxes)
Provide good error messages	Errors according to the type of error	True (Messages generated according to the type of error)	False (Generic message generated without specifying the type of error)
Allow users to use the keyboard or mouse	Generate shortcuts for methods	True (Shortcuts for the methods are generated)	False (Impossible to access to the methods through the keyboard)
	Generate shortcuts for tabs	True (Shortcuts for the tabs are generated)	False (It is not possible to Access to the tabs through the keyboard)
	Generate shortcuts for general menu	True (Shortcuts for the general menu are generated)	False (No access to the general menu through the keyboard)
Provide visual cues	Format data type information	True (The format of the data type is shown next to the attribute)	False (Only the name of the attribute is shown)
	Attribute data type information	True (Data type information of the attribute shown next to its name)	False (Only the name of the attribute is shown)

Most of the features of the Window and Input aspects have been included for educational purposes: they are used to show the learner how to apply design principles and generate the UI accordingly. An example in the 'Window aspects' is 'Generate shortcuts for tabs'. An example in the 'Input aspects' is 'Validate Empty data'. Other features have been included to give flexibility to the prototype generation process. Examples of such features are mainly in the 'Window aspects': 'Table pagination', 'Empty table', etc.

Designing the Feedback. The authors of [56] propose a framework to conceptualize the factors that need to be taken into account when automating feedback. FENIkS' feedback features are based on this framework. The feedback in FENIkS includes factors associated to the design and for automatically creating and delivering the feedback.

At the general level there are six most important factors for building the feedback: 1) Content Design, to represent the relevant factors for automatically designing the feedback content; 2) Delivery, to describe the relevant factors for automatically delivering feedback; 3) Context, the contextual aspects to consider for automatic feedback; 4) Usage, to describe the possible usages of feedback; 5) Impact: to express the factors that can be measured or observed to determine the impact of automated feedback and 6) Technique: the techniques, algorithms, etc. used or implemented for automating feedback [56]. The factors can be further broken down in several aspects.

The most important factors of the feedback provided by FENIkS are shown in Table 7. The goal of FENIkS is to improve the learning of UI design principles. Therefore, its feedback is oriented to help the student's in order to accomplish this goal.

Table 7. Applying the framework to FENIkS [7].

Factor	Aspect	FENIkS feedback
Content	Purpose	Corrective, explanatory, formative
	Level	Task-level
	Nature	Possitive and negative
	Domain	User Interface design principles
Delivery	Format	Textual and visual
	Timing	Anytime on demand to the student
	Learner control	Taken by the student
Context	Recipient	Individual learner
	Device	Desktop
	Learning task	Simple and complex tasks
	Educational setting	University
Usage		Check if the learning is on track
Impact		Measured by student's scores
Technique		Template-based MDE technique for the derivation of feedback from defined constraints about the compliancy of design principles showing the specific details of the error or the correct solution

The purpose of the feedback is corrective and explanatory: it provides knowledge about the correct response related to the application of the design principles. The feedback is formative: it informs the compliancy of the design principles with guidelines to improve the answers, or reinforce the correct answers. It is possible to revise the design while performing the learning task, allowing to change them and receiving new feedback. The feedback is provided at task-level, addresses how well tasks are understood, performed or applied. This feedback focuses on faults in the interpretation of design principles.

For a principle with feedback generation options FENIkS explains if all the guideline constraints have been satisfied or not and why. The principle is considered well applied if all the options associated to the principle have the correct value. If at least one guideline constraint is not satisfied, the principle is considered violated.

The chosen format is textual (factor delivery), with messages embedded in FENIkS. It is also visual when showing the generated UI and while interacting with the generated prototype. With regard to the timing the student can check it anytime. The level of learner control is taken by the student who decides when and where to see the feedback.

The recipient of the feedback is an individual learner (context factor). The used device is a desktop computer. The feedback is provided for simple and complex learning tasks. The educational setting is at university level. There are different possible usages for the feedback: it can be used for motivation purposes; for verifying learning progress, etc. The feedback helps the learner to check if the learning is on track and improve it. We chose to measure the impact factor by means of student's scores.

FENIkS builds the feedback with a template-based model-driven development technique according to two types of feedback to explain: 1) whether the design choices are compliant with design principles or not and why; and 2) why the UI is generated in a specific way tracing the application's appearance back to the presentation model [53]. The FENIkS feedback meta-model is shown in Fig. 3.

The main meta-class FeedbackModel is composed of two meta-classes that correspond to the two types of feedback FENIkS provides: for the compliancy of the design

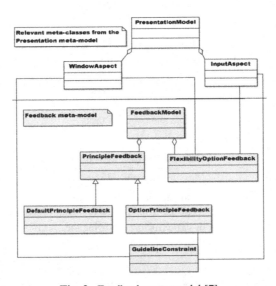

Fig. 3. Feedback meta-model [7].

principles (didactic purposes features) and for the options to give flexibility (flexibility features). The DefaultPrincipleFeedback meta-class represents the provided feedback about the principles automatically applied by default. The OptionPrincipleFeedback meta-class expresses the feedback is provided according to how the design principles have been correctly applied or not. To deliver this feedback it is necessary to check the constraints associated to the options of each principle (captured by Window or Input aspects) in the presentation model. The upper part of the figure includes the relevant meta-classes of the presentation meta-model, and shows how the GuidelineConstraints link InputApects to OptionPrincipleFeedback. The features related to the Window and Input aspects which give flexibility are used to build the FlexibilityOptionFeedback.

Example of FENIkS' Use. This section presents an example of the FENIkS' use. Figure 4 shows the class diagram of a student's grade system where teachers teach classes of certain subject. Students are enrolled in those subjects and obtain grades for each of them. Several grades can be obtained as the student is allowed at least two attempts, the best of which counts as final grade.

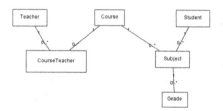

Fig. 4. Student's grade system class [7].

The UI designer elaborates the presentation model based on the diagram. The tab corresponding to the 'Input aspect' of the presentation model is shown in Fig. 5.

A UI Help option is included in the main menu of the generated prototype where the UI designer can check the UI feedback. In the first part of the help, the designer can see the preferences captured by the Window and Input aspects and the feedback given for the flexibility options. This feedback allows selecting the options and seeing why the UI is generated in certain way. The designer sees a preview of how the prototype will be generated according to the selected options. Before the generation the designer can also check the feedback on whether the UI design principles are satisfied by the options.

Presentation Model
Dialog to edit values of the Presentation Model

| General | Window Aspects | Input Aspects | Reports |

Show attribute type: ☐
Show format: ☑
Generate components by the attribute types: ☑
Way to show master: Table ▼
Validate boolean: ☑
Validate integer: ☐
Validate empty data: ☐
Error messages according to the type of error: ☑

Preview:

Object: Method
Attribute 1: ##-##-###-###
Attribute 2: ☐
Attribute 3: 0
Associated object

ID	Attribute 1	state	final	more...
0	Value 1	exists	false	view details
1	Value 1	ended	true	view details

Method   Cancel

Ok   Cancel

Fig. 5. Input aspects of the presentation model [7].

A second type of feedback about compliance with the UI principles is included in the UI Help. An example of this feedback is shown in Fig. 6. This feedback is split in two parts to show: 1) the principles the generated prototype is compliant with and the principles the generated prototype violates and 2) the principles the generated prototype implements by default. The rationale for (non-) compliance is always given.

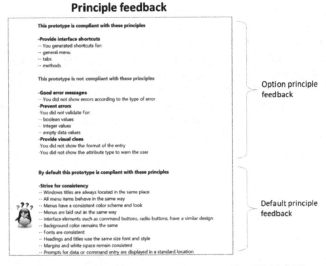

Fig. 6. Different types of feedback generated by FENIkS [7].

4.3 Implementation

As shown in Fig. 7, the transformation engine constitutes the heart of FENIkS. Using the conceptual domain and presentation models a transformation to the AUI model is executed. Then, transformation to the UI and application code are executed. Mapping rules define how to transform the domain model into the AUI model. This step combines the coding templates with the conceptual, presentation and AUI models, and generates the prototype. The code generator uses Java and Velocity Templates Engine.

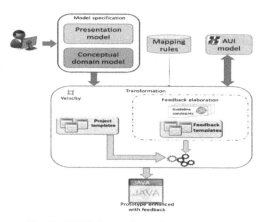

Fig. 7. FENIkS transformation process [7].

There are two kinds of templates: project templates for generating the application code and feedback templates to generate the feedback. The feedback messages are generated in the prototype using two templates. For the feedback associated to the compliancy of the design principles, the feedback shows the details of the error (why the principle is violated), or the correct solution. The other type of feedback shows the chosen preferences for the presentation model, what the consequences are for the generated prototype and how the preferences can be changed in the Window or Input aspects.

FENIkS extension has been implemented over a period of two years of non-fulltime work. Table 8 shows measures of volume of code. It required incorporating new classes to JMermaid and modifying existing classes. The modified classes are not shown.

Table 8. Measures of the implementation [7].

Project	Lines of code	Comment lines	Number of classes
JMermaid	44085	509	572
With FENIkS	50117	568	607
Code generator	10618	1458	35
Templates	27781	353	26

Principles are generally expressed at a high level of abstraction. Each principle needed to be translated into a more concrete form. We matched some principles and their guidelines to options for code generation while others to guidelines applied by default.

Table 9 reports on the complexity of the principles. To calculate the complexity we counted the number of guidelines applied by means of design options and those applied by default. A weight of 1 was given for each guideline with options. A weight of .5 was given for each guideline applied by default. The total complexity is the sum of the effort of implementing the guidelines (guidelines with options +.5*(guidelines by default)).

Table 9. Complexity of implemented principles [7].

Principle	'To actively observe'	'Observed by default'	Complexity
Prevent errors	4	2	5
Good error messages	1	4	3
Allow users to use the keyboard or mouse	3	0	3
Provide visual cues	2	2	3
Structure the UI		1	1
Strive for consistency		6	3
Offer informative feedback		1	1
Make things visible		2	1

5   Evaluation

This section presents the description of the performed evaluation of the FENIkS approach. Then discusses the limitations of the experimental evaluation.

5.1   Experimental Evaluation

During the first semester of the academic year 2015–2016 we performed a pilot usability experiment to assess FENIkS. Then, a full experiment was conducted during the second semester of the academic year 2016–2017. Table 10 shows details of both experiments.

The pilot experiment evaluated the perceived usability of FENIkS by 12 novel developers with no prior knowledge about the tool. We used the Computer System Usability Questionnaire [57]. The tool was perceived positively: the users believe FENIkS improves their design work and facilitates the creation of the presentation model. The quality of the information, the interface and the utility was well perceived as well [50].

A quasi-experiment was executed at the University of Holguin with 34 students of the Informatics Engineering program, 4th year. The goal was to assess the benefits of the feedback generated by FENIkS about design principles during a UI design course.

Table 10. Sequence of the experiments.

Experiment	Pilot usability CSUQ	Full experiment crossover design
Academic year	2015–2016	2016–2017
Participants	12 novice developers	34 students, 4th year, Informatics Engineering program
Details	Performed a set of tasks in FENIkS and filled CSUQ	UI design course - Lessons - Teach FENIkS - Randomized crossover design

The experiment used a crossover design. The dependent variable was the learning of design principles while the treatment consisted of creating a UI with FENIkS (starting with an already developed conceptual model). During the course, the students received lectures about UI design principles and learned how to use FENIkS. Then, in the same day, they completed Exercises A/B. Both exercises had the same goal: answering questions about specific choices in UI design, and whether these are in line with principles or not. Following the crossover design, students were randomly assigned to Group 1 or Group 2. Group 1 first made Exercise A without using FENIkS and then Exercise B with FENIkS, while Group 2 made first Exercise A with FENIkS and Exercise B without FENIkS [58]. Both tests were composed of equivalent sets of true/false questions about the design principles. The students were asked to motivate the answers.

The results of a paired t-test to determine if the support given by FENIkS was effective is shown in Table 11. The results shows a significant improvement for the scores obtained by the students when using FENIkS support, with 95% confidence interval. The results provide evidence that FENIkS is effective in helping the students understanding design principles. See [58] for the full experiment.

Table 11. Paired T-test for means of scores [7].

$\overline{X}$ score without	$\overline{X}$ score with	$\overline{X}$ difference	p-value
24.06	26.85	−2.79	.000

After the previous evaluation we assessed the perceived usefulness of FENIkS. Perceived usefulness is an important factor for contributing to user acceptance for computer-assisted learning environments [59]. In this research, we used a questionnaire composed of 15 items. The questionnaire collects information about the perceived usefulness of FENIkS for learning the application of design principles as a way to evaluate the usability of UIs. The items have 7-point Likert scales, anchored at the endpoints with the terms "Strongly disagree" for 1 and "Strongly agree" for 7. We assessed the reliability and validity of the acceptance measures using Cronbach's alpha (.93) and factor analysis, which indicated a high level of internal consistency for our scale.

At the end of the experiment presented in the previous section we asked the students to fill out the questionnaire. The results from the questionnaire used to collect the user acceptance are presented in Table 12.

Table 12. Questionnaire to measure perceived usefulness: items and scores.

Question statement	Mean	Std. dev	Mode
Using the prototype improves my understanding of UI principles	5.79	1.15	7
Using the prototype makes me understand UI principles much faster	5.70	1.09	6
Using the prototype improves my understanding of the relations between the conceptual model and the generated prototype components	5.64	1.04	6
Using the prototype makes me understand the relations between the conceptual model and the generated prototype much faster	5.21	1.25	6
Using the prototype improves my interpretation of usability results from the generated prototype	5.09	1.24	5
Using the prototype makes me interpret usability results from the generated prototype much faster	5.18	1.31	5
Previewing the UI facilitated the creation of the presentation model	5.09	1.33	5
Previewing the UI showed me the effects of the chosen options on the final UI, before UI generation	5.48	1.33	7
Previewing the UI helped me to decide better about design options	5.30	1.22	5
Previewing the UI allowed me to visualize how the generated UI will look like and assessing the result	5.21	1.34	6
Previewing the UI facilitated performing a "what-if" analysis	5.15	1.35	6
If had the choice, or opportunity I would use this tool to learn UI design principles	5.48	1.18	6
If I had to vote, I would vote in favor of using prototyping in the classroom	5.33	1.22	6
I am enthusiastic about using the prototyping in this kind of courses	5.33	1.22	6
Using the prototype was a positive experience	6.06	1.18	7

The scores per item rank well above 5 on 6, indicating a positive evaluation. The highest mean values were obtained for items 1 and 15: the students agree that using FENIkS was a positive experience and that it improves their understanding of UI principles. The lowest mean was obtained for items 5 and 7, although still high values. The mode represents what the majority of the participants score in of the participants in the test. The mode of only four items was 5, while for all the other items the mode was 6 or

7. After analyzing the results of the questionnaire it can be noticed that the proposed simulation method is suitable for novice UI designers.

5.2 Discussion

The experimental evaluation has some validity threats. Regarding to the internal validity we can say that a control group is not included. We took into account the psychological risk present in classroom studies where the students may worry about whether their participation or non-participation in the experiment will affect their grade. In this kind of experiment there is the risk of denying half of the group access to a tool that might improve their learning with is also impossible/unethical. In line with the ethical considerations, in this research we conducted a quasi-experiment instead of a classic experiment. To mitigate the problems we used a crossover design with two groups. The students did not receive feedback after completing the tests to avoid a maturation effect.

The validity of the results is limited to the course we described. However, the experiment's external validity improved by making the subject population similar to the target population: in this study, novice designers. We performed a power analysis on our experimental design parameters. The sample size was adequate to identify significant improvement on the learning of design principles, with a large effect size in the performed tests in general and a statistical power of 0.99 for the entire group.

6 Conclusions

This paper has presented FENIkS, a feedback enriched UI simulation MDE tool for improving the learning of UI design. With FENIkS is possible to define the conceptual and presentation models. These models are used for the generation of an AUI model and further used to generate a full working prototype, with the UI code integrated.

FENIkS combines the techniques most used in the literature for the automatic usability evaluation with the challenge of using MDE. In order to build FENIkS it was necessary to identify which usability principles and corresponding guidelines could be used in an automatic usability evaluation for a didactic approach. FENIkS supports the UI design process based on the following principles which have been empirically validated and can be translated into testable rules: *Prevent errors, Provide good error messages, Allow users to use the keyboard or mouse, Provide visual cues, Offer informative feedback, Strive for consistency, Make things visible* and *Structure the UI.*

FENIkS incorporates a feedback technique to assist novice UI designers during the learning of UI design. This paper presents the design of FENIkS' feedback. The used technique allows generating automatic feedback about UI design. The feedback can be seen while elaborating the models. The feedback explains if the options in the presentation model ensures compliancy with design principles. FENIkS incorporates a preview to simulate how the UI will be generated. This preview allows checking the consequences of the selected options in the presentation model. The feedback is also incorporated in the generated prototype. The feedback automation technique uses template-based code generation. It incorporates visual and textual feedback and helps understanding how the design principles have been applied and what the consequences are.

We performed an experimental evaluation with students. The results of the experiment prove FENIkS' effectiveness and improves their understanding of UI design principles. The tool was evaluated for its perceived usability and positively perceived by novice developers. We assessed the perceived usefulness of FENIkS for learning the application of design principles as a way to evaluate the usability of UIs novice UI designers by means of a questionnaire. After analyzing the results it can be noticed that the proposed simulation method is suitable for novice UI designers.

Besides applying usability principles, the proposed technique could be extended to other areas, such as programming or requirements engineering. A similar approach for other areas could be based on best practices reflecting either good or bad application of those best practices. Concrete and testable rules per practice should be formulated. The work we presented can be expanded to further develop the UI generation by:

- Incorporating more design options and new design principles to the presentation model to improve flexibility. This would allow providing new feedback.
- Specifying a user model: A user model is not taken into account in this version. It would allow enhancing the support for UI design in a way that novice learners can check the consequences of choices according to user's characteristics.
- Allowing the generation of UIs for other contexts of use: Currently, FENIkS generates a prototype for one context of use. The fact that FENIkS relies on MDE and already incorporates an AUI model it is possible to develop future versions for other contexts of use and new feedback can be generated for that.

References

1. Akiki, P.A., Bandara, A.K., Yu, Y.: Adaptive model-driven user interface development systems. ACM Comput. Surv. **47**(1), 2015. https://doi.org/10.1145/2597999
2. Shute, V.J.: Focus on formative feedback. Rev. Educ. Res. **78**(1), 153–189 (2008). https://doi.org/10.3102/0034654307313795
3. Merrill, M.D.: First principles of instruction. Educ. Technol. Res. Dev. **50**(3), 43–59 (2002). https://doi.org/10.1007/BF02505024
4. Benitti, F.B.V., Sommariva, L.: Evaluation of a game used to teach usability to undergraduate students in computer science. J. Usability Stud. **11**(1), 21–39 (2015)
5. Sutcliffe, A.G., Kurniawan, S., Shin, J.-E.: A method and advisor tool for multimedia user interface design. Int. J. Hum. Comput. Stud. **64**(4), 375–392 (2006). https://doi.org/10.1016/j.ijhcs.2005.08.016
6. Barrett, M.L.: A hypertext module for teaching user interface design. ACM SIGCSE Bull. **25**(1), 107–111 (1993). https://doi.org/10.1145/169073.169359
7. Ruiz, J., Snoeck, M.: Automatic feedback generation for supporting user interface design. In: 16th International Conference on Software Technologies (2021). https://doi.org/10.5220/0010513400230033
8. Deeva, G., Bogdanova, D., Serral, E., Snoeck, M., De Weerdt, J.: A review of automated feedback systems for learners: Classification framework, challenges and opportunities. Comput. Educ. **162**, 104094 (2021). https://doi.org/10.1016/j.compedu.2020.104094

9. Ormeño, Y.I., Panach, J.I., Condori-Fernández, N., Pastor, Ó.: A proposal to elicit usability requirements within a model-driven development environment. Int. J. Inf. Syst. Model. Des. **5**(4), 1–21 (2014)
10. Molina, P.J., Meliá, S., Pastor, O.: User interface conceptual patterns. In: Forbrig, P., Limbourg, Q., Vanderdonckt, J., Urban, B. (eds.) DSV-IS 2002. LNCS, vol. 2545, pp. 159–172. Springer, Heidelberg (2002). https://doi.org/10.1007/3-540-36235-5_12
11. Pastor, O., Molina, J.C.: Model-driven architecture in practice. In: A Software Production Environment Based on Conceptual Modeling, Springer, Berlin (2007). https://doi.org/10.1007/978-3-540-71868-0
12. Kitchenham, B., Charters, S.: Guidelines for performing systematic literature reviews in software engineering (2007)
13. Hedegaard, S., Simonsen, J.G.: Mining until it hurts: automatic extraction of usability issues from online reviews compared to traditional usability evaluation. In: Proceedings of the 8th Nordic Conference on Human-Computer Interaction: Fun, Fast, Foundational, pp. 157–166 (2014). https://doi.org/10.1145/2639189.2639211
14. Mateo Navarro, P.L., Hillmann, S., Möller, S., Sevilla Ruiz, D., Martínez Pérez, G.: Run-time model based framework for automatic evaluation of multimodal interfaces. J. Multimodal User Interfaces **8**(4), 399–427 (2014). https://doi.org/10.1007/s12193-014-0170-3
15. Jarraya, M., Moussa, F.: Proxy oriented approach for evaluating usability of a resilient life-critical interactive systems. In: 2018 IEEE 32nd International Conference on Advanced Information Networking and Applications (AINA), pp. 464–471 (2018). https://doi.org/10.1109/AINA.2018.00075
16. Kristoffersen, S.: A preliminary experiment of checking usability principles with formal methods. In: 2009 Second International Conferences on Advances in Computer-Human Interactions, pp. 261–270 (2009). https://doi.org/10.1109/ACHI.2009.26
17. de Oliveira, K.M., Lepreux, S., Kolski, C., Seffah, A.: Predictive usability evaluation: aligning HCI and software engineering practices. In: Proceedings of the 26th Conference on l'Interaction Homme-Machine, pp. 177–182 (2014). https://doi.org/10.1145/2670444.2670467
18. Santana, L.T.E., Pansanato, G.A.: Identifying usability problems in web applications through analysis of user interaction logs using pattern recognition. In: Proceedings of the IADIS International Conference WWW/Internet 2011, ICWI 2011, pp. 587–590 (2011).
19. Paternò, A., Schiavone, F., Conte, A.G.: Customizable automatic detection of bad usability smells in mobile accessed web applications. In: 19th International Conference on Human-Computer Interaction with Mobile Devices and Services, MobileHCI 2017 (2017). https://doi.org/10.1145/3098279.3098558
20. El-Halees, A.M.: Software usability evaluation using opinion mining. J. Softw. **9**(2), 343–350 (2014). https://doi.org/10.4304/jsw.9.2.343-349
21. Casas, S., Trejo, N., Farias, R.: AJMU: an aspect-oriented framework for evaluating the usability of wimp applications. J. Softw. Eng. **10**, 1–15 (2016). https://doi.org/10.3923/jse.2016.1.15
22. Shekh, S., Tyerman, S.: Developing a dynamic usability evaluation framework using an aspect-oriented approach. In: ENASE, pp. 203–214 (2009)
23. Chaudhary, N., Sangwan, O.P.: Multi criteria based fuzzy model for website evaluation. In: 2015 2nd International Conference on Computing for Sustainable Global Development (INDIACom), pp. 1798–1802 (2015)
24. Kallel, I., Jouili, M., Ezzedine, H.: HMI fuzzy assessment of complex systems usability. In: Abraham, A., Muhuri, P.K., Muda, A.K., Gandhi, N. (eds.) ISDA 2017. AISC, vol. 736, pp. 630–639. Springer, Cham (2018). https://doi.org/10.1007/978-3-319-76348-4_61

25. Molina, F., Toval, A.: Integrating usability requirements that can be evaluated in design time into model driven engineering of web information systems. Adv. Eng. Softw. **40**(12), 1306–1317 (2009). https://doi.org/10.1016/j.advengsoft.2009.01.018
26. do Amaral, L.A., de Mattos Fortes, R.P., Bittar, T.J.: A4U-an approach to evaluation considering accessibility and usability guidelines. In: Proceedings of the 24th Brazilian Symposium on Multimedia and the Web, pp. 295–298 (2018). https://doi.org/10.1145/3243082.3264666
27. Schiavone, A.G., Paternò, F.: An extensible environment for guideline-based accessibility evaluation of dynamic web applications. Univ. Access Inf. Soc. **14**(1), 111–132 (2015). https://doi.org/10.1007/s10209-014-0399-3
28. Benaida, A., Namoun, M.: Technical and perceived usability issues in Arabic educational websites. Int. J. Adv. Comput. Sci. Appl. **9**(5), 391–400 (2018). https://doi.org/10.14569/IJACSA.2018.090551
29. Khaddam, D., Bouzit, I., Calvary, S., Chêne, G.: MenuErgo: computer-aided design of menus by automated guideline review. In: IHM 2016 - Actes de la 28ieme Conference Francophone sur l'Interaction Homme-Machine, pp. 36–47 (2016). https://doi.org/10.1145/3004107.3004130
30. Dhouib, H.B., Trabelsi, A., Abdallah, A.: EiserWebs: an evaluation tool for interactive systems based on web services. In: 4th International Conference on Information and Communication Technology and Accessibility, ICTA 2013 (2013). https://doi.org/10.1109/ICTA.2013.6815297
31. Vigo, F., Leporini, M., Paternò, B.: Enriching web information scent for blind users. In: ASSETS'09 - Proceedings of the 11th International ACM SIGACCESS Conference on Computers and Accessibility, pp. 123–130 (2009). https://doi.org/10.1145/1639642.1639665
32. Dias, A.C.R., Paiva, F.: Pattern-based usability testing. In: 10th IEEE International Conference on Software Testing, Verification and Validation Workshops, ICSTW 2017, pp. 366–371 (2017). https://doi.org/10.1109/ICSTW.2017.65
33. Soui, M., Chouchane, M., Gasmi, I., Mkaouer, M.W.: PLAIN: PLugin for predicting the usAbility of mobile user INterface. In: VISIGRAPP (1: GRAPP), pp. 127–136 (2017)
34. Ivory, M.Y., Hearst, M.A.: The state of the art in automating usability evaluation of user interfaces. ACM Comput. Surv. **33**(4), 470–516 (2001). https://doi.org/10.1145/503112.503114
35. Ponce, A., Balderas, P., Peffer, D., Molina, T.: Deep learning for automatic usability evaluations based on images: a case study of the usability heuristics of thermostats. Energy Build. **2**(162), 111–120 (2018). https://doi.org/10.1016/j.enbuild.2017.12.043
36. Ruiz, J., Serral, E., Snoeck, M.: Evaluating user interface generation approaches: model-based versus model-driven development. Softw. Syst. Model. **18**(4), 2753–2776 (2018). https://doi.org/10.1007/s10270-018-0698-x
37. Galitz, W.O.: The Essential Guide to User Interface Design: an Introduction to GUI Design Principles and Techniques. Wiley, Hoboken (2007)
38. Folmer, E., Bosch, J.: Architecting for usability: a survey. J. Syst. Softw. **70**(1–2), 61–78 (2004). https://doi.org/10.1016/S0164-1212(02)00159-0
39. Kimball, M.A.: Visual design principles: an empirical study of design lore. J. Tech. Writ. Commun. **43**(1), 3–41 (2013). https://doi.org/10.2190/TW.43.1.b
40. Ruiz, J., Serral, E., Snoeck, M.: Unifying functional user interface design principles. Int. J. Human-Computer Interact. (2020). https://doi.org/10.1080/10447318.2020.1805876
41. Nielsen, J.: Enhancing the explanatory power of usability heuristics. In: Conference on Human Factors in Computing Systems, pp. 152–158 (1994). https://doi.org/10.1145/191666.191729
42. Shneiderman, B., Plaisant, C.: Designing the User Interface: Strategies for Effective Human-Computer Interaction, 5th ed. Pearson Addison-Wesley, Boston (2009)
43. Bastien, J.M.C., Scapin, D.L.: Ergonomic criteria for the evaluation of human-computer interfaces. Inria (1993)

44. Law, E.L.-C., Hvannberg, E.T.: Analysis of strategies for improving and estimating the effectiveness of heuristic evaluation. In: Proceedings of the third Nordic conference on Human-computer interaction, pp. 241–250 (2004). https://doi.org/10.1145/1028014.1028051

45. Bastien, J.M.C., Scapin, D.L.: A validation of ergonomic criteria for the evaluation of human-computer interfaces. Int. J. Human-Comput. Interact. **4**(2), 183–196 (1992). https://doi.org/10.1080/10447319209526035

46. Scapin, D.L., Bastien, J.M.C.: Ergonomic criteria for evaluating the ergonomic quality of interactive systems. Behav. Inf. Technol. **16**(4–5), 220–231 (1997). https://doi.org/10.1080/014492997119806

47. R. M. Baecker, Readings in Human-Computer Interaction: Toward the Year 2000. Morgan Kaufmann, San Francisco (2014)

48. Mariage, C., Vanderdonckt, J., Pribeanu, C.: State of the art of web usability guidelines. In: The Handbook of Human Factors in Web Design (2005)

49. Sedrakyan, G., Snoeck, M.: Feedback-enabled MDA-prototyping effects on modeling knowledge. In: et al. Enterprise, Business-Process and Information Systems Modeling. BPMDS EMMSAD 2013 2013. Lecture Notes in Business Information Processing, vol 147, pp. 411–425. Springer, Berlin (2013). https://doi.org/10.1007/978-3-642-38484-4_29

50. Ruiz, J., Serral, E., Snoeck, M.: UI-GEAR: User interface generation prEview capable to adapt in real-time. In: Modelsward, pp. 277–284 (2017). https://doi.org/10.5220/0006115402770284

51. Snoeck, M.: Enterprise Information Systems Engineering: The MERODE Approach. Springer, New York (2014). https://doi.org/10.1007/978-3-319-10145-3

52. Schlungbaum, E.: Model-based user interface software tools current state of declarative models. Georgia Institute of Technology (1996)

53. Ruiz, J., Serral, E., Snoeck, M.: Technology enhanced support for learning interactive software systems. In: Hammoudi, S., Pires, L., Selic, B. (eds.) Model-Driven Engineering and Software Development. MODELSWARD 2018. Communications in Computer and Information Science, vol. 991, pp. 185–210. Springer, Cham (2019). https://doi.org/10.1007/978-3-030-11030-7_9

54. Limbourg, Q., Vanderdonckt, J., Michotte, B., Bouillon, L., Florins, M.: USIXML: a user interface description language supporting multiple levels of independence. In: ICWE Workshops, pp. 325–338 (2004)

55. Ruiz, J., Sedrakyan, G., Snoeck, M.: Generating user interface from conceptual, presentation and user models with JMermaid in a learning approach. In: Interaction 2015 (2015). https://doi.org/10.1145/2829875.2829893

56. Serral Asensio, E., Ruiz, J., Elen, J., Snoeck, M.: Conceptualizing the domain of automated feedback for learners. In: Proceedings of the XXII Iberoamerican Conference on Software Engineering, CIbSE 2019 (2019)

57. Lewis, J.R.: IBM computer usability satisfaction questionnaires: psychometric evaluation and instructions for use, Boca Raton (1993)

58. Ruiz, J., Serral, E., Snoeck, M.: Learning UI functional design principles through simulation with feedback. IEEE Trans. Learn. Technol. **13**(4), 833–846 (2020). https://doi.org/10.1109/TLT.2020.3028596

59. Poelmans, S., Wessa, P.: A constructivist approach in an e-learning environment for statistics: a students' evaluation. Interact. Learn. Environ. **23**(3), 385–401 (2015)

Tales from the Code #2: A Detailed Assessment of Code Refactoring's Impact on Energy Consumption

Zakaria Ournani[1,2,3], Romain Rouvoy[2,3], Pierre Rust[1], and Joel Penhoat[1(✉)]

[1] Orange Labs, Rennes, France
{pierre.rust,joel.penhoat}@orange.com
[2] INRIA Lille Nord-Europe, Lille, France
{zakaria.ournani,romain.rouvoy}@inria.fr
[3] University of Lille, Lille, France

Abstract. Energy consumption has been a prominent question in the last decade that concerns both hardware and software dimensions. Source code refactoring is a widespread activity among developers that includes a set of well-known changes to improve the code quality without impacting the functional aspects. Hence, the concern of the impact that may those changes induce on the software energy consumption is legitimate, in order to identify whether and which refactorings have a significant impact on the evolution of the energy consumption. In particular, while the state of the art investigated the impact of some specific code refactorings on dedicated benchmarks, we miss an assessment that those apply to more comprehensive and complex software.

To address this threat, this paper studies the evolution of the energy consumption of 7 open-source software developed for more than 5 years. Then, by focusing on the impact on energy consumption of changes involving code refactorings, we intend to assess the effects induced by computational code refactorings. For all these software systems we studied, our empirical results report that the code refactorings we mined do not substantially impact energy consumption. Interestingly, these results highlight that *i)* structural code refactorings bring energy-preserving changes to the code, and *ii)* major energy variations seem to be related to computational code refactorings and/or functional changes.

Keywords: Software energy consumption · Code refactoring · Energy consumption evolution

1 Introduction

Software energy consumption has gained a substantial significance in the last decade, both for research and industrial contexts [5, 10, 27, 29, 34]. Hence, many researchers and practitioners started caring about the energy efficiency of software, beyond performance and hardware concerns [6, 19, 20, 26]. Being integrated into mobile or cloud environments, software systems are trying to minimize their resource consumption to reduce battery consumption or operational cost. Source code refactoring is one of the most

H.-G. Fill et al. (Eds.): ICSOFT 2021, CCIS 1622, pp. 94–116, 2022.
https://doi.org/10.1007/978-3-031-11513-4_5

famous and used software development techniques. It can be described as the application of acknowledged rules to improve one or many aspects of a software system, such as its clarity, maintenance, code smells, without impacting its functional behavior [2, 14].

Yet, code refactoring have also been considered as a mean to improve the performance and/or energy efficiency in a more or less automated way [3,4,6,7,12,21] Most of the works that investigated the impact of code refactoring on energy consumption [3,12,18,25] based their studies on predefined set of refactoring rules, design patterns, or code smells.

While this process may deliver interesting insights on the impact of specific code refactorings on the energy consumption of a code snippet, there is still no guarantee that the identified code refactorings are frequently applied during the lifespan of a software system. Some refactorings could be very advantageous but are rarely applied which limits their impact on the energy efficiency of the software. Moreover, most of these works [22] reported on a very small impact (usually less tan 5%) and concluded on the significance of those refactoring. However, this is not always valid, especially for server-side/desktop applications where jobs' energy consumption may significantly vary (more than %10) even on the same node/device [23].

In this paper, we extend our previous study [24] that explores an alternative way to study the impact of code refactorings on the energy efficiency of legacy software systems. We focus on acknowledged refactoring rules mostly issued from Martin Fowler's book [11], which are mostly structure-oriented rules (such as Extract Method) dealing with code architecture and organization for server-side applications. Instead of selecting a set of code refactorings *a priori* and evaluate them against some dedicated benchmarks, we extract these code refactorings from established open-source projects. More specifically, we mine the history of code refactorings that have been applied to these projects in the past, and we measure the impact of the commits that include acknowledged code refactorings on the overall energy consumption. This approach aims to detect the code refactorings that have been broadly applied, and their observable impact on energy efficiency in practice. By doing so, we believe that mined code refactorings are most likely to reflect an effective impact of code refactoring on energy consumption, compared to the study of a fixed set of refactoring candidates. Moreover, we investigate the total evolution of these legacy software systems' energy consumption to deduce the impact of structural code refactoring on this evolution. We also asses the impact of some than implementation and computation refactoring (such as Substitue Algorithm) to conclude on the impact of code refactoring on software energy consumption. This study, therefore, aims to answer the following research questions:

RQ 1: How do structural code refactorings contribute to the evolution of software energy consumption?

RQ 2: How does the energy consumption of software evolve over time?

The remainder of this paper is organized as follows. Section 2 introduces the experimental protocol (hardware, projects, tools, and methodology) we adopted in this study. Section 3 analyzes several experiments we conducted to mine the code refactorings and evaluate their impact on the energy consumption, as well as the results we observed during these experiments. Section 5 discusses the related work about source code refactoring contributions to reduce software energy consumption. Finally, Sect. 6 cover our conclusions.

2 Experimental Protocol

This section introduces our detailed experimental environment, including the hardware configuration, the studied projects/benchmarks and a detailed description of our experimental methodology.

2.1 Hardware Environment

We used during our experiments a Core i7 machine (i7-6600U CPU @ 2.60 GHz) with a total of 4 processing units to measure the energy consumption and an installed 18.04.4 LTS Ubuntu, with a 4.15.0-88-generic Linux kernel. We also used OPENJDK, version 1.8.0_242, to run most of our Java experiments except for the OkHttp project where we had to use OPENJDK, version 11.0.6. The execution environment has been configured according to guidelines [23] to mitigate the energy consumption variation and report on robust and accurate measurements, especially to measure small differences in energy consumption.

2.2 Projects Under Study

The main criterion of this study was to select well-known projects with a decent commit history, that have been existing for years, and with an active community. The study exclusively focuses on Java projects in order to unify the experimental protocol with no ambiguities due to languages/paradigms differences. The choice of the datasets also aimed at covering a large spectrum of features and operations such as: JSON and XML conversions, HTTP client, graph processing, data collections, etc. The advantage of choosing these projects is also related to them having an overall stable interface in which the main functionalities of the projects are non-ambiguously identified, so we can run our Longitudinal measurements across the many versions and releases.

Table 1 describes the projects that we considered for this study, including commits count and creation date. We note that all the projects we selected have been hosted on GitHub since at least 2015. The Git creation date only gives an overview of how long has the project been on GitHub and is different from the project creation date. Some projects, such as Gson, exists on GitHub since March 2015, but we still can checkout commits from 2003.

2.3 Methodology and Tools

Our experimental methodology is a process that includes extraction, evaluation, and validation steps. Figure 2 depicts the main steps we followed during our analysis. We start our process by cloning the public repository of the project from GitHub. Then, for

Table 1. List of selected open-source projects [24].

Project	Description	#commits	1st commit
OkHttp	Java HTTP client	4,684	05-2011
JGraphT	Graph objects and algorithms provider	3,158	07-2003
XStream	XML $\leftrightarrow$ Java objects serialization	2,736	10-2003
JFlex	Java lexical analyzer generator	1,741	02-2003
Gson	JSON $\leftrightarrow$ Java objects serialization	1,485	08-2008
Eclipse-Collections	Eclipse Java collections	1,374	12-2015
Google-Http	Google HTTP client library for Java	868	05-2011

each commit, we mine the code refactorings of the project using the REFACTORING-MINER. REFACTORINGMINER is an open-source tool [32,33] that analyses a project commit by commit and extracts the type and count of refactorings for each commit in a JSON format. The tool is capable of detecting up to 55 different types of refactoring in its version 2.0 (the later version by the time this study was conducted) used in this study.[1]

Once we extract the code refactorings that have been applied per commit on the master branch, we select the commits to be reproduced to measure their energy consumption. The selection method takes into account the refactorings count and types in each commit. We consider commits with at least 20 refactorings so we can expect a significant impact of the refactorings on the energy consumption. Figure 1 depicts the *cumulative distribution function* (CDF) that shows the frequency of commits per refactorings count (commits with more than 200 refactorings have been omitted for clarity). One can see that 20% of the commits have more than 20 refactorings on most of the studied projects, which constitutes a decent amount of commits on which code refactorings can be evaluated. The commits containing exclusively one type of refactoring are very rare. Thus, we will also consider commits containing different types of code refactoring even if it is not trivial to divide the recorded differences that we may record in our evaluation on the code refactorings.

The next step is to rebuild the project *Java archive* (JAR) for each of the previously selected commits in order to run them and measure the energy consumption before and after code refactoring. To be able to run and evaluate the compiled JAR, we need to provide a task to execute for each project. Unfortunately, we couldn't trust running the tests provided within each project. The reason behind this is that projects do substantially change and evolve from a commit to another, including the provided tests. Evaluating commits based on those tests might include/exclude functionalities that appear/disappear between commits, which does not constitute a fair comparison criterion. To remedy to this problem, we wrote our own JMH benchmarks "*Java Microbenchmark Harness for building, running, and analyzing nano/micro/milli/macro benchmarks written in Java and other languages targeting the JVM*".[2] for each project.

---

[1] https://github.com/tsantalis/RefactoringMiner.
[2] https://openjdk.java.net/projects/code-tools/jmh/.

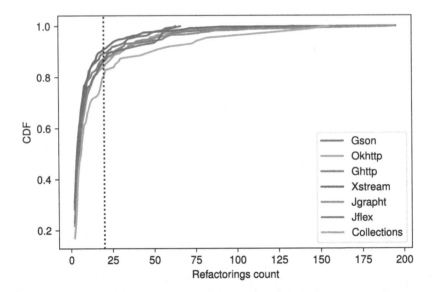

Fig. 1. CDF of code refactorings per commit [24].

Using JMH for writing benchmarks has many advantages, such as the easy management of run and warm-up iterations, and the prevention of dead code removal from the JIT using the concept of *blackhole* [30]. The purpose of each benchmark is to stress the main functionality of each project to ensure the same measurement conditions for all commits. Hence, through JMH benchmarking, we can deliver—for each project— experiments to compare the energy consumption of commits, while testing the main functionalities of the project. The main test functionality for **Gson** and **XStream** is JSON and XML to Java objects serialization and deserialization, respectively. For both **OkHttp** and **Google-Http** projects, we consider the core HTTP verbs (GET, POST, DELETE) with a local server to eliminate any network bias. For **JGraphT**, we consider the operations of graph creation, shortest path computation, max-flow computation, and discarding random edges. We also tested **JFlex** with lexical analyzer generation, and **Eclipse-Collections** with the core operations on the different mutable and immutable collections (lists, maps, sets), inspired from [27,31].

Once the JMH benchmark was written , we compute the coverage of the project by the benchmark using Jacoco (https://www.eclemma.org/jacoco). The purpose is not to cover all of the project classes and methods but only to test the main functionality of the project. Thus, only the commits with refactoring on the classes and methods that constitute the main functionality we are testing are considered for the evaluation. Of course, this operation requires applying additional checks to ensure that the changes of the commit x *are limited to the extracted refactorings and nothing else susceptible to affect the performance or the energy consumption*. Hence, this step ensures that the selected commits only contains refactoring that are being stressed by our benchmark.

The next step is to run the benchmarks for each of the JAR files compiled from relevant commits. To highlight the effect that code refactorings may have on energy consumption, we build and run the commit x that includes the code refactorings, but also the commit $x-1$ on the main branch, so we can compare the energy consumption and infer the impact of refactorings.

The percentage of reproduced commits, which designates the ratio of successfully built and ran commits in regards to the total count of selected commits (Gson: 95%, XStream: 80%, OkHttp V3 & V4: 90%, Google-Http: 15%, JGraphT: 25%, JFlex: 40%, Eclipse-Collections: 50%). Most of the unsuccessful projects' rebuilds are due to deprecated and invalid references.

During the execution of the experiments, we use Intel RAPL to report on the global energy consumption of CPU and DRAM consumption [8, 15]. We thus evaluate the energy consumption of every commit x and we compare it to its $x-1$ commit. We run every JMH benchmark for multiple iterations on a fixed amount of time (enough time to run the benchmark at least once), and we extract between 100 and 1,000 energy measurements depending on the duration of each iteration. The reason why we consider the energy consumption of iterations rather than the whole benchmark is to have an accurate estimation of the energy consumption of the execution rather than a fixed execution time that could represent a variable amount of iterations.

Then, we use the bootstrap method [9] to randomly build 100 subsets from the main set of measurements, and we compute the mean and standard deviation of these subsets. We end-up with 100 measures of averages and we use the median of these values for better accuracy and less bias.

The checked results are then used to build global statistics of the most efficient refactoring rules across the selected commits of all projects. We also pay special attention to the commits of each project that exhibit the most energy difference, when exceeding a threshold of 5%. This threshold is computed from the minimum CPU energy consumption variation and the computed standard deviation of the experiments [23].

This additional checks of those commits consists of applying a more detailed automatic and manual `git diff` analysis on the results of the previous step (using the code coverage that we computed earlier for the main functionalities) to understand every single occurrence of the detected refactorings and project the results and that there is no other changes that may affect the energy efficiency. Another check consists of an extra micro-benchmarking phase, where we prepare and execute the extracted refactorings to confirm and validate the effect they could have on the energy efficiency of the project/software. We also applied the Wilcoxon rank sum test (or Student test when possible) to check the statistical significance of the registered difference in the energy consumption between the commit x and the commit $x-1$, with a null hypothesis of the energy consumption of the commit x and $x-1$ being equal with a 5% certainty. During our experiments, we were careful not to fall in the benchmarking crimes described in [16], so we can conduct robust and reproducible experiments and evaluations with a focus on energy consumption.

Most of our experimental setup is made available on GitHub, including all the used JMH Benchmarks, JSON extraction results, micro-benchmarks, CSV of measurements, scripts, etc.[3]

---

[3] https://anonymous.4open.science/r/c3d38dca-1ab2-4814-ba07-b182120c5739.

3   Refactoring Impact Analysis

In this section, we aim at answering our research questions with a clear conclusion on whether refactoring has a substantial impact on the evolution of software energy consumption over time. We, therefore, conducted a set of experiments and validations to investigate the effect of structural refactoring on the evolution of software energy consumption.

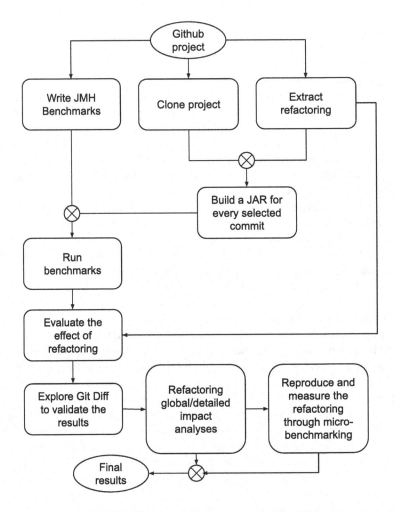

Fig. 2. Methodology of refactoring analysis [24].

4 Refactoring Rules Impact

To dive into the effective impact that code refactoring may have on software energy consumption, we further tracked and analyzed the evolution of the energy consumption on commits where code refactorings were detected. Thus, in our study, we consider the full commit history of 7 open-source projects, and we analyze the impact on energy consumption of commits including code refactorings, as described in Sect. 2.

Once we select commits with code refactorings and rebuild them, we run the JMH benchmarks that have been prepared for each project to compare the energy consumption of a commit x that came with the refactorings and the previous commit x−1 of the master branch.

Then, we report on global statistics from the raw measurements we obtained from each project, thus establishing a summary of the most used code refactorings and their impact.

Global Code Refactoring Statistics. The purpose of this step is to highlight the most used/impactful code refactorings. While it is easy to identify the most used code refactorings by counting the number of occurrences of each refactoring rule and the commits they appear in, there is no consensus on how to measure the effective impact of code refactorings on energy consumption, if any. The large majority of commits comes with a set of code refactorings of many types, and even if these refactorings can impact the energy consumption, there is no trivial way to isolate such an impact for each type of refactoring. Thus, we consider 3 indicators to capture the energy impact of refactoring. The first indicator, *Impact in Commits* (IC), is the ratio between the number of commits where the refactoring had a positive or negative impact—*i.e.*, the commit x containing this refactoring consume more or less energy than the previous commit x−1—and the total number of commits containing this refactoring. Equation 1 therefore computes IC for a rule $r \in R$ by exploring all the commit history C of a given project:

$$\text{IC}(r) = \frac{\sum_{c \in C} count\_positive\_negative(c, r)}{\sum_{c \in C} count(c, r)} \tag{1}$$

This indicator can be then enhanced by taking into account the occurrences—or weights—of each refactoring rule in a commit. In other words, considering the refactoring weight consists of using the number of occurrences of each refactoring type within a commit rather than only counting the commit as 1 if it contains at least a refactoring.

$$\text{WIC}(r) = \frac{\sum_{c \in C} count\_positive\_negative(c, w_r)}{\sum_{c \in C} count(c, w_r)} \tag{2}$$

Nevertheless, this indicator is not enough to evaluate the energy impact of refactoring. Indeed, including the weight of refactorings in commits supposes that all refactorings impact energy consumption equally, which may not be true, as we assume that the occurrence of a refactoring r_1 can have a bigger impact than many occurrences of a refactoring r_2.

The 2nd and 3rd indicators are $\delta\%$ and $\delta|\%|$ that indicate the mean of the energy consumption of every commit x containing the refactoring minus the energy consumption of commits x-1, and the mean of the absolute value of the energy consumption of every commit x containing the refactoring minus the energy consumption of commits x-1, respectively, $\|C_r\|$ being the commits in the commit history C where refactoring r occurred.

$$\delta\%(r) = \frac{\sum_{x=1}^{C_r}(E_x - E_{x-1})}{\|C_r\|} \tag{3}$$

$$\delta|\%|(r) = \frac{\sum_{x=1}^{C_r}|E_x - E_{x-1}|}{\|C_r\|} \tag{4}$$

where E_x and E_{x-1} represent the mean energy consumption of the commit x that includes at least the refactoring r, and the energy consumption of the commit x-1, respectively. These indicators are complementary to reflect the impact of the code refactorings on the energy consumption. Therefore, we consider an aggregate indicator that combines the previous indicators to capture the energy impact of refactorings across commits. This indicator, named *Refactoring Impact* (RI) builds on the previous indicators: the higher WIC and $\delta|\%|$, the most impactful the refactoring r is. However, if the difference $\delta|\%|-\delta\%$ is high, it means that the refactoring r has an unpredictable effect on the energy consumption and may affect the energy consumption positively or negatively. This is a negative effect and could mean that the refactoring does not have any impact at all. On the other hand, the more commits we have with the refactoring r, the more certain we are of the effect that it could have. Thus, we use the exponential function in Eq. 5 so the denominator cannot be null.

$$\text{RI}(r) = \frac{\text{WIC}(r) \times \delta|\%|(r)}{e^{\delta|\%|(r) - \delta\%(r)}} \times \|C_r\| \tag{5}$$

Table 2 shows the computed indicators for a total of 25 mined refactoring rules. We note that the commits that could not be reproduced and those where the refactorings are parts of classes that are not tested by our benchmark have already been discarded and not displayed in Table 2. Before analyzing the results we excluded all the code refactorings with a low number of occurrences and/or commits (less than 20 CountxCommits). For example, code refactorings that occurred only a couple of times and/or only in one or two commits cannot be faithfully studied due to insufficient data. Then, we highlight (in Cyan) the refactoring rules that have the best values for the previous indicators, which are very likely the refactorings with the most impact on energy consumption. The 4 refactoring rules with the most number of occurrences and commits, with a minimal IC of 30%, are "add method annotation", "rename parameter", "add class annotation", and "move class". These refactoring rules are also those that exhibit the highest RI, and thus, are most likely to be the most impactful on energy consumption. However, we still have to assess that these refactoring rules have an effective impact on the evolution of energy consumption. Thus, we conducted a more detailed study on the commits with the highest impact to validate the effect of code refactorings on energy consumption.

Table 2. The observed impact of mined refactoring rules [24].

Refactoring	Count	CountxCommits	IC	WIC	$\delta\%(r)$	$\delta|\%|(r)$	RI
add method annotation	10120	80960	30.77%	43.41%	1.13%	2.14%	7.34
change variable type	101	606	16.67%	14.95%	0.24%	1.32%	1.17
rename parameter	45	180	33.33%	71.69%	−0.07%	1.82%	5.12
change parameter type	42	168	11.76%	17.07%	−0.03%	1.20%	0.81
change attribute type	26	130	16.67%	9.39%	0.12%	1.35%	0.63
add class annotation	63	216	33.33%	63.53%	1.30%	2.20%	2.77
move class	40	120	30.00%	54.28%	0.77%	2.21%	3.55
change return type	28	112	14.81%	19.93%	0.14%	1.11%	0.88
move method	33	99	21.43%	19.10%	0.59%	1.76%	1.00
rename variable	21	84	25.00%	18.24%	0.46%	1.44%	1.04
move attribute	18	54	25.00%	18.81%	−0.07%	1.92%	1.06
extract method	37	37	20.00%	71.87%	0.08%	1.24%	0.88
pull up method	32	32	33.33%	38.90%	0.03%	1.97%	0.75
rename class	6	24	25.00%	13.71%	1.14%	1.51%	0.82
add attribute annotation	8	16	20.00%	15.12%	0.64%	1.14%	0.34
rename attribute	5	15	30.00%	8.77%	0.55%	1.62%	0.42
add parameter	6	12	16.67%	6.55%	0.82%	1.47%	0.19
merge parameter	6	6	100.00%	100.00%	6.00%	6.00%	6.00
extract class	2	4	33.33%	11.14%	0.72%	2.62%	0.57
extract variable	3	3	11.11%	10.52%	0.49%	0.91%	0.10
remove method annotation	1	1	11.11%	0.77%	0.71%	1.40%	0.01
rename method	1	1	11.11%	2.20%	0.32%	1.10%	0.02
modify method annotation	1	1	33.33%	7.99%	2.50%	2.50%	0.20
move & rename method	1	1	20.00%	13.17%	−0.32%	2.32%	0.30
merge attribute	1	1	100.00%	100.00%	6.00%	6.00%	6.00

Diving into the Most Impactful Commits. With the most impactful commits, we refer to commits where we observed the most substantial energy differences between the commits x and commit x−1. To select these commits, we fix a threshold of 5% in energy consumption difference. This threshold was fixed based on the CPU energy consumption variation [23] and the standard deviation of the many executions we ran on the same test, which is often around 4% to 5%. A total of 7 commits have been retrieved from the projects Gson, JFlex, Eclipse-Collections and JGraphT (no other refactoring commit with a minimal impact of 5% has been observed among the other projects).

We note that our experimental setup would highlight any effect that these refactoring could have caused on energy consumption. Indeed, the execution of a JMH code, which uses the compiled JAR for the commit x, is composed of numerous warmup and standard iterations. Each iteration itself consists of running the benchmark many thousands of times for several seconds, so the effect that difference between the commits x and x−1 could be noticed, if any.

Table 3 reports on the most impactful commits including code refactorings. For each commit, we can see the type and number of refactorings extracted using REFACTOR-INGMINER [32,33], the measured energy consumption difference, a short description of the refactoring-related changes that have been observed within the commits, and the computed p-value of the Wilcoxon test.

First, the commit ID is the first 6 digits of the git hash that can be used to access the commit and reproduce our experiments/results. The *energy consumption* (EC) difference represents the percentage of differences between the average measure of commits x and x−1 (after applying the bootstrapping as we compute the average of multiple subsets built from the main set of values). The next 2 columns contain the extraction results of the REFACTORINGMINER tool. They include the type and count of each refactoring the tool was able to extract. We notice that the rules that we identified as most impactful in the previous phase (add method annotation, rename parameter, add class annotation, and move class) are—most of the time—part of the extracted rules in theses commits that have shown the highest differences in energy consumption, with add annotation and move class being the most common. Sometimes, they are the only detected code refactorings, that we could suspect to be responsible for the energy consumption variation, as in commit #b9dfbc of Eclipse Collections.

We apply 3 different validation measures to confirm whether the impact is effectively caused by the refactoring. The first validation is through detailed git di checks of the 7 selected commits to assess that the refactorings have been faithfully applied. We remind that we already made sure that these refactorings only concerns classes and methods that are being stressed by the JMH benchmarks, and do not contain other changes that can be responsible for the energy consumption difference. For example, we do not suspect adding some code documentation to alter the energy consumption, yet we do suspect changing a data structure, a loop, or a code snippet to do so.

In the second validation step, we conduct a statistical validation through Wilcoxon rank sum test (as Student test could not be applied due to variables not following a Gaussian distribution) to compare the commits x and x−1 averages. With a risk of 5%, we reject the null hypothesis of the means of the executions of commits x and x−1 being equal. For the p-value commit #f1074b being higher than 0.05, we cannot reject the possibility that the average is equal in both commits. The same goes for the commits #033164, #b34361, #b9dfbc where we cannot accept that the means of the commits x and x−1 are statistically different.

The remaining commits—being #827717, #45bf2d, and #298b7a—mainly contain the add annotation and move class refactorings. We thus achieve our third validation step through dedicated micro-benchmarking. We first build a micro-benchmark to check the effect that every encountered annotation may have (@override,@SuppressWarnings("unchecked"), @SuppressWarnings

Table 3. A deeper look into the most impactful commits [24].

Project	Commit ID	EC diff	Refactoring	Count	Git diff	p-value
Gson	#82771f	5.5%	add method annotation	23	Adding @SuppressWarnings(``unused'') and @SuppressWarnings(``unchecked'') to methods, classes and variables that appear in the call trace of the JMH code with no other changes that might impact the energy consumption.	0.018
			Add class annotation	3		
			Modify method annotation	1		
			Add attribute annotation	1		
	#45bf2d	6.8%	Add method annotation	3	Adding @SuppressWarnings(``unchecked'') to methods and moving classes (project reorganization) that appear in the call trace of the JMH code.	0.000
			Move class	30		
JGraphT	#033164	6%	Merge attribute	1	Some code restructuring, reorganization and class movement that that appear in the call trace of the JMH code. No other changes suspected of impacting the energy consumption were detected	0.056
			Change parameter type	1		
			Rename parameter	9		
			Move method	22		
			Rename class	1		
			Extract class	1		
			Move attribute	15		
			Move class	8		
			Merge parameter	6		
			Change variable type	19		
			Change attribute type	1		
	#f1074b	5%	Add method annotation	1	Adding @Override annotation and the renaming of some attributes/parameters. However these changes does not appear in the call trace of the JMH code.	0.2
			Add class annotation	60		
			Rename class	2		
			Rename attribute	1		
			Change variable type	16		
			Rename parameter	4		
JFlex	#b34361	5%	Add method annotation	53	Adding @Override annotation to methods that appear in the call trace of the JMH code with no other changes that might impact the energy consumption.	0.054
			Move & rename method	1		
			Rename class	1		
Eclipse Collections	#b9dfbc	6%	Add method annotation	9944	Adding @override annotation to methods that appear in the call trace of the JMH code with no other changes.	0.4
	#298b7a	5%	Add method annotation	73	Adding @override annotation to methods that appear in the call trace of the JMH code, but too many changes unrelated to refactoring were found.	0.01

("unused")) and ran hundreds of millions times each, on classes, methods and variables to check whether it has an effect on the energy consumption. The results—as expected—did not have any effect (about 1% difference that we cannot consider due to CPU energy variations [23]) on energy consumption, as annotations are not supposed to have a substantial impact on the generated bytecode that would be executed by the JVM. This would invalidate the fact that the observed energy consumption difference is mainly related to the add annotation refactoring in the commits that only contain this type of refactoring, such as #827717, #b9dfbc, and #298b7a. The second micro-benchmark concerns the move class refactoring, where we measured the energy consumption for several scenarios, after moving some classes/interfaces around and reorganizing the structure of the micro-benchmark. The results showed a difference in energy consumption of up to 8%, with an average standard deviation of 5%. The move class refactoring—which is often accompanied with the rename refactorings—indicates a code reorganization that might have an impact. While the observed impact through the JMH experiments or with micro-benchmarking might not be substantial, it would be beneficial to be aware that restructuring/reorganizing a project could have an impact on energy consumption, and thus compare the before/after energy consumptions to track that effect. Unfortunately, we could not detect any specific pattern or guidelines on when the code reorganization or restructuring would impact positively or negatively the energy consumption. Hence, we can only faithfully retain the commit #45bf2d of the Gson project among the commits of Table 3, where the 30 move class refactoring could have been responsible of 2% of energy consumption difference as the standard deviation of the measures is 5%.

We finally conclude that structure-oriented refactoring has no substantial impact on the energy consumption of the main functionality of 7 projects that have been existing for at least 5 years with a total of 16,046 commits. We argue that it could be applied to improve the code quality with no negative impact on software energy consumption. Although, comparing the energy consumption before and after the changes is always a good practice to keep track of its evolution.

> To answer RQ1, we conclude that code refactoring rules are mostly "safe" operations that have **no substantial impact** on software energy consumption. Developers should not fear structure-oriented refactorings, especially regarding how little is the impact they could have compared to the real energy consumption evolution of projects, registered while answering RQ1.

4.1 Software Energy Consumption Evolution

The first step is to investigate the evolution of software energy consumption over time. Figure 3 depicts the evolution of energy consumption for the projects Google-Http, XStream, JGraphT, and Eclipse Collections, for which we run the main releases and report on the energy consumption measured over time, by focusing on the main functions stressed by our JMH benchmarks.

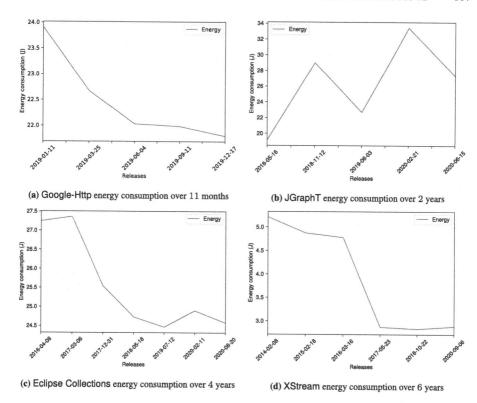

(a) Google-Http energy consumption over 11 months

(b) JGraphT energy consumption over 2 years

(c) Eclipse Collections energy consumption over 4 years

(d) XStream energy consumption over 6 years

Fig. 3. Energy consumption evolution of Google-Http, XStream, JGrapht, and Eclipse Collections [24].

Except for JGraphT, one can observe that energy consumption tends to decrease over time for most of the projects. One can mention a 10% decrease in 12 months for the Google-Http project (cf. Fig. 3a), a 10% decrease in 4 years for the Eclipse Collections project (cf. Fig. 3c), and a very substantial decrease of 50% in 6 years for the XStream project (cf. Fig. 3d).

Then, to have a more concrete look on the evolution of energy consumption per commit, we select the Gson project to reproduce the evolution of its energy consumption along the full commit history. Given the large number of involved commits, we consider the full set of commits of the Gson project (12 years) with a span of 25— *i.e.*, we build, run, and measure the energy consumption every 25th commits. Figure 4 depicts the evolution of energy consumption for the Gson project with a total of 57 successfully reproduced commits, out of 60. The line plot validates and confirms the results shown in Fig. 3. Most notably, one can observe a reduction of 82% from the highest to the lowest consumption commit within 12 years of the project's lifespan— *i.e.*, the energy consumption became 5 times lower.

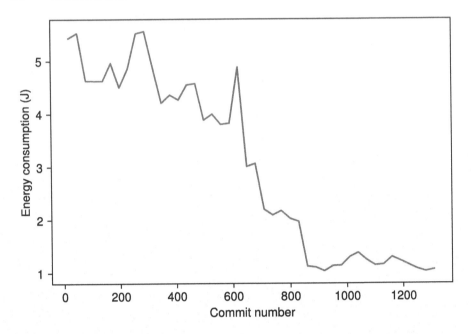

Fig. 4. Gson energy consumption across for every 25th commit [24].

One can also see a more sudden energy consumption reduction between commits 600 and 850. To investigate this, we thus run a similar experiment to measure the energy consumption of a all commits between 600 and 850 depicted in Fig. 5. The results clearly show that the decrease in energy consumption of the Gson project is not linear across commits, but is rather due to some specific commits. In fact, two specific commits are responsible of dropping the energy consumption of the Gson project tested functionality. These two commits (626 and 691) decrease the energy consumption from 4.5 J to 3.0 J and from 3.0 J to 2.0 J respectively.

In order to understand the kind of changes that can be responsible of such reduction in energy consumption, we meticulously analyzed one of the two previous commits (commit 691 for-which the test consumed 2686 KJ) and compared it to the previous commit (commit 690 for-which the test consumed 3563 KJ). Hence, we analyzed the Git diff of the commit 691 to spot the main changes. The analysis results showed that the changes are mainly related to the serialization Jsonwriter method, called in the TypdeAdapter class as shown Fig. 6. Concretely, the 690th commit uses a parser that is responsible for handling a buffer of objects and recursively (for arrays and complex objects) parse them as string to be written, while the 691st commit uses a more straightforward Jsonwriter and JsonElementWriter methods with a call to the Stringwriter method, to write objects one-bye-one with a simple cast to Json primitive Types.

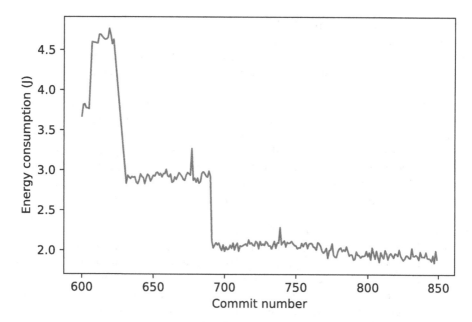

Fig. 5. Gson energy consumption for commits between 600 and 850.

```
import com.google.gson.JsonElement;
import com.google.gson.JsonIOException;
import com.google.gson.internal.Streams;
import com.google.gson.reflect.TypeToken;
import com.google.gson.stream.JsonReader;
import com.google.gson.stream.JsonWriter;

import java.io.IOException;
import java.io.Reader;
import java.io.StringReader;
@@ -56,13 +54,10 @@ public abstract class TypeAdapter<T> {

  public JsonElement toJsonElement(T src) {
    try {
      StringWriter stringWriter = new StringWriter();
      JsonWriter jsonWriter = new JsonWriter(stringWriter);
      JsonElementWriter jsonWriter = new JsonElementWriter();
      jsonWriter.setLenient(true);
      write(jsonWriter, src);
      JsonReader reader = new JsonReader(new StringReader(stringWriter.toString()));
      reader.setLenient(true);
      return Streams.parse(reader);
      return jsonWriter.get();
    } catch (IOException e) {
      throw new JsonIOException(e);
    }
```

Fig. 6. Git diff main changes of the Gson commit 691.

To prove the impact of this change on the Jsonwriter on the energy consumption of the Gson serialization, we use an asynchronous code profiler.[4] The purpose of the

---

[4] https://github.com/jvm-profiling-tools/async-profiler.

profiler is to frequently sample the Java execution stack to collect stack traces and to track memory allocation. The expected result is thus to see the Jsonwriter method executed much longer with the 690th commit compared to the 691st as it is the only section that has been modified between commits to achieve 25% reduction in energy consumption.

We thus draw two flame-graphs to illustrate and compares the stack traces of the 690th and 691st commits tests, shown in Fig. 7a and Fig. 7b respectively.

One can see that the Jsonwriter method lasted 7 times more in the commit 690 than 691 (in blue in both flame-graphs). In fact, the profiler recorded 138 samples of Jsonwriter method against using the Gson Commit 690, and only 20 samples for tr commit 691. The Jsonwriter was thus responsible of 30% of the energy consumption for the commit 690 against only 6% for the commit 691. The flame-graphs prove that the changes on the Jsonwriter method are responsible for about 25% of extra energy consumption on the commit 690 compared to 691st commit.

This kind of code changes are not structure-oriented refactoring but computational refactorings such as algorithm/method substitution. In the previous example, we recorded 25% reduction in energy consumption by substituting the logic to write the Json data. To showcase this, we run another experiment with Javax.Crypto library[5] to decrypt a 1.5 GB file using different read methods issued from multiple classes (IOStream: java.io.InputStreamReader, Channel: java.nio.FileChannel, FileReader: java.io.FileReader, BIOStream: java.io.BufferedInputStream and NIOF: java.nio.Files). The results in Fig. 8 clearly show that substituting different read methods can result in up to 100% in energy consumption to read the same data. Computational refactoring can thus have a substantial impact on the energy consumption of software, and should be wisely monitored. In fact, such changes should be either validated and widely adopted (to extract changes pattern that can be applied to other code portions within the software of other software) or seriously questioned if they decrease or increase software energy consumption respectively.

> To answer RQ1, we can conclude that software energy consumption can **evolve drastically** over time. For the analyzed target systems, in spite of fluctuations, the energy consumption has decreased non-negligibly for 4 systems and grown for one.
>
> Moreover, computational refactoring can have a substantial impact on energy consumption. Monitoring the energy consumption after such changes is very important to spot any increase or decrease in software energy consumption.

Given the previous results reported by the literature, the remainder of this paper aims to closely study and assess the impact of code refactoring on such observed evolutions.

---

[5] https://docs.oracle.com/javase/7/docs/api/javax/crypto/package-summary.html.

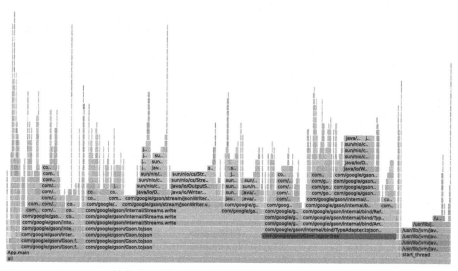

(a) Stack trace flame-graphs of the test execution on commit 690

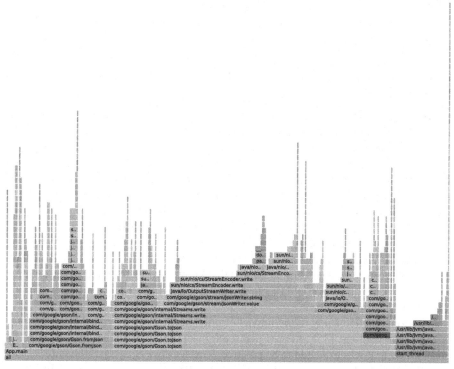

(b) Stack trace flame-graphs of the test execution on commit 691

Fig. 7. Stack trace flame-graphs of the test execution on commits 690 and 691.

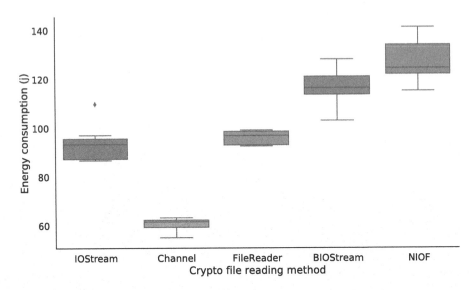

Fig. 8. Energy consumption of the Java Crypto library to decrypt a 1.5 GB file using different I/O methods.

5   Related Work

In this section, we review the state of the art of green software design efforts related to code refactorings.

Desktop Applications. Achieving software energy efficiency through refactorings has been studied for desktop applications and server-side applications. Pinto *et al.* discuss 12 contributions taken from the state of the art on the refactoring that can be applied to improve software energy efficiency [28]. This literature review was conducted on the papers that were published in 8 of the top software engineering conferences prior to 2015 such as ICSE and ASPLOS. It summarizes some interesting information and practices relating to CPU offloading, HTTP requests, I/O operations, DVFS techniques, etc. Sahin *et al.* studied the impact of 6 different refactoring rules on a total of 197 selections from 9 Java applications. Their results showed that the impact of applying the refactoring could be statically significant, but is not very consistent across the software and platform versions. They suggested that knowledge on the energy consumption impact of refactoring rules could be integrated within IDEs to help developers building less energy-bleeding software.

In a more detailed study of the impact of only one refactoring rule *"inline method"* on 3 Java applications, [35] reported that the impact on the execution time and energy consumption that was expected to be positive, was not always energy efficient.

Rather than looking for green refactoring rules reducing software energy consumption, some practitioners chose to conduct wider studies that apply on a much larger set of refactorings to capture a subset of "green" rules. This is exactly what the authors of [13] pursued: They prepared C++ micro-benchmarks of 63 refactoring techniques/design patterns suggested by Martin Fowler [1], then ran experiments and isolated a set of green refactoring rules based on the micro-benchmarks for C++. However, the conclusion cannot even be generalized on C++ applications, as they were built on specific tests that were executed on specific microbenchmarks.

The authors of [17] focused on investigating the impact of Java coding practices, which include primitive data types, operations on strings, usage of exceptions, loops, and arrays. Using RAPL [15], they measure the energy consumption of code snippets and micro-benchmarks and presented some minor observations, such as string concatenation consuming less than `StringBuilder` and `StringBuffer`, static variables consume 60% more energy compared to instance variables, etc.

Mobile Applications. In another context, the reduction of software energy consumption through refactoring actions has also been explored in the context of mobile applications. EARMO proposes a multi-objective refactoring approach to automatically improve the architecture of mobile applications [21]. The authors conducted an empirical study to measure the negative impact of 8 anti-patterns on 20 open-source applications. They then used a multi-objective search-based approach, called EARMO, to correct up-to 84% of the anti-patterns on the tested applications and increase the battery lifespan by up-to 29 min. However, their statistical analyses with a significance level of 5% only showed that half of the rules can impact energy efficiency in some cases. Moreover, the CPU/chip energy variation has not been taken into account for the significance level of the comparaisons.

Other works also considered energy efficient refactoring for mobile applications [12]. In particular, the authors of [29] presented some early experiments on different micro-benchmarks and discussed many coding aspects with a focus on implementation techniques, such as how to iterate on a matrix, avoid operations with immutable data types, evaluating strings, or the use the more specific numeric data types to save battery life. Anwar *et al.* [3] also gave concrete examples on how to save some battery time through refactoring. They achieved a maximum of 10% of energy savings by refactoring the DuplicatedCode and TypeChecking code smells.

In the same context, Cruz *et al.* [7] studied the effect of 8 of the best performance-based practices on the energy efficiency of 6 Android applications. The results of the experiments showed that some patterns, such as ViewHolder, DrawAllocation, Wake-Lock, ObseleteLayoutParam need to be taken into account for a better design of energy-efficient applications, with a reported impact of 4.5% for the Writeily Pro app. The authors also proposed the LEAFACTOR tool to improve the energy efficiency of Android applications by automatically refactoring the source code to fix the above patterns [6]. The process was applied on a set of 140 open-source Android applications and yielded a total of 222 refactorings, which were submitted as pull requests, with 16 successfully merged pull requests.

6 Conclusion

This paper introduces an investigation of the effective impact of code refactoring on software energy consumption. The investigation includes the analysis of at least 7 Java open-sources well-established projects with more than 10k commits, and deals with 55 different types of source code refactoring.

The results showed that structure-oriented refactorings have no substantial impact on the energy consumption of Java server-side software. Which means that structure-oriented code refactorings can be safely applied to improve source code maintainability and readability with no significant drawbacks on the energy consumption. However, functional and computational oriented code refactoring showed to play a significant role and can substantially impact software energy consumption. We argue that developers' efforts should be directed towards these refactorings (such as the choice of data structures, algorithms, I/O methods, etc.) rather than structure-oriented refactorings to reduce energy consumption. Such Computational refactorings can alter the energy consumption of software by a large margin in a positive or a negative way and should be wisely monitored. We were able for instance to register up to 100% of energy consumption differences just by refactoring/substituting the I/O read method for the Java Crypto library.

We believe that our approach is the major contribution of this paper, as it allows a more concrete way to study the impact of code refactoring rules on the energy consumption of real projects. This can also be extended to other projects and programming languages. Most importantly, this should motivate future works to validate that refactorings can be safely applied with no drawbacks on the energy consumption, yet investigate the commits and the nature of code changes that increase/decrease energy consumption.

References

1. Refactoring: Improving the Design of Existing Code. Addison-Wesley Longman Publishing Co., Inc. (1999)
2. Abid, C., Alizadeh, V., Kessentini, M., do Nascimento Ferreira, T., Dig, D.: 30 years of software refactoring research: a systematic literature review. CoRR abs/2007.02194 (2020). https://arxiv.org/abs/2007.02194
3. Anwar, H., Pfahl, D., Srirama, S.N.: Evaluating the impact of code smell refactoring on the energy consumption of android applications. In: 2019 45th Euromicro Conference on Software Engineering and Advanced Applications (SEAA), pp. 82–86. IEEE, Kallithea-Chalkidiki, August 2019. https://doi.org/10.1109/SEAA.2019.00021
4. Bree, D.C., Cinnéide, M.Ó.: Inheritance versus delegation: which is more energy efficient? In: ICSE 2020: 42nd International Conference on Software Engineering, Workshops, Seoul, Republic of Korea, 27 June–19 July 2020, pp. 323–329. ACM (2020). https://doi.org/10.1145/3387940.3392192
5. Chowdhury, S.A., Hindle, A., Kazman, R., Shuto, T., Matsui, K., Kamei, Y.: GreenBundle: an empirical study on the energy impact of bundled processing. In: Atlee, J.M., Bultan, T., Whittle, J. (eds.) Proceedings of the 41st International Conference on Software Engineering, ICSE 2019, Montreal, QC, Canada, 25–31 May 2019, pp. 1107–1118. IEEE/ACM (2019). https://doi.org/10.1109/ICSE.2019.00114

6. Cruz, L., Abreu, R., Rouvignac, J.: Leafactor: improving energy efficiency of android apps via automatic refactoring. In: 2017 IEEE/ACM 4th International Conference on Mobile Software Engineering and Systems (MOBILESoft), pp. 205–206, May 2017. https://doi.org/10.1109/MOBILESoft.2017.21

7. Cruz, L., Abreu, R.: Performance-based guidelines for energy efficient mobile applications. In: 4th IEEE/ACM International Conference on Mobile Software Engineering and Systems, MOBILESoft@ICSE 2017, Buenos Aires, Argentina, 22–23 May 2017, pp. 46–57. IEEE (2017). https://doi.org/10.1109/MOBILESoft.2017.19

8. Desrochers, S., Paradis, C., Weaver, V.M.: A validation of DRAM RAPL power measurements. In: Proceedings of the Second International Symposium on Memory Systems, MEMSYS 2016, pp. 455–470. Association for Computing Machinery, New York (2016). https://doi.org/10.1145/2989081.2989088

9. Efron, B.: The bootstrap and modern statistics. J. Am. Stat. Assoc. **95**(452), 1293–1296 (2000)

10. Fonseca, A., Kazman, R., Lago, P.: A manifesto for energy-aware software. IEEE Softw. **36**(6), 79–82 (2019). https://doi.org/10.1109/MS.2019.2924498

11. Fowler, M.: Refactoring: Improving the Design of Existing Code. Addison-Wesley, Boston (1999)

12. Gottschalk, M., Jelschen, J., Winter, A.: Energy-efficient code by refactoring. Softwaretechnik-Trends **33**(2), 23–24 (2013). https://doi.org/10.1007/s40568-013-0030-4

13. Park, J.-J., Hong, J.-E., Lee, S.-H.: Investigation for software power consumption of code refactoring techniques. In: SEKE (2014)

14. Kerievsky, J.: Refactoring to Patterns. Pearson Higher Education (2004)

15. Khan, K.N., Hirki, M., Niemi, T., Nurminen, J.K., Ou, Z.: RAPL in action: experiences in using RAPL for power measurements. ACM Trans. Model. Perform. Eval. Comput. Syst. **3**(2), 1–26 (2018)

16. van der Kouwe, E., Andriesse, D., Bos, H., Giuffrida, C., Heiser, G.: Benchmarking crimes: an emerging threat in systems security. CoRR abs/1801.02381 (2018)

17. Kumar, M., Li, Y., Shi, W.: Energy consumption in Java: an early experience. In: 2017 Eighth International Green and Sustainable Computing Conference (IGSC), pp. 1–8. IEEE, Orlando, October 2017. https://doi.org/10.1109/IGCC.2017.8323579

18. Linares-Vásquez, M., Bavota, G., Bernal-Cárdenas, C., Oliveto, R., Di Penta, M., Poshyvanyk, D.: Mining energy-greedy API usage patterns in Android apps: an empirical study. In: Proceedings of the 11th Working Conference on Mining Software Repositories - MSR 2014, pp. 2–11. ACM Press, Hyderabad (2014). https://doi.org/10.1145/2597073.2597085

19. Manotas, I., et al.: An empirical study of practitioners' perspectives on green software engineering. In: Proceedings of the 38th International Conference on Software Engineering - ICSE 2016, pp. 237–248. ACM Press, Austin (2016). https://doi.org/10.1145/2884781.2884810

20. Manotas, I., Sahin, C., Clause, J., Pollock, L., Winbladh, K.: Investigating the impacts of web servers on web application energy usage. In: 2013 2nd International Workshop on Green and Sustainable Software (GREENS), pp. 16–23. IEEE, San Francisco, May 2013. https://doi.org/10.1109/GREENS.2013.6606417

21. Morales, R., Saborido, R., Khomh, F., Chicano, F., Antoniol, G.: EARMO: an energy-aware refactoring approach for mobile apps. IEEE Trans. Software Eng. **44**(12), 1176–1206 (2018). https://doi.org/10.1109/TSE.2017.2757486

22. Moreira, E., Correia, F.F., Bispo, J.: Overviewing the liveness of refactoring for energy efficiency. In: Conference Companion of the 4th International Conference on Art, Science, and Engineering of Programming. pp. 211–212. ACM, Porto, March 2020. https://doi.org/10.1145/3397537.3397538

23. Ournani, Z., Belgaid, M.C., Rouvoy, R., Rust, P., Penhoat, J., Seinturier, L.: Taming energy consumption variations in systems benchmarking. In: Proceedings of the ACM/SPEC International Conference on Performance Engineering, ICPE 2020, pp. 36–47. Association for Computing Machinery, New York (2020). https://doi.org/10.1145/3358960.3379142

24. Ournani, Z., Rouvoy, R., Rust, P., Penhoat, J.: Tales from the code #1: the effective impact of code refactorings on software energy consumption. In: Fill, H., van Sinderen, M., Maciaszek, L.A. (eds.) Proceedings of the 16th International Conference on Software Technologies, ICSOFT 2021, Online Streaming, 6–8 July 2021, pp. 34–46. SCITEPRESS (2021). https://doi.org/10.5220/0010517900340046

25. Palomba, F., Nucci, D.D., Panichella, A., Zaidman, A., Lucia, A.D.: On the impact of code smells on the energy consumption of mobile applications. Inf. Softw. Technol. **105**, 43–55 (2019). https://doi.org/10.1016/j.infsof.2018.08.004

26. Pinto, G., Castor, F., Liu, Y.D.: Understanding energy behaviors of thread management constructs. In: Proceedings of the 2014 ACM International Conference on Object Oriented Programming Systems Languages & Applications - OOPSLA 2014, pp. 345–360. ACM Press, Portland (2014). https://doi.org/10.1145/2660193.2660235

27. Pinto, G., Liu, K., Castor, F., Liu, Y.D.: A comprehensive study on the energy efficiency of Java's thread-safe collections. In: 2016 IEEE International Conference on Software Maintenance and Evolution (ICSME), pp. 20–31. IEEE, Raleigh, October 2016. https://doi.org/10.1109/ICSME.2016.34

28. Pinto, G., Soares-Neto, F., Castor, F.: Refactoring for energy efficiency: a reflection on the state of the art. In: 2015 IEEE/ACM 4th International Workshop on Green and Sustainable Software, pp. 29–35. IEEE, Florence, May 2015. https://doi.org/10.1109/GREENS.2015.12

29. Rodriguez, A.: Reducing energy consumption of resource-intensive scientific mobile applications via code refactoring. In: 2017 IEEE/ACM 39th International Conference on Software Engineering Companion (ICSE-C), pp. 475–476. IEEE, Buenos Aires, May 2017. https://doi.org/10.1109/ICSE-C.2017.33

30. Rodriguez-Cancio, M., Combemale, B., Baudry, B.: Automatic microbenchmark generation to prevent dead code elimination and constant folding. In: Proceedings of the 31st IEEE/ACM International Conference on Automated Software Engineering, ASE 2016, pp. 132–143. Association for Computing Machinery, New York (2016). https://doi.org/10.1145/2970276.2970346

31. Hasan, S., King, R., Hafiz, M.: Energy profiles of java collections classes. In: ICSE (2016)

32. Tsantalis, N., Ketkar, A., Dig, D.: RefactoringMiner 2.0. IEEE Trans. Softw. Eng. (2020). https://doi.org/10.1109/TSE.2020.3007722

33. Tsantalis, N., Mansouri, M., Eshkevari, L.M., Mazinanian, D., Dig, D.: Accurate and efficient refactoring detection in commit history. In: Proceedings of the 40th International Conference on Software Engineering, ICSE 2018, pp. 483–494. ACM, New York (2018). https://doi.org/10.1145/3180155.3180206

34. Verdecchia, R., Procaccianti, G., Malavolta, I., Lago, P., Koedijk, J.: Estimating energy impact of software releases and deployment strategies: the KPMG case study. In: 2017 ACM/IEEE International Symposium on Empirical Software Engineering and Measurement (ESEM), pp. 257–266 (2017). https://doi.org/10.1109/ESEM.2017.39

35. Silva, W.G.P., Brisolara, L., Corrêa, U.B., Carro, L.: Evaluation of the impact of code refactoring on embedded software efficiency. Unpublished (2010). https://doi.org/10.13140/2.1.1481.8249

Towards Power Consumption Optimization for Embedded Systems from a Model-driven Software Development Perspective

Marco Schaarschmidt[1]([⊠])[ID], Michael Uelschen[1][ID], and Elke Pulvermüller[2]

[1] Faculty of Engineering and Computer Science, Osnabrück University of Applied Sciences,
Osnabrück, Germany
{m.schaarschmidt,m.uelschen}@hs-osnabrueck.de
[2] Software Engineering Research Group, University of Osnabrück,
Osnabrück, Germany
elke.pulvermueller@uos.de

Abstract. A power consumption optimization for battery-powered and resource-constrained embedded systems is typically performed on the hardware layer while the application layer is often neglected. Because software applications affect the hardware behavior directly, power-related optimizations can result in major application design and workflow changes. Such in-depth modifications should be considered in early design phases, where they are most effective. For embedded software development, current trends in software engineering such as *Model-Driven Development* (MDD) can be used for an early power consumption analysis and optimization even if the hardware platform is not yet finalized. However, power consumption aspects on the application layer are currently not sufficiently considered in MDD. In this paper, we present an approach to abstract hardware components of an embedded system using the *Unified Modeling Language* (UML) and annotate UML-based models with power characteristics. Additionally, we define a novel UML profile to capture the dynamic behavior of hardware components while interacting with software applications. With our approach, energy profiles can be derived to make the impact of software on power consumption in early design stages visible. Energy profiles are also suitable for software optimization and energy bug detection, which is demonstrated using a sensor node use case example.

Keywords: Model-Driven Development · Embedded systems · UML · MARTE · Power consumption · Energy bug

1 Introduction

As forecasts show, the ongoing trends of *Internet of Things* (IoT) and *Industrial Internet of Things* (IIoT) will lead to a high increase of embedded systems deployed. A study presented in [23] expects a growth from 8 billion devices in the year 2020 to more than 25 billion until the year 2030. Another forecast published by Gartner [20] predicts the number of IoT-connected devices to reach tens of billions by the year 2023. For the same year, Cisco [11] forecasts IoT devices to represent 50% of all networked devices

© Springer Nature Switzerland AG 2022
H.-G. Fill et al. (Eds.): ICSOFT 2021, CCIS 1622, pp. 117–142, 2022.
https://doi.org/10.1007/978-3-031-11513-4_6

while using short-range technologies, such as WiFi, Bluetooth, and Zigbee [22]. The standby energy consumption of all IoT-connected devices is expected to reach 46 TWh in 2025 [15]. Typically, embedded systems in IoT and IIoT are used in environmental monitoring, smart cities, agriculture, and smart factories applications [1,14,45] with an expected operational lifetime between weeks and decades. If those devices are battery-powered and placed in harsh environments or buried underground [19,44], the supply of power is a major challenge. In many cases, maintenance (e.g., recharging or replacing batteries) is not possible, impractical, or results in higher costs.

At the hardware level, power consumption is well-addressed by developers and researchers resulting in more energy-efficient hardware components. However, this topic is often neglected at the software level because software developers are in many cases unaware of how energy-efficient applications may be specified, implemented, and evaluated [34,36]. However, especially for battery-powered devices, power-related *Non-Functional Requirements* (NFRs) are gaining importance. In addition to the increased functionality of modern software applications and the growing complexity of algorithms, the variety of *microcontroller units* (MCUs), sensors, actuators, and communication interfaces lead to additional challenges for software developers when power-related NFRs need to be specified and evaluated. Furthermore, the detection and elimination of energy bugs are also important while analyzing software applications. As described in [6], an energy bug is defined as a behavior causing an unexpected energy drain that is not necessary to perform the actual task. Typical sources for energy bugs are complex software-hardware interactions, incorrect use of peripheral devices, and flaws in the software design [6,35]. While conventional software bugs are causing errors in the program flow or system crashes, energy bugs do not necessarily lead to the misbehavior of the software itself. Because field or burn-in tests are not able to detect such application-based misbehavior [40], energy bugs have to be addressed during early development stages using accurate simulations or detailed power consumption measurements on a fully functional hardware platform in a laboratory setting.

When battery-powered devices are used, the energy consumption of software applications can be a significant bottleneck [5] causing up to 80% of the total energy consumption through software-hardware interactions [16]. Since the impact of the software application on energy consumption is often unknown, it is essential to consider power-related NFRs in early design phases, where changes are more effective [42]. Typically, a power consumption analysis is carried out at the end of the development process when the software application and hardware platform are close to their final states. While the hardware platform is often not modified at this late stage of the development process, the software application is going into a re-design and optimization phase, causing time delays and increasing costs. Additionally, there exist no approaches or tool support to evaluate the software application regarding power-related NFRs, to estimate the power consumption, and to detect possible energy bugs in early design phases where the hardware platform may not be available or defined yet.

Model-Driven Development (MDD) allows multiple levels of abstraction when used in software engineering and reduces the overall complexity of software applications to its essential complexity. In general, software models are not bound to the underlying implementation by definition. This can help to overcome some of the aforementioned challenges during software development. The *Unified Modeling Language* (UML) [31] is typically used to describe aspects like the general structure and behavior of the software application. Software developers using MDD can focus on applications logic, behavior, and program flow. By this, most of the aforementioned sources of energy bugs are already taken into account. Code generators can be used to transform UML models into source code for the specific target platform. By this, automatic processes can be used to generate energy-optimized source code, which increases the quality of software applications. As an extension for UML, the *Modeling and Analysis of Real-time and Embedded systems* (MARTE) profile [32] describes *Non-Functional Properties* (NFPs) like time behavior or schedulability and provides power consumption and dissipation modeling for hardware components in a simplified way. However, stereotypes provided by MARTE are not sufficient to model dynamic power consumption and power-related behavior in a granular way. To the best of our knowledge, there exists no approach to combine software application models with hardware models to obtain an early and straightforward power consumption estimation for given hardware configurations. Furthermore, current MDD tools do not provide any analysis of energy bugs. This work addresses the gap of power consumption estimation in MDD and tries to answer the following *Research Questions* (RQs):

RQ1: How can hardware behavior be abstracted and described using UML?
RQ2: How can hardware models be coupled with the software model?
RQ3: How can hardware models be annotated with energy-related NFPs?
RQ4: How can software-hardware interactions be simulated in MDD?

Furthermore and beyond answering RQ 1–4, this paper extends the work in [37] and comes with a set of novel contributions that can be summarized as follows:

- An extended description of the model transformations used in this approach.
- A revised description of how our concepts can be integrated into MDD.
- A more detailed evaluation of the hardware component modeling concepts and the proposed UML profile.

The remainder of this article is organized as follows: Sect. 2 discusses related research and their conceptual differences compared to our approach. Section 3 introduces the overall methodology and the tools used to answer RQ 1–4. Section 4 describes the concept of *hardware component models*, while Sect. 5 provides an overview of our UML profile for a power consumption estimation. Section 6 describes the model transformation process, while Sect. 7 deals with the integration of our approach into the MDD workflow. Section 8 describes the evaluation of our approach. Finally, Sect. 9 covers the discussion of our approach and Sect. 10 concludes our work.

2   Background and Related Work

In this section, related work to our approach is introduced. With a focus on power consumption analysis and estimation, this includes approaches for hardware component and systems modeling as well as NFR modeling.

Concepts for power consumption estimation have been proposed in a set of research approaches based on workflow models [47], Petri nets [2], and mathematical models [9,28,46]. Unfortunately, the authors do not consider the impact of software applications and the integration into software development. In [4], a low-level device modeling and power estimation solution is described. The approach uses the IP-XACT standard [25] to describe hardware models, while state machines define power-related behavior. In MDD however, low-level hardware component models (e.g., clock generators) are not suitable for an evaluation of software application models in early design phases, due to the high complexity and amount of submodels needed to specify a model of a sensor or MCU. Especially if the analysis has to take the interaction and impact of the software application on single components (e.g., sensors) or the entire system into account. Moreover, their approach does not consider the dynamic behavior of peripheral devices. Due to the requirement of high-level knowledge about architectures and lengthy simulation times, low-level approaches such as *Instruction-level Power Analyses* (ILPA) are generally not suitable for an evaluation of software application models in early design phases. For ILPA, platform-dependent assembly code is required for estimating the cost of each instruction and is therefore not close to the abstraction level of UML-based models [27]. Additionally, these approaches are primarily used to simulate processors, which makes them also not suitable for a system-wide analysis.

Several approaches are using UML and MARTE to model software applications and hardware aspects of embedded systems for a power consumption estimation. The work presented in [26] describes an approach for a model-driven energy-aware timing analysis based on UML and MARTE. Design models are obtained through a reverse engineering process, where source code is transformed to UML classes and operations. MARTE is used to annotate the software model with timing and power-related properties. Afterwards, the UML model is transformed into a timing-energy analysis model, where UML classes are mapped to tasks and UML operations to runnable representations. In the final step, this model is used for power analysis. The approach takes only the processor of the system into account and does not consider peripheral devices. Additionally, UML models are derived by a reverse engineering process, which is not applicable in early design phases because the source code used as an input for the reverse engineering process does not exist yet. A multi-view power modeling approach for different functional and structural system views based on UML, SysML, and MARTE is proposed in [17]. Unfortunately, the authors focused on connections between views and do not consider a power analysis of single components nor the impact of software applications.

Other works proposed extensions for MARTE to improve modeling and analysis of power characteristics. The authors in [3] defined a UML profile based on MARTE to model system-wide dynamic power management aspects of embedded systems. For each hardware component, a state machine is defined and states are annotated with power specifications to represent supported operation modes. Additionally, the concepts of power modes and power configurations are introduced. Power modes are mapped to power configurations and describe the application behavior. As a property of the execution platform, power configurations are composed of a set of hardware component states which remain active as long as the configuration is selected. Use cases allocating configurations are defined to generate and analyze workflows. However, the presented concept assumes hardware configurations to be constant for a power mode. Therefore, dynamic behavior is not taken into account. A MARTE-based power consumption analysis profile with new stereotypes to specify power-related characteristics is introduced in [21]. The profile is used in simulations to find an optimal power solution when taking dynamic voltage scaling into account. The annotation of processors includes switching capacitance, leakage power consumption, as well as voltage and frequency parameters while tasks are annotated with their execution interval, the worst-case execution time, and worst-case execution cycles.

However, when modeling and analyzing power consumption, the aforementioned works focus on hardware-centric approaches. Software application aspects are simulated by using tasks and predefined use cases with fixed execution times. Software developers have hardly any possibilities to quantify the impact of a software model on power consumption. Furthermore, a power-related software optimization is not possible and energy bugs remain undetected. In contrast, our approach is integrated into the development process while focusing on software execution and software-hardware interactions.

3   Methodology and Tools

This chapter describes the methodology of our approach for a power consumption optimization of software applications in MDD. Furthermore, the tools used to model and analyze software applications are introduced. Our approach aims to combine software and hardware models to achieve an early power consumption optimization in MDD. As shown in Fig. 1, application requirements can be used as one of many sources to deduce the structure and behavior of the software application model. Hardware properties, taken from data sheets, existing drivers, and APIs, are used to derive basic *hardware component models*, which are extended with power consumption aspects. *Hardware component models* are defined as a combination of a UML class for the basic structure and a state machine used as a behavior model. To extend the behavior model with power-related properties, we implemented a UML profile (c.f. Sect. 5) which is also used in the analysis process. In our approach, *hardware component models* are

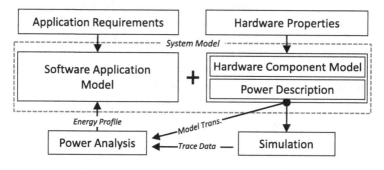

Fig. 1. Overview of the approach to optimize power consumption in MDD [37].

represented as black boxes and only those behavior aspects are modeled, which have a direct impact on the power consumption and can be accessed or influenced by the software application model. The combination of software and hardware models is defined as a *system model*, which is not limited to a specific group of hardware components. By using UML as a description for both system aspects, *hardware component models* can be completely integrated into the software domain which addresses RQ 1–3. To make the impact of the software application on the system visible and answer RQ4, the *system model* can be used to derive *energy profiles* when simulated. An *energy profile* describes the power-related impact of the software application on an embedded system. Software developers may utilize *energy profiles* to optimize the workflow and design of the application as well as the used algorithms. Additionally, *energy profiles* may also be used as an indicator for energy bugs. Moreover, by providing detailed feedback, the concept of energy transparency [16] can lead to energy-aware decisions to meet power-related requirements.

As an MDD tool, IBM Engineering Systems Design Rhapsody - Developer[1] [24] in Version 9.0 is used. IBM Rhapsody also provides a simulation environment for UML-based models which is used in our approach for the defined software and hardware models. The analysis is done with MathWorks MATLAB R2020a [43]. For this, extensions were developed to parse *hardware component models* (c.f. Sect. 6) and process traces (c.f. Sect. 8.2).

4 Hardware Component Models

To address RQ 1–3, this section describes the concept of *hardware component models* for a model-based power consumption optimization of embedded systems. This includes the abstraction of hardware components and dynamic behavior modeling. Section 4.1 gives a brief overview of the formal definition of *hardware component models*. Section 4.2 addresses the integration of hardware models into the software model domain and describes the realization of software-hardware interactions.

4.1 Formal Definition of Hardware Component Models

In [28, 47], the dynamic behavior for different system states with varying levels of power consumption has been analyzed. Furthermore, according to [7, 46], each hardware component may be described with a set of states defining operating modes and transitions to switch between modes. This concept can be described as a power state machine [7, 12], where the states and transitions are annotated with meta-information related to power consumption. As a formal notation in our approach, we denote *hardware component models* of an embedded system as H^{Sys} with the tuple (SM, OP, A), defined as:

- SM: Finite set of all states S, transitions T, and events E of a hardware component described as $\{S, T, E\}$. States S represent a list of operation modes, transitions T a list of possible state changes, triggered by events of the event list E.

---

[1] To improve readability, the abbr. *IBM Rhapsody* is used for the rest of this article.

- OP: Finite set of operations used by a software model, e.g., to change the configuration and trigger events.
- A: Finite set of attributes defining the inner state of the hardware component.

A state change of the *hardware component model* H_n^{Sys} from a state $s1 \in S_n$ to state $s2 \in S_n$ can be achieved by executing the transition $t_{12} \in T_n$, triggered by and event $e_{12} \in E_n$, so that $s1 \xrightarrow{t_{12}|e_{12}} s2$. In general, SM corresponds to the previously mentioned power state machine, containing all states, transitions, and events to model the power-related behavior of a hardware component. However, our approach extends these concepts by including dynamic power characteristics in states and transitions. For this, attributes in A are used, representing the current device configuration. To model hardware components in MDD, we are using UML class elements. Power state machines can be directly mapped to UML behavioral state machines [31] which in turn can be applied as classifier behavior to UML class elements. Due to this, a UML class element C^{hw} is suitable to represent a *hardware component model* so that $H^{Sys} \rightarrow C^{hw}$. Software models can interact with hardware representations and simulate real hardware accesses. By this, our approach is able to take the interaction of software models and hardware representations into account and enables a simulation of real hardware accesses as a crucial part of the power consumption estimating process [16].

4.2 Integration into the Software Model Domain

The integration of hardware models into the software model domain is an important step to evaluate software models in terms of power consumption and to detect energy bugs. In early development phases, the evaluation can be performed by software developers without fully finalized and existing hardware platforms. Figure 2 shows the proposed concept to integrate hardware component models into the software model domain. As a central interface between the software models and *hardware component models*, the *system model* (c.f. Fig. 1) is extended with an instance of the *SystemBuilder* class to manage and monitor all hardware models of the embedded system. All hardware models are derived from one of the two abstract device base classes *PeripheralDevice* and *ProcessingUnit*. To provide a minimal interface for software application models, the introduced predefined classes provide basic power-related operations. This type of generalization follows the *Hardware Proxy Pattern* described in [13]. *PeripheralDevice*

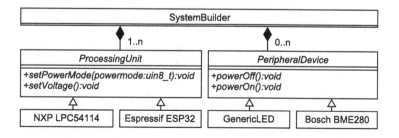

Fig. 2. Concept of *hardware component model* integration [37].

is used, e.g., for sensors, actors, and communication interfaces. To extend the provided interface and make specific functionalities of a hardware component accessible for the software model, existing driver descriptions can be considered as a source for function signatures, data types, and parameter names. By this, a *Hardware Abstraction Layer* (HAL) is defined. If source code is generated by MDD tools in later steps, *hardware component models* can be replaced with existing driver implementations due to identical function signatures while the generated source code of the software model does not require additional manual adjustments.

Each MCU family provides a different number of operating modes and strategies when CPU cores, flash units, SRAM banks, and oscillators are powered, throttled, or tuned off. Because of this, the consideration of MCUs is a special challenge, and *hardware component models* representing MCUs require further abstraction. Unlike peripheral devices, changing the power mode of an MCU directly affects the execution time and life cycle of the software model. Secondly, to keep the software model platform-independent, a HAL for MCUs must be implemented. To provide a consistent interface for software application models, the abstract class *ProcessingUnit* offers a set of predefined power states, namely:

- *ACTIVE*: Normal state with all configured peripherals powered.
- *SLEEP*: The system clock is stopped, no instructions are executed. Peripherals are powered and can generate interrupts. If configured, registers, SRAM and flash modules, DMA, and GPIOs are maintained.
- *DEEP_SLEEP*: Like *SLEEP* mode but with disabled main and peripheral clocks. Flash modules are put in standby mode or turned off.
- *DEEP_POWER_DOWN*: With exception of the *Real Time Clock* (RTC), the MCU is completely turned off and can be waked up by RTC generated interrupts. SRAM and registers are not maintained.
- *OFF*: The MCU is completely turned off.

Each power mode has to be mapped to an existing power mode of the specific MCU. Because of this, a HAL implementation for an MCU must at least support the aforementioned power modes.

5   Power Analysis Profile (PAP)

This section describes the UML profile which is used to extend *hardware component models* (c.f. Sect. 4) with power-related properties. For a power consumption optimization of embedded systems in MDD, existing model descriptions have to be extended with the required information (e.g. non-functional aspects). UML can be used for object and component-based modeling but the specification lacks the ability to express NFPs. MARTE makes use of the UML extension mechanism and provides a UML profile specifically to describe real-time-related aspects of embedded systems. The specification also provides descriptions of software and hardware execution platforms, including non-functional properties to address power consumption aspects. In general, MARTE has only limited support for power-related characteristics and does not provide accurate descriptions of important base and derived SI metrics like voltage and electrical current.

As a first step toward the *Power Analysis Profile* (PAP), we extended MARTE for a more detailed and dynamic characterization of hardware behavior when used from a software perspective. Based on the MARTE specification [32, 39], Fig. 3 shows the descriptions of the defined metrics and the corresponding NFP types. The *ElectricCurrentUnitKind* measurement unit in Fig. 3 represents the SI metric for current with the physical base dimension *I*. As a derived SI metric, the *VoltageUnitKind* consists of the base dimensions for mass (*M*), length (*L*), time (*T*), and electric current (*I*). The tags *baseUnit* and *convFactor* in the upper part of Fig. 3 can be used for conversions within the same unit. With *NFP_Voltage* and *NFP_Current*, additional data types for the two measurement units are defined and added to the *NFP_Types* section of the MARTE library. *NFP_Types* can be used for tag specifications of stereotypes, which are later applied on states and transitions of *hardware component models* to describe non-functional aspects such as current consumption in a dynamic and detailed manner. Figure 4 gives an overview of the PAP. While the profile is based on MARTE, it extends the specification by adding new tags specifically to describe dynamic behavior and power consumption, as well as using the introduced *NFP_Types* shown in Fig. 3. The profile is divided into two main packages *HardwareAbstraction* and *HardwareBehavior*. Stereotypes of the *HardwareAbstraction* package are designed to describe abstract hardware components while stereotypes of the *HardwareBehavior* package can be used to express power-related behavior. A UML class can be annotated with the *HardwareDeviceAbstraction* stereotype of the *HardwareAbstraction* package if it corresponds to a base representation of a *hardware component model* H^{Sys}, expressed as C^{hw}. By this, general properties such as the supply voltage and supported frequencies can be added to the model description. With *HWBehavioralImpact* and *HWPowerAttribute* of the *HardwareAbstraction* package, operations and attributes can also be annotated, if these elements are influencing the hardware behavior in terms of power consumption. To realize behavior changes of hardware components as defined in Sect. 4.2, software models can change the configuration or single attributes annotated with the *HWPowerAttribute* stereotype. By this, the connection between software models and the *hardware component models* is defined.

Stereotypes of the *HardwareBehaviour* package (c.f. lower part of Fig. 4) can be applied on state machines (*HWDeviceBehavior*), states (*HWDeviceBehavioralState*), and transitions (*HWDeviceBehavioralTransition*) to extend the modeled behavior with power-related characteristics. For tags like *current* and *execTime*, the *Value Specification Language* (VSL) [32, 39] is used to take dynamic behavior into account. However, the basic VSL concept was slightly adapted to express relations between tags of the stereotypes provided by our profile. In general, values for *NFP_Types* of the MARTE specification are expressed as the tuple *(value, expr, unit, source, precision, statQ, dir)* [32], where:

- *value*: Contains the actual value expressed as numerical quantity or string.
- *expr* (optional): Contains a *VSL_Expression*, if expressions instead of fixed values are used.
- *unit*: Contains the physical measurement unit.
- *source* (optional): Describes the origin of the value (e.g. measured, estimated, calculated).
- *precision* (optional): Defines the standard deviation of the measurement to obtain the value.

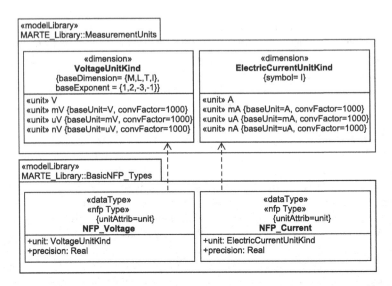

Fig. 3. Voltage and electrical current descriptions as extensions for MARTE [37].

- $statQ$ (optional): Used to qualify the value for statistical analyses (e.g., max, min, mean).
- dir (optional): Used to enable a qualitative comparison between values of the same type.

As a basic example for the tuple notation, the tagged value *current* (c.f. Fig. 4) can be expressed as $(value = 5, unit = mA)$, $(5, -, mA, -, -, -, -)$, or $(5, mA)^2$ as a shortened notation. In related approaches described in Sect. 2, a fixed number is used to describe the power, execution time, and other tagged values within states and transitions. However, changing the number of repeated measurements to obtain an average value may affect the power consumption for a specific state or transition of a sensor. As another example, if the software application varies the amount of data to be transmitted by a communication interface, the execution time for the transmission state is affected. Due to the usage of expressions to model dynamic behavior, our approach does not have this limitation. Modifiable configurations are supported so that software-hardware interactions can be evaluated. If an expression is used, the tag $hasDynamicConsumption = true$. Expressions are composed of elements from the sets V, C, and O, where:

- V: Contains all variables used to express dynamic behavior for a given state or transition.
- C: Represents a list of constants.
- O: Represents a finite set of mathematical operators.

---

[2] For a better readability, the shortened notation $(value|expr, unit)$ is used in the following sections.

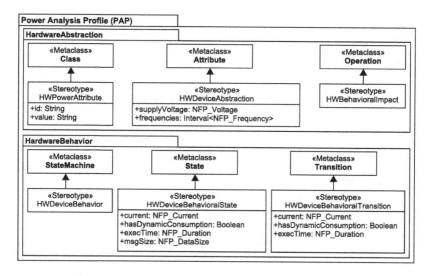

Fig. 4. Power Analysis Profile packages with stereotypes and basic tags [37].

While variables in V are still based on VSL and use the *Variables* type from the *VSL::Expressions* package [32,39], their definition and usage are slightly adapted and differ from the MARTE specification to enable cross-references between tags of UML elements of a class C^{hw} (e.g., states, transitions, attributes). The MARTE specification describes a methodological rule, that analysis tools have to compute the *VSL::Expressions::Variables* and return them to the UML model at the start of a VSL evaluation. As a first difference, whenever tagged values are modified during simulation, affected expressions are re-evaluated. Instead of explicit declarations for *VSL::Expressions::Variables*, our approach uses a specific naming scheme to achieve a linkage between the variable definition and the tagged value it is linked to. Examples for the use of the implicit naming scheme are:

- $\$ \ll tag \gg$: Denotes a tagged value for a tag in the scope of the current UML element.
- $\$SM. \ll NameOfState \gg . \ll tag \gg$: Represents a tag of a state within a state machine.
- $\$SM. \ll NameOfTransition \gg . \ll tag \gg$: Represents a tag for a transition within a state machine.
- $\$ATTR. \ll attributeId \gg$: Denotes an attribute annotated with *HWPowerAttribute*. The tagged value *id* must match $\ll attributeId \gg$.

Figure 5 introduces an example of a *hardware component model* for a *DimmableLED* to demonstrate the basic concepts and the usage of the PAP. The upper part of Fig. 5 shows the class definition of the *DimmableLED*, derived from the base class *PeripheralDevice* (c.f. Sect. 4.2). The behavior is expressed as a state machine and described in the lower part of Fig. 5. The class definition includes an internal attribute *brightnessLevel* as a configuration parameter of the current brightness and a method

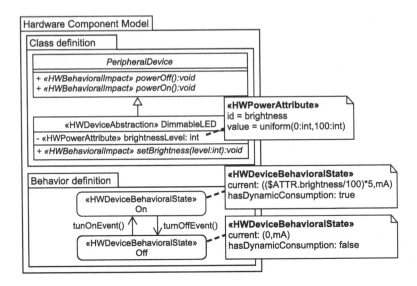

Fig. 5. Basic example of a *hardware component model* annotated with PAP [37].

to change the *brightnessLevel*. The stereotype *HWDeviceAbstraction* is applied to the attribute *brightnessLevel* to define a unique id as well as a specification about the value range and probability distribution, which may be used by simulation environments if return values have to be generated. When the functions *powerOff()* and *powerOn()* are executed, events are emitted initiating state transitions. The state machine consists of two states *Off* and *On*, which are extended with the *HWDeviceBehavioralState* stereotype. For the *Off* state, the tagged value of the *current* tag is set to a fixed value. Since the actual consumption depends on the *brightnessLevel*, the *current* tagged value of the *On* state is defined as an expression. The value of the *brightnessLevel* can be included in the expression by using the aforementioned implicit naming scheme resulting in the variable name $\$ATTR.brightness$. The value for the tag *current* of the *On* state can thereby be declared as $((\$ATTR.brightness/100) \cdot 5, mA)$. As a result, the value can vary between 0.05 and 5 mA. By calling the method *setBrightness*, this attribute can be modified by software models, which affects the power consumption when the *DimmableLED* is enabled.

6   Model Transformation

UML is able to define and describe *Platform Independent Models* (PIMs). A PIM defines a highly abstract model and contains the formal specification of the structure and functionality of a system while being independent of any specific implementation technologies. A *Platform Specific Model* (PSM) on the other hand defines a model using a specific technology to implement the functionalities defined by a PIM [33]. The transformation process between models, e.g., PIM to PIM and PIM to one or more PSMs, represents an important feature of MDD and is called *model-to-model* (M2M) transformation or model mapping. According to [10], the model m of the system s described with the formalism (metamodel) f can be defined as $m(s)/f$. The transformation from a source model $m_s(s)/f_s$ into a target model $m_t(s)/f_t$ can be written as $m_s(s)/f_s \rightarrow m_t(s)/f_t$. In MDD, this process is used to transform PIMs (e.g., UML models) into language-specific PSMs (e.g., C/C++), which, in turn, are translated into an executable program using model-to-text transformations. For this approach, we perform an exogenous transformation $m(s)/UML \rightarrow m(s)/MATLAB$ of *hardware component models* (c.f. Sect. 4) annotated with the PAP (c.f. Sect. 5) from a UML-based MDD tool (e.g., IBM Rhapsody) to an analysis tool (e.g., MATLAB) for a power consumption optimization of the software model based on trace analysis. The transformation of UML classes and state machines in this work does not cover the complete definition and is limited to elements defining the behavior, power-related tagged values, and attributes of *hardware component models*. For the transformation of UML-based models like classes and state machines, we provide a lightweight JSON-based interchange format [29].

```
1   "Statemachines": [{
2     "Name": "DimmableLED",
3     "Attr": {
4       "brightnessLevel": {
5         "Id": "brightness",
6         "Type":"Integer",
7         "Value": "uniform(0.0,100.0)"
8       }, [...]
9     },
10    "States": {
11      "ON": {
12        "Id": "6917cdb7-f8a3-4c78-835b-2150a3da38f6",
13        "Behavior":{
14          "Current": "(($ATTR.brightness/100)*5,mA)",
15          "ExecTime": "",
16          "HasDynamicConsumption": true
17        }
18      }, [...]
19    },
20    "Transitions": {
21      "1": {
22        "DefaultTransition": false,
23        "FromState": "ed4869b3-5e1b-4dfd-8ce8-56f1adda58e3",
24        "ToState": "6917cdb7-f8a3-4c78-835b-2150a3da38f6",
25        "Behavior":{
26          "Current": "(0, uA)",
27          "ExecTime": "(0, ms)",
28          "HasDynamicConsumption": false
29        },
30      }, [...]
31    }
32  }]
```

Fig. 6. Example of a JSON-based *hardware component model* [37].

Figure 6 shows a basic example description of a single *hardware component model* for the *DimmableLED* introduced in Sect. 5. To take the dynamic behavior of hardware components into account, the description includes the basic state machine structure, power-related tagged values, and class attributes, structured as follows:

- *Name*: The name of the hardware component.
- *Attr*: Contains all attributes annotated with the stereotype *HWPowerAttribute*. The inner structure of a single attribute is not fixed but may contain the following elements:
  - *Id*: The attribute's unique id used for variables in equations.
  - *Type*: The data type of the attribute.
  - *Value (optional)*: Probability distribution provided by the MARTE *NFP_CommonType* [32, 39]. Used if values have to be generated, e.g., as external input or to define test cases.
- *States*: Contains operational states of a hardware component. Every state can be described with the following elements:
  - *Id*: The attribute's unique id.
  - *Behavior*: Describes the energy-related behavior of the state. The *hasDynamicConsumption* flag indicates if the power consumption of the transition is static (e.g., fixed value) or dynamic (e.g., equation). The execution time (*execTime*) can be a fixed value, equation, or left empty if a state change is not initialized automatically.
- *Transitions*: Contains state transitions of a hardware component. Every transition can be described as follows:
  - *DefaultTransitions*: True, if the current transition is a default transition, false otherwise.
  - *FromState*: The unique id of the source state. Not defined if the transition is a default transition.
  - *ToState*: The unique id of the destination state.
  - *Behavior*: Describes the energy-related behavior of the transition. The *hasDynamicConsumption* flag indicates if the power consumption of the transition is static (e.g., fixed value) or dynamic (e.g., equation). The execution time (*execTime*) can be a fixed value, equation, or 0 if the transition is instantaneous without any delays.

For the evaluation of our approach (c.f. Sect. 8), we implemented an extension for IBM Rhapsody to map a *hardware component model* to the JSON-based interchange description. The algorithm of the extension is described in the UML activity diagram in Fig. 7. In case of the *hardware component model* for the *DimmableLED* (c.f. Fig. 5) introduced in Sect. 5, the JSON-based description shown in Fig. 6 can be generated. For this, the UML class definition of the *DimmableLED* is analyzed and metadata like the name are temporally stored. In the next step, all attributes annotated with the *HWPowerAttribute* are analyzed and the content of the tags *id*, *type*, and *value* are saved. Afterwards, the algorithm checks if a state machine with the *HWDeviceBehavior* exists. If a corresponding state machine is found, the analysis of states and transitions is performed. In the last step, the JSON-based interchange description based on the stored information is generated. If no state machine exists, the algorithm terminates without producing an output.

The resulting JSON file is used in MATLAB for tracing purposes. For other UML-based MDD tools, this process might be different.

7 Model-Driven Development Workflow Integration

This section discusses the integration of our approach (c.f. Sect. 4–6) into an MDD workflow. In Fig. 8, the extended MDD workflow is described using a UML activity diagram. The workflow starts with the definition of functional and non-functional requirements for the software application model. The next steps 2–5 can be processed simultaneously by the software developer. In step 2, the software model is defined while in step 3 all hardware components are identified, which can be accessed or influenced by the software model, e.g., MCUs, sensors, actuators, and communication interfaces. To allow the reuse of hardware models in future projects, *hardware component models* can be stored in model libraries. If no hardware model exists for the specific component, software developers may use data sheets to derive *hardware component models* (c.f. Sect. 4) (steps 4(a)–4(b)). Those models are annotated with PAP (c.f. Sect. 5) to add power and execution time properties and are automatically stored in the model library (steps 4(c)–4(d)). As described in step 5(a), MDD tools like IBM Rhapsody or Enterprise Architect [41] can be used to query model libraries for existing *hardware component model* descriptions. Model libraries can be private, community-driven, or vendor-specific, where *hardware component model* descriptions are provided as a package along with drivers and data sheets. In step 6, both models are linked together by integrating function calls of the *hardware component model* interface into the software model, e.g., as opaque behavior. Since the function signatures provided by *hardware component models* should be identical with the driver implementations, hardware models can be replaced by driver implementations when the software model is transformed into platform-specific source code. By this, no further code adjustments of the resulting software application are required. A logging extension is added for both models in step 7 to provide basic information for power analysis by externals tools. Depending on the MDD tool used, the extension process can be executed automatically. The intermediate model resulting from the actions in steps 6–7 also contains a system builder class (c.f. Sect. 4.2), which is used in simulation environments to instantiate *hardware component models* and make those models accessible for the software model. The system builder is also responsible for capturing event logs, which can be provided to external power analysis tools via *Comma-Separated Values* (CSV) files or a socket connection, to achieve an analysis in real-time. In step 8, an M2M transformation is performed and in step 9, the simulation of the software application model is executed. Afterward, the software developer can use the results to check whether the requirements defined in step 1 are met. If not, the software model can be optimized and the simulation repeated. This procedure can lead to several iterations until requirements are met and energy bugs fixed.

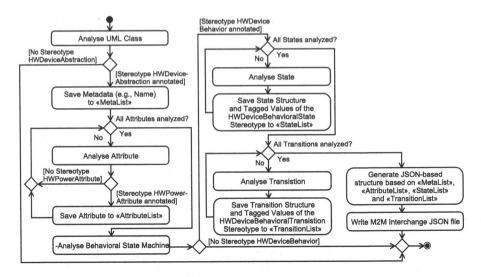

Fig. 7. Sequence of the JSON-base interchange file creation process.

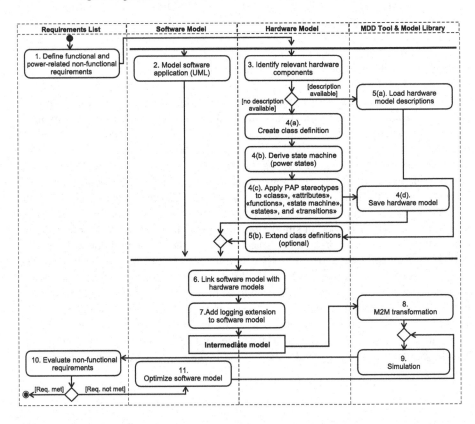

Fig. 8. Extended MDD workflow as UML activity diagram.

8   Evaluation

Based on the methodology described in Sect. 3, our approach is elaborated in this section by obtaining an *energy profile* of a software application for a typical sensor node example in an early design phase. As shown in Fig. 9, the evaluation is designed as a three-step process. The definition and development of the use case example as the first step is described in Sect. 8.1. This includes a description of the hardware components the embedded system is composed of, the derived *hardware component models*, and the exemplary software application model. Section 8.2 covers the simulation part and introduces the structure of trace logs and addresses the M2M transformation. Finally, the analysis results and the *energy profile* are presented in Sect. 8.3.

8.1   Development

To evaluate our approach described in Sect. 4, 5 and 6, we defined an exemplary hardware platform typical for a sensor node used in IoT use cases. The hardware system consists of an NXP LPC54114 [30] MCU, a Bosch BME280 environmental sensor [8], and a standard LED. The NXP LPC54114 is composed of an ARM Cortex-M4 and ARM Cortex-M0+ co-processor. To keep this use case simple while focusing on the evaluation of the proposed modeling concepts, the co-processor is unused and has been disabled. While the standard LED represents a visual output, the Bosch BME280 is used to measure the temperature, barometric pressure, and humidity of the surrounding. The following Table 1 gives an overview of the hardware devices used including provided operation modes with their expected current consumption. Values for the NXP LPC54114 are taken from a configuration with a voltage supply of 3.3 V, a clock rate of 96 Mhz, and a powered flash module. All hardware models are derived from their corresponding data sheets [8, 30]. Figure 10 shows the state machine for the NXP LPC54114. For this use case, only the states *Active*, *Sleep*, and *Deep Sleep* are used by the software application. As shown in Table 1, the current consumption in each state of the MCU is defined as a static value. For the states *Active*, *Sleep*, and *Deep Sleep* the values are set

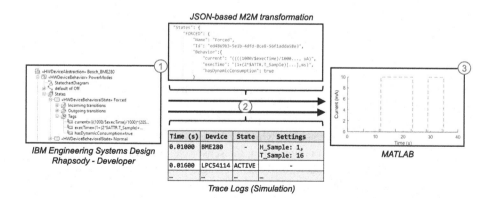

Fig. 9. Evaluation process of our approach.

Table 1. Hardware devices with operational states and electric current values.

Device	Operational state	Current
NXP LPC54114	Active	9.9 mA
	Sleep	3.0 mA
	Deep sleep	18 μA
	Deep power down	450 nA
	Off	0.0 mA
Bosch BME280	Normal	*dynamic*
	Forced	*dynamic*
	Sleep	0.1 μA
	Off	0.0 mA
Standard LED	On	5.0 mA
	Off	0.0 mA

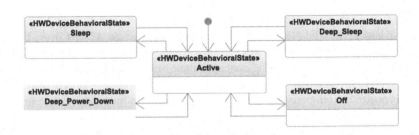

Fig. 10. NXP LPC54114 state machine [37].

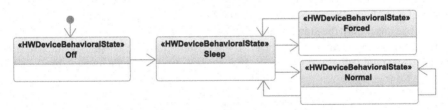

Fig. 11. Bosch BME280 state machine [37].

to 9.9 mA, 3 mA, and 18 μA respectively. Since the software application model itself initiates all state changes of the MCU, the tag *execTime* for each state is left empty. The *hardware component model* of the Bosch BME280 is shown in Fig. 11. The *Sleep* state defines the default state of the sensor, which is automatically entered after the sensor is powered. Depending on the configuration, the sensor can be configured dynamically by the software application model, to perform a single measurement (*Forced* state) or to continuously take measurements (*Normal* state). The dynamic consumption for the Bosch BME280 in the operation states *Normal* and *Forced* (c.f. Table 1) depends on the current configuration of the sensor. A software application model can change the over-

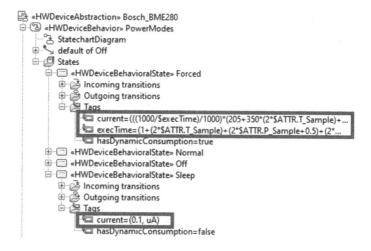

Fig. 12. Bosch BME280 state machine in IBM Rhapsody [37].

sampling rate of each sensor provided by the Bosch BME280 during runtime, which directly impacts the amount of electric current and the measurement time. To take this dynamic behavior into account, class attributes for the oversampling rate of each sensor (e.g., temperature, pressure, humidity) have been defined as configuration parameters and extended with the stereotype *HWPowerAttribute* following our concept proposed in Sect. 4–5. For the tag *id* of the stereotype, the values *T_Sample*, *P_Sample*, and *H_Sample* have been defined, which are used in the value fields of the *current* and *execTime* tags provided by the *HWDeviceBehavioralState* stereotype, as shown in Fig. 12. By re-evaluating the equations during simulation, configuration changes initiated by the software application model can be taken into account. For the software-hardware interaction between the BME280 *hardware component model* and the software application, we abstracted the existing sensor driver implementation[3]. We furthermore applied *HWBehavioralImpact* stereotypes on each operation affecting the power-related behavior. The state machine of the LED will not be discussed in detail due to its simplicity. Besides the definition of *hardware component models*, we also implemented an exemplary software application model. The software application is based on a typical use case for smaller IoT systems, where temperature values are measured and evaluated. As pictured in Fig. 13, the software model is based on a state machine with four different states:

– *Input*: A single measurement of the Bosch BME280 (*Forced*) is performed.
– *Process*: In this state, the measurement is processed. Measurement values are compared against a threshold and if the threshold exceeds, the application will switch to the *Output* state and to the *Sleep* state otherwise. Active outputs will be disabled before entering the *Sleep* state.
– *Output*: As a visual output, the LED will be enabled and the system will switch to the *Sleep* state afterwards.

---

[3] https://github.com/BoschSensortec/BME280_driver.

– *Sleep*: In this state, the MCU is set to a low power mode for a fixed amount of time before re-entering the *Input* state automatically.

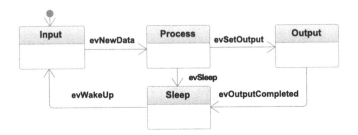

Fig. 13. Software application model [37].

In the state *Sleep*, it is expected, that the MCU is set into the *Deep Sleep* state. For the evaluation of our approach, we prepared the software application with an energy bug. If the LED is powered in the *Output* state, the event *evOutputCompleted* will be triggered. Because of a faulty event handling in the *Sleep* state of the software model, the MCU is set to the *Sleep* mode instead, consuming more power than expected. Since there exists no functional error in the application logic nor on the code level, this energy bug may be hard to detect with normal existing debugging methods.

8.2 Simulation

IBM Rhapsody is used for a continuous simulation of UML-based models and associated state machines. The simulation environment has been extended to be capable of generating event logs for software-hardware interactions and state changes of hardware models. All logs are aggregated and stored in a CSV file, where each entry has the same structure and consists of the following elements:

– *Timestamp*: The simulation time in milliseconds of the event.
– *Device*: The name of the affected hardware component.
– *State*: New operational state of the devices. Required for behavior messages.
– *Settings*: List of affected attributes of a configuration change expressed as a JSON structure. Required for configuration messages.

We defined two different message types for behavior and configuration-related messages. A state change of a hardware component represents a typical example of a behavior-related message and can be written as *Timestamp;Device;NewState;*. An example for a configuration-related message with two changed parameters can be expressed as *Timestamp;Device;;Settings:{ "ParamA": "NewStringValue", "ParamB": NewIntValue}*. For the proof of concept, a plugin for IBM Rhapsody has been developed to import and export *hardware component models* using the proposed M2M interchange format definition (c.f. Sect. 6). As a preparation for the simulation, a measurement series with the Bosch BME280 was performed. The measured values are passed back to the software model when the hardware model of the sensor is set into a measurement state.

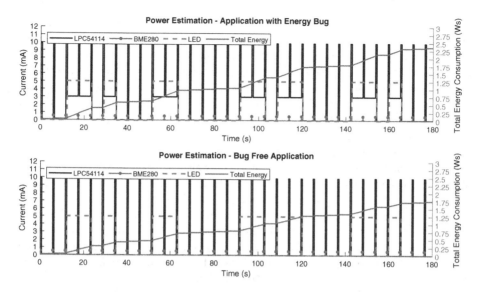

Fig. 14. Energy profile of the software application model [37].

8.3 Analysis

In this section, we evaluate our approach and obtain an *energy profile* of the software application model in an early design phase. The analysis in MATLAB is based on the recorded event logs and the M2M transformation of the *hardware component models*. The information provided by the M2M transformation are used in Matlab as a lookup table so that lists containing all states, transitions, and attributes are generated and used to calculate the power consumption of the current and active state for each hardware component. Figure 14 shows the resulting energy profiles of the software model interacting with the defined hardware components. The simulation was executed for a total of 180 s. The upper part of Fig. 14 shows the power estimation and accumulated energy consumption for the software application containing the energy bug. The resulting *energy profile* after the software developer has changed the software model and fixed the energy bug is shown in the lower part of Fig. 14. As a result of the fixed energy bug, the total consumption could be reduced by 25 % from approx. 2.36 Ws to 1.76 Ws. It must be mentioned that the error adds up over time, resulting in a more significant impact when the system is operated for a longer period.

9 Discussion

The approach presented in this article can be used by software developers to estimate and optimize power consumption for a software application model in early design phases. Our novel UML-based profile enables fine-grained modeling of hardware components and dynamic hardware behavior. Hardware models can be linked with the software application model to make software-hardware interactions visible. By this, we were able to address RQ1–3. To answer RQ4, we extended the simulation environment with the capability to provide event logs that are used for trace analysis in MATLAB. The trace analysis and the presented M2M transformation are used to derive energy profiles and to identify energy bugs of software application models in early design stages. The evaluation has shown that our approach can analyze software-hardware interactions. The impact of energy-related software design patterns [38] on the entire system may also be analyzed with the presented approach. Additionally, sub-systems, individual program sequences, test cases, and power-related NFRs, e.g., total peak power or battery capacity, may be evaluated, which can lead to early design changes in the application's workflow. The presented concept may also be used to perform exploration methods [18] and evaluate the best software-hardware configuration based on power and use case related factors. The presented concepts are tool independent. Hardware models may be exchanged between tools and reused in different projects due to the lightweight interchange format, resulting in increased developer productivity. The visualization of possible energy bugs is also useful to improve the quality of the application. With a focus on the software developer perspective, we also presented a concept focusing on the integration of our approach into an MDD workflow.

There exist also limitations that can impact the results when our approach is used. The accuracy of models decreases with the level of abstraction. A highly accurate simulation of an MCU, for example, must take all components (ADCs, timer, GPIOs) into account and use intermediate code as an input. The transformation of UML-based models into intermediate code representations for specific platforms can be a time-consuming manual endeavor and is therefore unsuitable for early design stages. Additionally, parameters for tagged values of the PAP are currently derived from data sheets or have been previously measured in specific environments (e.g., temperature), resulting in another loss of accuracy. The last limitation addresses the simulation environment of current MDD tools, where the execution time does not match the runtime of generated code directly executed on an embedded system.

Overall, our approach offers valuable feedback for software developers. Furthermore, the overall development time and costs can be reduced by performing an energy-related re-design and optimization of the software application in early design phases.

10   Conclusion

The work presented in this article represents an important step towards an energy transparent software application in MDD. Our concept offers a novel approach to provide power estimations for software applications in early design phases by considering software-hardware interactions and dynamic power-related behavior of hardware components. Based on UML and MARTE, we created *hardware component models* as an abstraction of the embedded system environment and included dynamic power characteristics in their descriptions. Hardware accesses initiated by the software applications can be traced using simulations environments of MDD tools while MATLAB was used for the analysis and evaluation steps. By this, software applications of embedded systems can be evaluated in early design stages without the need for real hardware components. To improve the quality of software applications further, our approach may also be used to track down energy bugs of software applications.

Future work includes the comparison of our approach with physical measurements on real hardware platforms for accuracy evaluations. Furthermore, we are planning to extend our concepts to include energy sources and communication interfaces. We are also planning to provide a simulation and analysis environment for deriving *energy profiles*, detecting energy bugs, and evaluating NFRs.

References

1. Abd El-Mawla, N., Badawy, M., Arafat, H.: IoT for the failure of climate-change mitigation and adaptation and IIoT as a future solution. World J. Environ. Eng. **6**(1), 7–16 (2019). https://doi.org/10.12691/wjee-6-1-2
2. Andrade, E., Maciel, P., Falcão, T., Nogueira, B., Araujo, C., Callou, G.: Performance and energy consumption estimation for commercial off-the-shelf component system design. Innovations Syst. Softw. Eng. **6**(1–2), 107–114 (2010). https://doi.org/10.1007/s11334-009-0110-7
3. Arpinen, T., Salminen, E., Hämäläinen, T.D., Hännikäinen, M.: Marte profile extension for modeling dynamic power management of embedded systems. J. Syst. Archit. **58**(5), 209–219 (2012). https://doi.org/10.1016/j.sysarc.2011.01.003
4. Atitallah, Y.B., Mottin, J., Hili, N., Ducroux, T., Godet-Bar, G.: A power consumption estimation approach for embedded software design using trace analysis. In: Proceedings of the 41st Euromicro Conference on Software Engineering and Advanced Applications, Madeira, Portugal, 26–28 August 2015, pp. 61–68 (2015). https://doi.org/10.1109/SEAA.2015.34
5. Banerjee, A., Chattopadhyay, S., Roychoudhury, A.: On testing embedded software. In: Advances in Computers, vol. 101, pp. 121–153. Elsevier (2016)
6. Banerjee, A., Chong, L.K., Chattopadhyay, S., Roychoudhury, A.: Detecting energy bugs and hotspots in mobile apps. In: Proceedings of the 22nd ACM SIGSOFT International Symposium on Foundations of Software Engineering, FSE 2014, Hong Kong, China, 16–21 November 2014, pp. 588–598 (2014). https://doi.org/10.1145/2635868.2635871. ISBN 978-1-450-33056-5
7. Benini, L., Bogliolo, A., de Micheli, G.: A survey of design techniques for system-level dynamic power management. IEEE Trans. Very Large Scale Integr. (VLSI) Syst. **8**(3), 299–316 (2000). https://doi.org/10.1109/92.845896
8. Bosch Sensortec GmbH: BME280 - Data sheet, Version 1.9. Document Number BST-BME280-DS001-18. https://www.bosch-sensortec.com/media/boschsensortec/downloads/datasheets/bst-bme280-ds002.pdf (2020). Accessed 09 Jul 2021
9. Bouguera, T., Diouris, J.F., Chaillout, J.J., Jaouadi, R., Andrieux, G.: Energy consumption model for sensor nodes based on LoRa and LoRaWAN. Sensors **18**(7), 2104 (2018)
10. Caplat, G., Sourrouille, J.L.: Considerations about model mapping. In: Bezivin, J., Gogolla, M. (eds.) Workshop in Software Model Engineering (WiSME) at the 6th International Conference of the Unified Modeling Language, Modeling Languages and Applications (UML 2003), San Francisco, CA, USA, 21 October 2003
11. Cisco Systems: Cisco annual internet report (2018–2023). White Paper C11-741490-01. https://www.cisco.com/c/en/us/solutions/collateral/executive-perspectives/annual-internet-report/white-paper-c11-741490.html (2020)
12. Danese, A., Pravadelli, G., Zandonà, I.: Automatic generation of power state machines through dynamic mining of temporal assertions. In: Proceedings of the 2016 Conference on Design, Automation & Test in Europe, Dresden, Germany, DATE 2016, 14–18 March 2016, pp. 606–611. EDA Consortium, San Jose (2016). ISBN 9783981537062

13. Douglass, B.P.: Design Patterns for Embedded Systems in C: An Embedded Software Engineering Toolkit. Newnes/Elsevier, Oxford and Burlington (2011)
14. Elijah, O., Rahman, T.A., Orikumhi, I., Leow, C.Y., Hindia, M.N.: An overview of internet of things (IoT) and data analytics in agriculture: benefits and challenges. IEEE Internet Things J. **5**(5), 3758–3773 (2018)
15. Friedli, M., Kaufmann, L., Paganini, F., Kyburz, R.: Energy efficiency of the internet of things: technology and energy assessment report prepared for IEA 4e EDNA (2016). https://www.iea-4e.org/document/384/energy-efficiency-of-the-internet-of-things-technology-and-energy-assessment-report
16. Georgiou, K., Xavier-de Souza, S., Eder, K.: The IoT energy challenge: a software perspective. IEEE Embed. Syst. Lett. **10**(3), 53–56 (2018)
17. Gomez, C., DeAntoni, J., Mallet, F.: Multi-view power modeling based on UML, MARTE and SysML. In: Proceedings of the 2012 38th Euromicro Conference on Software Engineering and Advanced Applications, Cesme, Turkey, 05–08 September 2012, pp. 17–20 (2012). https://doi.org/10.1109/SEAA.2012.66
18. Gries, M.: Methods for evaluating and covering the design space during early design development. Integr. VLSI J. **38**(2), 131–183 (2004). https://doi.org/10.1016/j.vlsi.2004.06.001
19. Grunwald, A., Schaarschmidt, M., Westerkamp, C.: LoRaWAN in a rural context: Use cases and opportunities for agricultural businesses. In: Roer, P. (ed.) Proceedings of the Mobile Communication-Technologies and Applications; 24. ITG-Symposium, ITG-Fachbericht, 15–16 May 2019, pp. 134–139. VDE-Verl. GmbH, Osnabrück, Germany (2019)
20. Gupta, A., Tsai, T., Rueb, D., Yamaji, M., Middleton, P.: Forecast: internet of things: endpoints and associated services, worldwide, vol. 2017 (2017). https://www.gartner.com/en/documents/3840665/forecast-internet-of-things-endpoints-and-associated-ser
21. Hagner, M., Aniculaesei, A., Goltz, U.: UML-based analysis of power consumption for real-time embedded systems. In: Proceedings of the 10th International Conference on Trust, Security and Privacy in Computing and Communications, 16–18 November 2011, pp. 1196–1201. IEEE, Changsha, HN,China (2011). https://doi.org/10.1109/TrustCom.2011.161. ISBN 978-1-4577-2135-9
22. Holst, A.: Number of internet of things (IoT) connected devices worldwide from 2019 to 2030 (2021). https://www.statista.com/statistics/1183457/iot-connected-devices-worldwide/
23. Holst, A.: Number of internet of things (IoT) connected devices worldwide from 2019 to 2030, by communications technology (2021). https://www.statista.com/statistics/1194688/iot-connected-devices-communications-technology/
24. IBM: IBM Engineering Systems Design Rhapsody - Developer (2021). https://www.ibm.com/products/uml-tools. Accessed 12 July 2021
25. IEEE SA: IEEE Standard for IP-XACT, Standard Structure for Packaging, Integrating, and Reusing IP within Tool Flows. Document Number IEEE 1685–2014. https://standards.ieee.org/standard/1685-2014.html (2014)
26. Iyenghar, P., Pulvermueller, E.: A model-driven workflow for energy-aware scheduling analysis of IoT-enabled use cases. IEEE Internet Things J. **5**(6), 4914–4925 (2018). https://doi.org/10.1109/JIOT.2018.2879746
27. Julien, N., Laurent, J., Senn, E., Martin, E.: Power consumption modeling and characterization of the TI c6201. IEEE Micro **23**(5), 40–49 (2003). https://doi.org/10.1109/MM.2003.1240211
28. Martinez, B., Monton, M., Vilajosana, I., Prades, J.D.: The power of models: modeling power consumption for IoT devices. IEEE Sens. J. **15**(10), 5777–5789 (2015). https://doi.org/10.1109/JSEN.2015.2445094

29. Nurseitov, N., Paulson, M., Reynolds, R., Izurieta, C.: Comparison of JSON and XML data interchange formats: a case study. In: Che, D. (ed.) Proceedings of the 22nd International Conference on Computer Applications in Industry and Engineering (CAINE), 4–6 November 2009, pp. 157–162. ISCA, San Francisco, CA, USA (2009)
30. NXP Semiconductors: LPC5411x - Product data sheet, Rev. 2.5. Document identifier LPC5411x. https://www.nxp.com/docs/en/data-sheet/LPC5411X.pdf (2019). Accessed 07 Sep 2021
31. Object Management Group: Unified Modeling Language, Version 2.5.1. OMG Document Number formal/17-12-05. https://www.omg.org/spec/UML/2.5.1/ (2017)
32. Object Management Group: A UML Profile for MARTE: Modeling and Analysis of Real-Time and Embedded Systems, Version 1.2. OMG Document Number formal/19-04-01. https://www.omg.org/spec/MARTE/1.2/ (2019). Accessed 07 Sep 09 2021
33. Object Management Group (gG): Model Driven Architecture (MDA): MDA Guide rev. 2.0. OMG Document Number ormsc/2014-06-01. https://www.omg.org/cgi-bin/doc?ormsc/14-06-01 (2014). Accessed 07 Sep 2021
34. Pang, C., Hindle, A., Adams, B., Hassan, A.E.: What do programmers know about software energy consumption? IEEE Softw. **33**(3), 83–89 (2016)
35. Pathak, A., Hu, Y.C., Zhang, M.: Bootstrapping energy debugging on smartphones: a first look at energy bugs in mobile devices. In: Proceedings of the 10th ACM Workshop on Hot Topics in Networks, HotNets-X, Cambridge, MA, USA, 14–15 November 2011, 6 p. (2011). https://doi.org/10.1145/2070562.2070567. Article No. 5. ISBN 978-1-4503-1059-8
36. Pinto, G., Castor, F., Liu, Y.D.: Mining questions about software energy consumption. In: Proceedings of the 11th Working Conference on Mining Software Repositories, MSR 2014, 31 May–1 June 2014, pp. 22–31. ACM, Hyderabad, India (2014). https://doi.org/10.1145/2597073.2597110. ISBN 978-1-4503-2863-0
37. Schaarschmidt., M., Uelschen., M., Pulvermüller., E.: Power consumption estimation in model driven software development for embedded systems. In: Proceedings of the 16th International Conference on Software Technologies - ICSOFT, 6–8 July 2021, pp. 47–58. INSTICC, SciTePress, Online Streaming (2021). https://doi.org/10.5220/0010522700470058. ISBN 978-989-758-523-4. ISSN 2184-2833
38. Schaarschmidt, M., Uelschen, M., Pulvermüller, E., Westerkamp, C.: Framework of software design patterns for energy-aware embedded systems. In: Proceedings of the 15th International Conference on Evaluation of Novel Approaches to Software Engineering - ENASE, 5–6 May 2020, pp. 62–73. INSTICC, SciTePress, Online Streaming (2020). https://doi.org/10.5220/0009351000620073. ISBN 978-989-758-421-3, ISSN 2184-4895
39. Selic, B., Gérard, S.: Modeling and analysis of real-time and embedded systems with UML and MARTE: Developing cyber-physical systems. Morgan Kaufmann, Waltham (2014)
40. Silicon Labs: Energy debugging tools for embedded applications. Technical Report (2010)
41. SparxSystems: Enterprise architect (2020). https://sparxsystems.com/products/ea/index.html. Accessed 12 Jul 2021
42. Tan, T.K., Raghunathan, A., Jha, N.K.: Software architectural transformations: a new approach to low energy embedded software. In: Design, Automation, and Test in Europe Conference and Exhibition, 7 March 2003, pp. 1046–1051. IEEE Computer Society, Munich, Germany (2003). https://doi.org/10.1109/DATE.2003.1253742. ISBN 978-0-7695-1870-1
43. The MathWorks Inc: MATLAB (2021). https://www.mathworks.com/products/matlab. Accessed 12 Jul 2021
44. Vuran, M.C., Salam, A., Wong, R., Irmak, S.: Internet of underground things in precision agriculture: architecture and technology aspects. Ad Hoc Netw. **81**, 160–173 (2018). https://doi.org/10.1016/j.adhoc.2018.07.017

45. Zanella, A., Bui, N., Castellani, A., Vangelista, L., Zorzi, M.: Internet of things for smart cities. IEEE Internet Things J. **1**(1), 22–32 (2014)
46. Zhou, H.Y., Luo, D.Y., Gao, Y., Zuo, D.C.: Modeling of node energy consumption for wireless sensor networks. Wirel. Sens. Netw. **03**(01), 18–23 (2011). https://doi.org/10.4236/wsn.2011.31003
47. Zhu, Z., Olutunde Oyadiji, S., He, H.: Energy awareness workflow model for wireless sensor nodes. Wirel. Commun. Mob. Comput. **14**(17), 1583–1600 (2014). https://doi.org/10.1002/wcm.2302

Materializing Microservice-oriented Architecture from Monolithic Object-oriented Source Code

Pascal Zaragoza[1,2]([✉]), Abdelhak-Djamel Seriai[1]([✉]), Abderrahmane Seriai[2]([✉]), Anas Shatnawi[2]([✉]), Hinde-Lilia Bouziane[1]([✉]), and Mustapha Derras[2]([✉])

[1] LIRMM, CNRS and University of Montpellier, Montpellier, France
{zaragoza,seriai,bouziane}@lirmm.fr
[2] Berger-Levrault, Paris, France
{abderrahmane.seriai,anas.shatnawi}@berger-levrault.com

Abstract. Following the evolution of Cloud Computing and Service-Oriented Architecture (SOA), microservices (MS) have naturally emerged as the next trend due to the advantages they provide. These advantages include increased maintainability, better scalability, and an overall better synergy with DevOps techniques. This makes migrating legacy software towards a microservice-oriented architecture (MSA) an attractive prospect for organizations. The migration process is a complex and consequently risky endeavor that can be decomposed into two phases (1) the microservice-based architecture recovery phase and (2) the transformation (i.e. materialization) phase. Several studies have been done to automate the microservice architecture recovery phase. However, to the best of our knowledge, no work has been completed to automate the transformation phase. In this paper, we propose a systematic approach to refactor the existing code of an object-oriented monolithic application towards an MS-oriented one by using the target architecture from the recovery phase as a guide. By defining and applying a set of transformation patterns, we are able to generate a set of deployable microservices. Finally, we validate our approach by automating it through our tool MonoToMicro, and we apply it to a set of monolithic Java applications to generate a set of MSAs.

Keywords: Microservices · Monolith · Modernization · Reverse engineering · Refactoring · Transformation · Software architecture

1 Introduction

Over the past decade, there has been a significant paradigm shift towards cloud computing. As organizations try to keep up with the latest organizational, conceptual and technological trends and avoid accumulating technical debt, there has been a demand for shifting legacy systems to the Cloud [22]. From this shift, the microservice-oriented architecture (MSA) is a recent architectural style that has emerged to take advantage of the Cloud [27]. In an MSA, applications are

© Springer Nature Switzerland AG 2022
H.-G. Fill et al. (Eds.): ICSOFT 2021, CCIS 1622, pp. 143–168, 2022.
https://doi.org/10.1007/978-3-031-11513-4_7

developed as a suite of small services, each running in its own process and communicating through lightweight interfaces [20,23]. Individually, each microservice is technologically independent, and functionally autonomous while guaranteeing its autonomy with regard to their manipulated data. As a consequence, this results in a more manageable codebase as each microservice can be managed by a smaller team [6,32]. These small manageable services used in conjunction with popular DevOps techniques enable quick deployment and better scalability on the Cloud.

Meanwhile, enterprise application are often built in three parts: the client-side user interface (UI), a server-side application that handles the business logic, and the database [20]. In the MSA style, the server-side application is divided into a group of microservices. In contrast, the monolithic architecture style builds the server-side application as a single logical executable unit (i.e., monolith) [20]. Initially, the development of monolith is relatively simple. However, as product requirements change and grow, they become large and complex and thus harder to maintain. Furthermore, any change to the application requires rebuilding and redeploying the entire monolith [30]. After deployment, these monolith are rigid as increasing the workload requires duplicating the entire application. The duplication of instance is resource-intensive, as every part of the application must be replicated even when only one feature is utilized [29].

For these reasons, companies are increasingly interested in migrating their existing monolithic legacy systems towards a microservice-based one. Realistically, the migration process is a two-step process. The first step of the process involves recovering the microservice architecture from the existing application. In the second step, the extracted microservice architecture is then used to materialize (i.e., transform) the source code of the MSA.

Several approaches address the first step of the migration process by partitioning the OO implementation of a given monolithic application into clusters of classes that can later be used in the materialization step [4,5,10,11,17,18,21,24,26,28]. However, they either do not address the materialization step or complete this step manually. Although the recovered clusters help understand the target MSA, the source code must be transformed to conform to the MSA style (service-based, message-oriented communication, etc.).

Concretely, the goal of the materialization step is to transform the existing monolithic source code to create functional microservices that conform to the recovered microservice architecture, while preserving the business logic of the application. With regards to monolithic applications following the object-oriented paradigm, the difficulty of the materialization step is to transform the OO dependencies present between the identified clusters of classes into MSA-type dependencies (i.e. services). In addition, these transformation must adhere to the refactoring principles (i.e. preserve the business-logic) without degrading the performance of the overall system. However, despite the importance of the second step of the migration, and to the best of our knowledge, no approach have been proposed to automate it.

In this article, we propose a systematic approach to transform an OO application from the monolithic style to an MSA one based on a set of transformation
patterns. This set of transformation patterns create microservice-based communication mechanisms that preserve the semantic of the monolith while conforming to the principles of the MSA (e.g. message-based and data-oriented).
Furthermore, we propose an automated process, and a tool, that applies our
systematic transformation approach. Finally, we apply our approach on a set
of monolithic applications to determine whether this approach is able to refactor the code while preserving the business logic and not negatively affect the
performance of the application.

This article is an extension of the work presented in the ICSOFT 2021 proceedings [33]. In this extension, we present another set of transformation patterns
to address the exception handling mechanism found in object-oriented languages.
Furthermore, we enriched the related works to present a greater view of the existing literature with regards to the migration process as a whole. We extend the
evaluation of our approach to take into consideration the transformation patterns concerning the exceptions handling mechanism. Additionally, we expand
the research questions regarding the syntactic and semantic correctness of our
transformation approach, as well as the applicability of our approach on different
OO applications.

The remainder of this paper is organized as follows. Section 2 and 3 describe
the problem statement through an illustrative example and the overall migration approach. Section 4 and 5 describe the transformation patterns proposed
to automatically refactor the inter-microservice OO dependencies to materialize
fully-encapsulated microservices. While Sect. 6 presents the refactoring order of
all the identified encapsulation violations. Section 7 presents the tool developed
to make the approach proposed in this paper a reality, as well as the experimentation to demonstrate the validity of the approach. Section 8 and 9 provide the
related work, a conclusion and future directions.

2   The Migration Towards an MSA: A Two-step Problem

The overall goal of the migration towards an MSA is to create structurally,
behaviorally, and operationally-correct microservices. Especially, we define a
microservice as one that follows the commonly accepted definitions which include
structural and behavioral characteristics such as *"structural & behavioral autonomy"*, *"small and focused on one functionality"*, and *"data autonomy"* [20].
Furthermore, operational characteristics include *"communicate with lightweight
mechanisms"*, *"running on its own process"*, and *"automatically deployed"* [20].
Later, we use these characteristics to guide the migration process.

The process of migrating a monolithic application towards an MSA is a two-
step process involving (1) the recovery of a microservice architecture from a
monolithic OO source code and (2) the transformation of the source code to
conform to the recovered architecture. Next, we propose an example application,
followed a step-by-step migration using this example to motivate the difficulties
of each migration step.

2.1 Motivating Example: Information Screen

In this paper, we illustrate the problems we encounter during the migration process with a display management system (e.g., an airport information display). This application contains a *DisplayManager* class whose responsibility is to handle the information and display it through the *Screen* class (see Fig. 1). The information is handled using the *ContentProvider* class which handles content such as the current time (i.e., *Clock* instances) or incoming messages (i.e., *Message* instances). Finally, The *Clock* class uses an instance of the *Timezone* class to get the time based on its GPS location.

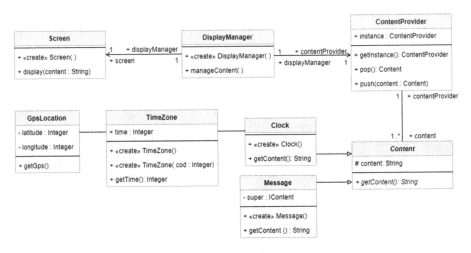

Fig. 1. Information screen class diagram inspired [2].

2.2 Microservice-based Architecture Recovery

The goal of the MSA recovery step is to partition a monolith's classes into a set of clusters that forms the basis of a **structurally and behaviorally-valid** microservices. Several approaches have been proposed to partition classes to maximize the quality of each microservice based on these characteristics. They often work to maximize the cohesiveness of the classes within a microservice while minimizing the coupling between microservices [5,29], or [18].

The results of applying a microservice recovery approach in *Information Screen* are shown in Fig. 2. In Fig. 2, five clusters are recovered. In this recovered architecture, the microservice candidate **MS1** manages and displays the content on a screen, through its classes *DisplayManager* and *Screen*. Each class can be placed into two different categories: internal classes and edge classes. An **internal class** can be defined as being a class that does not contain any inbound or outbound dependencies with a class belonging to another cluster. This is the case for *Screen* and *GpsLocation*. While an **edge class** is defined as a class which has at least one dependency with a class belonging to another cluster. These dependencies can be of any type (e.g. method invocation, constructor calls, or inheritance).

2.3   OO Source Code Transformation Towards an MSA One

The architecture recovery step's identified MSA is materialized in the transformation step. It entails converting object-oriented source code into MSA source code. Each recovered cluster of classes is then deployed into its own microservice during this step (i.e., **microservice encapsulation**).

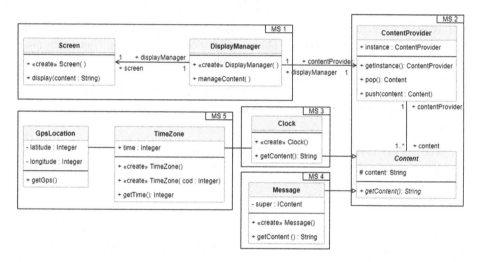

Fig. 2. Recovered microservice architecture for the information screen application.

Yet, edge classes (e.g., *DisplayManager* and *Clock*) by definition have dependencies with classes belonging to another cluster. These direct structural dependencies between the classes of different microservices are called **microservice encapsulation violations**, and they must be handled before a microservice can be fully encapsulated. Indeed, all violations must be handled by refactoring methods that convert all OO-type dependencies into MS-type dependencies before a microservice can be generated.

During this step, the operational characteristic of an MSA to use message-oriented communication between different microservices is considered. In other words, method invocations between classes belonging to different clusters (e.g. the method calls between *DisplayManager* and *ContentProvider*) must be restricted to a set of provided and required interfaces that define both the web services it provides and those it consumes. In addition, inter-process communications (IPC) calls between microservices are limited to value-based communication. In other words, only primitives and serialized data are exchanged between microststrvices. However, a procedural call in an OO system may pass object references between the invoking object and the invoked one. To encapsulate microservices, the instance sharing mechanism between microservice candidates must be resolved.

Besides these explicit OO dependencies, implicit dependencies between clusters must be addressed to fully encapsulate the microservice candidates. Inheritance mechanism and exception handling are the two main implicit OO mechanisms must be addressed. Particularly, an inheritance violation is defined as a class that has a super-class that belongs to another clusters (e.g., between *Message* and *Content*). The exception handling violation is defined as a class throwing an exception that is caught by a class belonging to another cluster. Both of these OO mechanisms must be addressed and transformed into MS-type dependencies.

Lastly, MSA generated after the transformation step must adhere to 2 additional operational characteristics: (1) microservices must run on their own process and (2) they must be automatically deployable. To conform to these operational characteristics, each microservice must define an independent project that must be configured for Cloud deployment. Both of these characteristics must be addressed during the generation of the source code for each microservice.

3   MonoToMicro: A Semi-automated Refactoring Approach

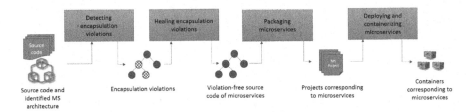

Fig. 3. The transformation process using the MonoToMicro tool [33].

In this paper, we propose a systematic way of transforming a monolithic OO application into an MSA application with a set of transformation patterns. The purpose of this approach is to transform monolithic object-oriented source code into an MSA by encapsulating the clusters discovered during the initial migration step. To do so, we define a process composed of four steps as presented in Fig. 3 which consist of: (1) detecting encapsulation violations, (2) healing encapsulation violations, (3) packaging microservices, and (4) deploying and containerizing microservices.

3.1   Detecting Encapsulation Violations

Each recovered cluster of classes is encapsulated in its own microservice to materialize the recovered microservice candidates from the source of object-oriented software. On the other hand, encapsulation prevents OO dependencies between clusters (i.e., encapsulation violations). Therefore, they must be transformed into MS-type dependencies. However, before the transformation can take place these encapsulation violation must be identified. To facilitate the detection of these encapsulation violations, a set of encapsulation violation rules are proposed to analyze the monolith:

(**Rule 1:**) if a cluster's method invokes a method belonging to a class from another cluster then it is a method invocation violation.
(**Rule 2:**) if a cluster's method accesses an attribute belonging to a class from another cluster then it is an access violation.
(**Rule 3:**) if a cluster's class contains a reference targeting a class from another cluster then it is an instance violation.
(**Rule 4:**) if a cluster's class inherits a class belonging to another cluster then it is an inheritance violation.
(**Rule 5:**) if a cluster's method throws, catches or declares an exception defined in another cluster then it is a thrown exception violation.

These rules are applied on the AST representation of the OO source code. Initially, the target architecture description is used to partition the AST nodes that represent the classes in the OO source into clusters. Then, each node is parsed for references towards class nodes belonging to another cluster using the aforementioned detection rules. After all the violations have been detected, the process of resolve all these violations can take.

3.2   Healing Encapsulation Violations

The violations detected in the preceding step must be healed using transformation rules in order to encapsulate the microservices. These transformations must either fully heal or reduce a violation to a solvable type. Previously, the identification of encapsulation violation covered (1) method invocation, (2) attribute access, (3) instance handling, (4) inheritance, and (5) exception handling. In this paper, we present a set of transformation rules to heal the encapsulation violations identified in the first step. Particularly, we separate these violations into two categories: explicit and implicit. As a general rule, microservice should obfuscate their internal structure and behavior while exposing a clearly-defined interface. Violations that break this rule are considered explicit (e.g., attribute access, instance handling, and method invocation). While implicit violations are related to the implicit dependency between microservices caused by OO mechanism (e.g., inheritance and exception handling). Therefore, we present the transformation rules related to explicit violations in Sect. 4, and the transformation rules related to implicit violations in Sect. 5. Finally, as most of the proposed transformation rules would create different additional violations, a transformation order is presented in Sect. 6 to resolve all violations.

3.3   Packaging and Deployment of an MSA

Once the MSA source code has been generated, it must be packaged and made deployable. In step (3), the violation-free microservices are packaged. To accomplish this, each microservice has its own project where the source code is generated. The file structures and project dependencies are then automatically constructed. The microservice projects are then containerized in step (4) by generating instantiable images. An image description file is created for each microservice. A composition file is also created, which arranges and delivers all of the microservices at the same time.

In this work, we concentrate on the first two steps of the transformation phase, which comprise the major scientific roadblocks previously highlighted, and leave the last two steps for the implementation in 7 as they comprise more technical roadblocks. Next, we present the set of transformation patterns based on the encapsulation type (see Sect. 4 and 5).

4   Explicit Encapsulation Violation Resolution

After fragmenting the monolithic code into different microservices (i.e. clusters of classes), some classes are instanced in one microservice and used (i.e., invoked, referenced, accessed) in others. To remove these type of violations, it is necessary to provide adequate answers to the following questions: (1) How do we access attributes of objects belonging to another microservices? (2) How do we invoke a method existing in a class belonging to another microservice? (3) How do we create an instance of a class belonging to another microservice? (4) When a given instance is referenced in several microservices, how do we ensure the sharing of this instance while preserving the business logic of the application? All of these questions must be answered to properly heal all explicit violations.

4.1   Attribute Access

The attribute access violation can be reduced to a method invocation violation by applying the getter/setter pattern, limiting the attribute access to the class, and refactoring the internal code to replace all access with the appropriate method.

4.2   Method Invocation

The method invocation between two classes (e.g., *ContentProvider* and *DisplayManager*) belonging to different clusters is the only violation that can be refactored without creating additional violations. To remove these encapsulation violation, the set of methods from the invoked class (i.e., *ContentProvider*) are extracted into a set of required and provided interfaces that are placed in the appropriate clusters. The outgoing methods calls from *DisplayManager* are then refactored to invoke the interface instead. This transformation allows us decouple the two classes while providing an interface for future communication.

Nevertheless, after the encapsulation towards an MSA the invoked class (e.g., *ContentProvider*) cannot be reached by the invoker (e.g., *DisplayManager*) via the required interface. Indeed, as microservice communicate exclusively through lightweight mechanism (e.g., RPC or events), a technological layer must be implemented. Therefore, the provided interfaces must be implemented, or exposed, as a web service in the microservice containing the invoked class (e.g., *ContentProvider*). In Fig. 4, a *WebService* class is generated to expose the methods of *ContentProvider*. To achieve this goal, a method is created in the *WebService* for every public method of *ContentProvider*, to act as a proxy to receive a request. The proxy method then calls the appropriate method and returns its result. From the invoking microservice, a *WebConsumer* class is generated to implement the required interface and handle the network calls to its corresponding *WebService class*.

4.3   Instance Handling

Regarding the questions surrounding the creation and sharing of instances of a class between multiple microservices, we propose a combination of design patterns to recreate the constructor calls and the sharing of instances. More specifically, we apply a Factory pattern to decouple the creation of instances between classes belonging to different cluster. For instance, we replace the instantiation of *ContentProvider* by the class *DisplayManager* with an interface acting as an object factory. For simplicity, the same provided/required interfaces used

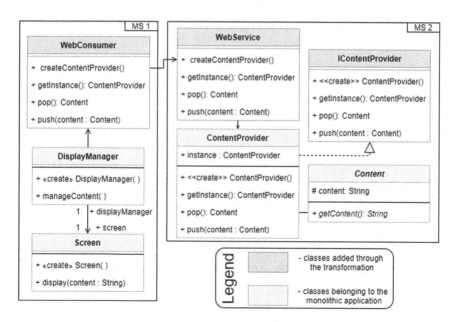

Fig. 4. Decoupling method invocations with interface-based calls and class instantiation with the factory pattern.

to decouple method invocations between microservices are used to define these object factory methods. In Fig. 4, this requires adding a factory method in the required/provided interface (i.e., method *createContentProvider()*), and implementing the corresponding methods in the *WebConsumer* & *WebService*.

Applying a Proxy Pattern is the next step in transforming the instance creation violation. According to [16], the proxy pattern is used to provide a surrogate for another object to control access to it. Figure 5 illustrates the proxy pattern applied on the class *ContentProvider* to propose a surrogate (*ContentProviderProxy*) and handle all method invocations from *DisplayManager*. In this scenario, the proxy class acts to decouple the object referenced in one microservice which is defined in another microservice. Therefore, a proxy class is created for any class referenced in one microservice and defined in another. This proxy class will have the same public methods and the same public constructors. However, the proxy class implementation is rewritten to use the *WebConsumer* class to interact with the real class definition.

Furthermore, upon the instantiation of the proxy class, the real class' instance is created. To differentiate, between the proxy class and the real class, the instances of the proxy class are called proxy instances, and instances of the real class are called concrete instances. However, after instantiating a proxy instance, there needs to be a mechanism to link the proxy instance to the concrete instance. Indeed, a proxy instance should reference its concrete instance. Therefore, we propose that a proxy instance references its concrete instance via the same unique reference, and any operation on a proxy instance is transferred to its concrete instance. Finally, whenever the concrete instance is exchanged between microservices, the unique reference is passed instead of the concrete instance.

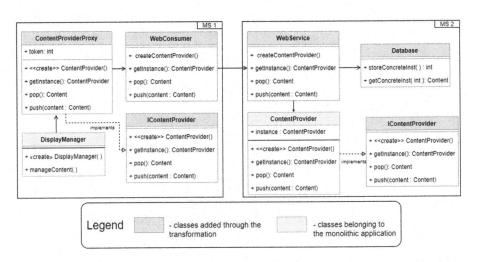

Fig. 5. Replacing access to an object with the proxy pattern.

Concretely, there needs to be a mechanism to keep the state of the concrete instance between methods calls. Therefore, we implement a class to store and manage all concrete instances created in a microservice. Whenever a factory is called to create a concrete instance, it sends the object to a storage class (e.g., the *Database class in Figure* 5 to preserve it. In return the storage class returns a token for accessing the object. The factory method returns the token via its web service implementation to the proxy instance which stores it for later method invocations. Later, when a proxy-instance method is invoked, it transfer the request along with the token to the appropriate web service method. The token adds the required context for the web service to load the concrete instance and invoke the correct method.

Another thing to consider is that complex objects may be passed as a parameter between microservices. While primitives or data classes can be easily serialized, certain objects and their states cannot be serialized without losing information. Since microservices are limited to lightweight communication, we need to transform the exchange of complex objects while preserving the consistency of the application's business logic. For instance, a microservice may receive or send an object of a class which it does not define. Whether the sender holds a proxy or a concrete instance, it must be able to produce a token to represent it. In the case of the receiver, it must be able to handle a token whether the receiver holds the concrete instance or not. With this token mechanism, complex objects can be passed between microservices as tokens, while the owner of the class manages the instances. A microservice is able to instantiate the proxy instance whenever it receives a token. When a microservice receives a token, it is able to instance the appropriate proxy class to access the concrete instance.

5   Implicit Encapsulation Violation Resolution

In the previous section, we covered explicit encapsulation violations and how to resolved them. In this section, we cover the implicit encapsulation violations relating to the inherent OO mechanisms. Particularly, we address the inheritance relationship between classes, and exception handling.

5.1   Inheritance Relationship

Whenever a class inherits from another class belonging to a different microservice, it is considered an inheritance violation. To heal this encapsulation violation, inheritance must be decomposed into its different mechanisms and then transformed as to preserve all of the mechanisms. This includes (a) the extension of the child class definition through the parent class, (b) the subtyping mechanism, and (c) polymorphic assignment. To do so, we propose a three-step transformation inspired from [2]: (i) Uncoupling the child/parent inheritance with a double proxy pattern, (ii) Recreating subtyping via interface inheritance, and (iii) recreating the polymorphic assignment through interface inheritance.

Child/Parent Definition Extension. The first mechanism that must be transformed is the extension of the definition of the parent by the child. A child class has access to the parent's attributes and methods. Furthermore, it may override the parent's methods. Finally, both child and parent method definitions may access each other's methods through the use of reference variables to the parent object or itself. To preserve the this mechanism, we propose a double-proxy pattern inspired by the work presented in [2]. In their paper, the authors propose a double delegate pattern to preserve the inheritance between class placed in different components [2].

When a child object is created, a parent object is also created as an attribute within the child object. However, the child class is refactored to implement any parent method that is not redefined. These methods delegate any invocation to the parent method through the stored parent object. Inversely, the parent object store the child object and acts as a delegate and preserves the dynamic calling of overridden methods. This transforms the inheritance encapsulation violation into a set of instantiation violations and a method invocation violations which can be healed using the transformation patterns proposed previously. In the case of an abstract parent class, [2] apply a proxy pattern so that the proxy class inherits from the parent class and it can be instantiated by the child class. However, since we later heal the instantiation violations with a proxy pattern, this is already handled.

Furthermore, the double-delegate pattern of [2] refactors the internal code of the child and parent class. This requires informing the developer to use the delegate pattern instead of the native inheritance implementation. Instead, we proposed a revised version that treats inheritance as a service and reduced the refactoring of the internal classes.

Concretely, we propose a double-proxy pattern to reproduce the inheritance link between the child and parent classes without significantly refactoring the child/pattern classes. First, a parent proxy class (e.g., *ContentConsumer*) is created and implements the methods defined by the interface extracted from the parent (e.g., *IContent*). Then, the child class (e.g., *Message*) is refactored to extend the parent proxy (e.g., *ContentConsumer*). Finally, child proxy class (e.g., *MessageConsumer*) is defined to extend the parent class, and acts as the child proxy for the parent class. Figure 6 illustrates the transformation of the inheritance link between the child (e.g., *Message*) and the parent class (e.g., *Content*).

Recreating Subtyping Through Proxy Inheritance. To preserve the internal logic created through subtyping, the proxy classes are exposed as web services (as seen in Sect. 4). This results in the creation of two web services (Fig. 6). Upon the creation of a child object (e.g., *Message*), the parent proxy's constructor (e.g., *ContentConsumer*) is called to consume the Parent web service. This has the effect of initializing the child proxy (e.g., *MessageConsumer*) that inherits naturally from the parent class (e.g., *Content*). Whenever a method defined by the parent class (e.g., *Content*) is invoked by the child object (e.g., *Message*), the parent object will be invoked via the parent web service. Furthermore, when the parent class (e.g., *Content*) references the instance, it will invoke the child object through the child proxy (e.g. *MessageConsumer*) object.

Recreating Polymorphic Assignment Through Interface Inheritance. Finally, to recreate the polymorphic mechanism, a child interface (e.g., *IMessage*) is defined to extend the parent interface (e.g. *IContent*). The child class implements the child interface, allowing for the polymorphic assignment of the child objects (see Fig. 6).

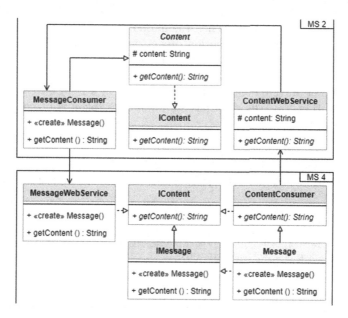

Fig. 6. Polymorphic assignment can be recreated by applying an interface inheritance between the parent interface and the child interface [33].

5.2 Source Code Transformation to Heal Exception Throwing and Catching Violations

The exception handling encapsulation violation involves create, throwing, and catching exception objects across microservices. To ensure a well-contained throwing & handling of exceptions we propose a two-step transformation process: wrapping the exception response and transforming the exception-handling source code.

Wrapping the Exception Response. Normal methods have two different types of responses. They may return the normal intended type response, or an exception response. However, Web service methods are not intended to throw exception objects. When a method is exposed as a service, this limitation must be circumvented by introducing a class that acts as a wrapper return type which can hold either the normal response type, or an exception response type. Every method's return type is replaced by this wrapper class.

Transforming the Exception-Handling Source Code. To prepare the wrapper type, a web service operation surrounds the method invocation with a try and catch. When the method returns the normal response type, it safely adds the value in a dictionary. When the method returns an exception response type, it safely captures the exception object, stores it for later use, and adds its corresponding access token to access the dictionary. Listing 13 illustrates an example of a web service method wrapping the normal *IContent* response type, or catching either an *EmptyContentStackException* or a *FullContentStackException* object. Either way, the object is stored and its token is placed in a JSON node and returned.

```
1  public class ContentProviderWebService {
2      public JsonNode pop(int proxy_id){
3          JsonNode return_node = new JsonNode();
4          IContentProvider contentprovider = InstanceDB.getContentProvider(
   proxy_id);
5          try{
6              return_node.put("return", InstanceDB.addContent(contentprovider.
   pop()));
7          } catch(EmptyContentStackException e){
8              return_node.put("EmptyContentStackException", InstanceDB.
   addEmptyContentStackException(e));
9          }
10         return return_node
11     }
12 }
```

Listing 1.1. Surrounding the method which throws an error with a try and catch.

Upon receiving the response from the service, the proxy must check the response with a series of if/else. If the wrapper contains the normal response then it returns it. If, on the other hand, it contains one of the exception responses, then it extracts the token corresponding to the exception response, associates it with a new proxy exception object, and finally throws the latter. Listing 23 illustrates how the JSON sent in Listing 13 is handled. If the JSON contains a value designating any of the keys that correspond to an exception type, then the corresponding exception proxy is created. Otherwise, it is assumed that the normal response was stored in the return key of the JSON.

```
13 public class ContentProviderConsumer {
14     public IContent pop() throws EmptyContentStackExceptionImpl {
15         JsonNode return_node = getProxy().pop(contentprovider_id);
16         if(return_node.get("EmptyContentStackException" != null){
17             throw new EmptyContentStackExceptionImpl(return_node.get("
   EmptyContentStackException"));
```

```
18    } else {
19        return new IContentImpl(return_node.get("return").asInt());
20    }
21  }
22 }
```

Listing 1.2. Surrounding the network call with an if/else statement to unwrap either the normal response or the exception response.

6   Violation Resolution Order

For every type of encapsulation violation identified in this approach, transformation rules have been proposed. However, some transformation rules produced additional violations. Such is the case with the inheritance violation which creates additional instance violations. Therefore, to systematically fully resolve all encapsulation violations in one iteration, we propose a violation resolution order which is presented in 7.

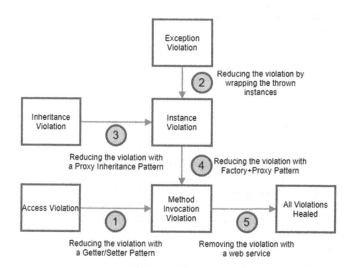

Fig. 7. The transformation order of each microservice encapsulation violation.

The order is as follows:

1. The attribute access violation is reduced as it adds public methods to its class that may be further refactored by inheritance violation.
2. The thrown exceptions are reduced to instance violations.
3. The inheritance violations are reduced to an instance violation so all instance violations can be healed together.
4. The instance violations are reduced to method invocation violations.
5. The remaining method invocations violations are transformed into a set of web services.

In the next section, we apply this transformation order when resolving the encapsulation violations identified on a set of applications.

7 Evaluation

To evaluate our approach we implemented a tool to apply our approach. Furthermore, we migrated to various degree a set of monolithic applications of various sizes. We extracted an initial list of 19 applications that were used in nine different articles in the field of MSA recovery. We selected 6 applications based on whether the source code was open-source and object-oriented. The seventh application (*Omaje*), is a closed-source legacy application by Berger-Levrault, an international software editor. This application was designed over 10 years ago by a team of 4 developers to handle the distribution of software licenses between Berger-Levrault and its clients. Metrics on the seven applications are available in Table 1.

Table 1. Applications on which the experiment was conducted (originally in [33]).

Application name	No of classes	Lines of code (LOC)
FindSportMates[1]	21	4.061
JPetStore[2]	24	4.319
PetClinic[3]	44	2.691
SpringBlog[4]	87	4.369
IMS[5]	94	13.423
JForum[6]	373	60.919
Omaje	1.821	137.420

[1]https://github.com/chihweil5/FindSportMates.
[2]https://github.com/mybatis/jpetstore-6.
[3]https://github.com/spring-petclinic/spring-framework-petclinic.
[4]https://github.com/Raysmond/SpringBlog.
[5]https://github.com/gtiwari333/java-inventory-management-system-swing-hibernate-nepal.
[6]https://github.com/rafaelsteil/jforum2/.

7.1 Data Pre-processing: Microservice Identification

To evaluate the transformation approach, we must first use recover the microservice architecture. We use the semi-automatic approach proposed in [29] to recover an MSA as a cluster of classes but other identification approaches can be used. These clusters along with the source code of the applications are used as input for our approach.

7.2 Research Questions and Their Methodologies

We conduct an experiment with the goal of answering the three following research questions regarding our approach.

RQ1: Is the Mono2Micro Approach Applicable for Different Types of OO Applications?

Goal. The goal of this research question is to test the applicability of Mono2Micro on a set of different applications. By selecting a several applications of varying size and implementation, we aim to demonstrate that this approach is applicable in real use cases.

Method. To answer RQ1, we applied our approach on the set of applications found in Table 1. For each case study, we compiled the packaged target code. We consider that the transformations proposed in our approach materialize the encapsulation characteristic in the case where Mono2Micro is able to successfully heal the encapsulation violations detected in the different types of applications, and no compilation or execution error is revealed within all 7 applications.

RQ2: What Is the Precision of Mono2Micro Approach When Materializing a Microservice-oriented Architecture?

Goal. The goal of this research question is to evaluate the syntactic and semantic correctness of the microservice architecture. We aim to demonstrate that we are able to transform the source code of a monolithic application while preserving its business logic.

Method. We measure the precision of our approach based on the syntactic and semantic correctness of the transformed microservices. It stands to reason that if the resulting MSA applications behaves in the same way as the monolithic applications then the business logic was preserved.

We consider that microservices have a correct syntax if there is no compilation errors. To measure the semantic correctness, we rely on whether the transformed microservices produce the same results compared to the functionalities of the original the monolithic applications at run-time. To do so, we identify a set of execution scenarios that can be used in both applications. We compare the outputs of the monolithic application with its microservice counterpart for each execution scenario. We consider that the transformation has a semantic correctness when the outputs generated by the monolith and the MSA are identical based on the same inputs.

When possible, the identification of execution scenarios is based on test cases defined by the developers of the monolithic applications (e.g. JPetStore). When test cases are not available, we identify a set of features and sub-features for each monolithic application (e.g. FindSportmates, IMS). From these features, we establish a set of user scenarios that cover all features of each application. These user scenarios are performed on the monolithic application and the results are saved. Then, these user scenarios are performed on the MSA, and the results are compared with those of the monolithic application. When they are identical we consider this as a passed test. Otherwise, they are marked as a failed test.

The precision is calculated by taking the number of tests passed by both architectures and dividing by the number of the tests passed by the MSA.

Due to time constraints related to the application packaging that is highly dependent on the technology of the monolith working with Spring, we study this research question with the *FindSportMates*, *JPetStore*, and *InventoryManagementSystem* applications. For *JPetStore*, we ran the Selenium tests provided with the monolithic application. For *FindSportmates* and *Inventory Management System*, we manually ran these user scenarios.

RQ3: What Is the Recall of Mono2Micro Approach When Materializing a Microservice-oriented Architecture?

Goal. This RQ is similar to *RQ2*, but aims to evaluate the recall of our Mono2Micro approach

Method. Similarly to **RQ3**, we perform the same procedure. However, we calculate the recall by taking the number of tests passed by both architectures and dividing it by the number of tests passed by the monolith.

RQ4: What Are the Impacts of Mono2Micro on the Performance?

Goal. The overall goal of our approach is to migrate while preserving the semantic behavior of an application. Moreover, an important aspect of the migration is that it must preserve the semantic without degrading drastically the runtime performance of the application. Therefore the primary goal of this RQ is to evaluate whether the performance impacts resulting from the migration of the monolithic application to microservices are negligible when compared to the original application.

Method. To answer RQ4, we rely on the execution time of user requests. The execution time measures the delay between the time when the request is sent and the time when the response is received by the user. We compare the execution time of both the monolith and the MSA.

We establish a user scenario using *Omaje* to compare the performance of the monolithic application with its microservice counterpart. We chose *Omaje* for this evaluation because its business logic is the most complex of all 7 applications. To evaluate the performance, we simulate an increasing number of users connecting to both the MSA and the monolith, using JMeter[1] to simulate user load. As the number of user increases, we increase the number of instances of the microservice for both the monolith and the MSA. For the monolith, this involves duplicating the application. For the MSA, this involves duplicating the microservices involved in the current scenario. We consider that the refactoring results improve or maintain the quality and performance of the original code if the execution time difference between both architectures is negligible for the average user while the resource utilization is optimized. For our test we use a computer with an i7-6500U @ 2.5 GHz and 16 GB of ram.

---

[1] https://jmeter.apache.org/.

7.3   Results

RQ1: Is the Mono2Micro Approach Applicable for Different Types of OO Applications?

Table 2 displays the number of violations detected and resolved. A violation is defined as a class that is dependent on a class belonging to a different microservice. Note that we have manually transformed two encapsulation violations in relation to the use of the Java reflexivity mechanism (e.g. Class.forName(className), proxyClass.getConstructor().newInstance()). This type of violation is not yet addressed in our approach. Table 3 highlights the different violations detected. The distribution of the type of violations can be explained by the relatively low amount of inheritance and exception classes found in these applications. The number of class inheritance is low in these applications as the frameworks used emphasizes simpler class relations. Exception-type violations are not present in FindSportMates, JPetStore, and IMS as they do not contain exception class definitions. As a result of the refactoring process, we observed that the execution of the seven applications, in their two versions, monolithic and microservices, was completed without compilation or runtime errors. Based on the analysis of these results, we answer **RQ1** as follows: The proposed transformations make it possible to remove direct dependencies between the clusters which constitute violations of the encapsulation characteristic of the corresponding microservices. Therefore, our approach guarantees the encapsulation characteristic of microservices over a variety of applications.

Table 2. Data on the applications being transformed (originally in [33]).

Application	No. MSs	No. data classes	No. violations
Findsportmates	3	2	9
JPetStore	4	9	21
PetClinic	3	7	26
SpringBlog	4	8	104
IMS	5	18	113
JForum	8	37	1031

RQ2: What Is the Precision of Mono2Micro Approach When Materializing a Microservice-oriented Architecture?

Table 4 shows the results of **RQ2**. The results show that our approach has a 100% precision for *FindSportMates*, *JPetStore* and *InventoryManagementSystem* in terms of syntactic and semantic correctness. Therefore, our approach is able to preserve the business logic with a high precision.

Table 3. Type of violations caused by OO-type dependencies between microservices (originally in [33]).

Application	No. Instances	No. Inheritances	No. Exceptions
Findsportmates	9	0	0
JPetStore	20	0	0
PetClinic	24	2	0
SpringBlog	95	7	2
IMS	110	3	0
JForum	1013	16	2

RQ3: What Is the Recall of Mono2MMicro Approach When Materializing a Microservice-oriented Architecture?

Table 4 shows the results of **RQ3**. The results show that our approach has a 100% recall for *FindSportMates*, *JPetStore* and *InventoryManagementSystem*. The proposed transformation did not create a side-effect that was detected by failed functional tests that otherwise passed for the monolith. Therefore, our approach is able to preserve the business logic with a high recall. However, it should be noted that for *JPetStore* the Selenide test "testOrder" failed for both the monolithic version and the MSA version, as both checked the pricing notation using a period as a decimal separator while the testing was performed on a computer which defaults to using a comma instead.

Table 4. Number of tests performed for each application and the resulting precision and recall from these tests (originally in [33]).

Application	No. Test	Precision	Recall
Findsportmates	7	100%	100%
JPetStore	34	100%	100%
IMS	36	100%	100%

RQ4: What Are the Impacts of Mono2Micro on the Performance?

Fig. 8 illustrates the number of users per scenario with the different architecture configurations. We can see, there is a small gain in performance upon the introduction of scaling for the microservice-oriented architecture.

The proposed transformations from Mono2Micro does not negatively affect the performance of the application. Our expectations were that by introducing additional network calls the performance of the migrated application would be affected negatively. However, in this scenario it was not the case. This was likely due to the parallelization aspect of scaling the requested service. By adapting the number of instances of microservices, the MSA was able to handle the increased requests and compensate for the additional network layer. In fact, as the number of parallel requests increased, the MSA performed better (on average) compared to its monolith counterpart.

7.4 Threats to Validity

Our study may be concerned by internal and external threats to validity. We discuss below these two kinds of possible threats:

Internal Threat to Validity. The first threat to validity is that our transformation approach uses static analysis to detect and transform the existing source code. Indeed, static analysis cannot detect dynamic binding and polymorphism when identifying instance encapsulation violations. However, this can be avoided by taking into consideration the worst case by creating an instance dependency for every sub-type. Another risk is that static analysis, unlike dynamic analysis, does cannot detect unused source code. This results may result in detecting more dependencies than necessary. However, this can be mitigated in well-maintained applications. Another solution is to perform a hybrid analysis during the detection step. However, dynamic analysis requires instrumenting and providing a thorough set of test cases, which is not always available or feasible in a large industrial code-base. Also, we consider our approach to be adequate for source code that is not reliant on a strong framework (e.g. Spring for JAVA). We do not consider, dependency injection which is one of the properties of this type of framework. Finally, our approach does not consider the reflexivity of certain languages, thus in our experiment we identified and manually resolved these types of encapsulation violation.

External Threat to Validity. One external threat of validity we considered is the use of a specific architecture recovery approach (e.g., [29]) to have an impact of the transformation phase. Indeed, the number of identified dependencies and the overall performance are highly dependent on the results of the architecture recovery phase. However, our goal was not to analyze the impact of our transformation on the produced architecture, but whether we are able to migrate applications while preserving the intended behavior (business-wise and performance-wise) of the application. Another threat we considered is that our monolithic application are all implemented in JAVA. However, the obtained results can be generalized for any OO language. We argue, just as most architecture recovery approaches, that generalization is possible since all OO languages (e.g., C++, C#) are structured in terms of classes and their relationships are realized through the same general mechanisms (e.g. method invocations, field access, inheritance, etc.).

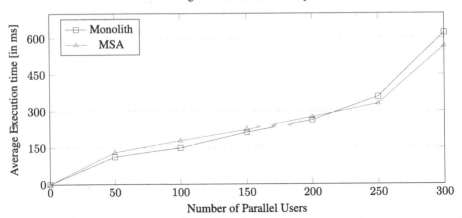

Fig. 8. Average execution time of Omaje based on the number of users and the corresponding architecture (originally in [33]).

8   Related Work

We present related work in relation to the two phases of a migration process.

8.1   Microservice-based Architecture Recovery

Architecture recovery is fundamental to promote software reuse, increase software comprehension and support software evolution. Previously, architecture recovery as focused on recovering components. Particularly, [8,9] focus on recovering a component-based architecture from a object-oriented system. More generally, several surveys have been proposed to cover component recovery [7,12].

Recently, many works have been done on the process of extracting an MSA from an OO software, and several systematic reviews have been published on the subject and microservices in general [14,15,25]. Several have presented methodologies or techniques to decompose and identify microservices within a monolithic application [4,5,10,11,17–19,21,28]. Chen et al. present a dataflow-driven approach to extracting microservices [10]. The authors of [4] present a clustering technique from business processes. Jin et al. propose a microservice extraction method that focuses on functional independence, and use 5 different metrics to measure the functional independence quality of the extracted microservices [18]. [19] proposes an ad-hoc method to decompose a monolithic application starting with a triple (F,B,D) where F is a set of facades, B is a set of business functions, and D is a set of database tables. In [17], the authors present a service decomposition tool known as *Service Cutter* which assists software architects when making design decisions. The authors of [5] present an automated tool that analyses the OpenAPI interface of an application to extract its microservices. Other tools use various clustering methods such as [21] which represents the monolith with a graph where a class is represented by a node and the edge between nodes has a weight function that is related to the coupling between two classes. Or [28], which uses a semi-automated approach based on architect's recommendations and a hierarchical clustering method with a fitness function. Another technique for microservice discovery is the function-splitting heuristics proposed in [11].

8.2 Transformation Towards a Microservice-oriented Application

The goal of refactoring is to extend the lifetime of an existing software product while preserving its functional behavior via code transformation to improve the structure of the source code. To the best of our knowledge, there does not exist any work in the transformation towards microservice that attempts to automate this process. However, there exists works towards refactoring existing OO code towards component-based architecture. Particularly, [2,3] have proposed a transformation approach to seamlessly refactor existing OO source code into a component-based architecture. Similarly, [1] transforms java applications into OSGi-type components. However, contrary to [2,3] they do not treat component instantiation.

Both a systematic mapping study [25] and a systematic review [15] on the subject of microservice migration, indicate a lack of tool to support the migration towards microservices. [31] proposes a technique for extracting modules from monolithic software architectures based on a series of refactoring to modularize concerns through the isolation of code fragments. [31] proposes a technique for extracting modules from monolithic software architectures based on a series of refactoring to modularize concerns through the isolation of code fragments. However, they don't focus on the transformation of modules that can be independently deployed as microservices, and therefore does not solve the main problems with encapsulating a microservice (i.e. uncoupling classes belonging to different modules by creating web services). Furthermore, the authors present an approach to isolate concerns into modules, however they do not explicitly focus on modularizing all of the monolith.

Besides, several works offer insights on the manual transformation such as [13,27], and [4]. [13] presents an experiment report where the authors share their migration process on an example. [4] propose an extraction method accompanied by a manual transformation to validate their approach.

9 Conclusion

The migration of OO monolithic applications towards a microservice-oriented one is a complex two-step process. In Sect. 2.1, we have exposed the particular difficulties in the transformation step in which we must transform existing OO-type dependencies between microservice candidates before they can be encapsulated. Furthermore, we have presented a set of transformation patterns to refer the different OO-type dependencies into microservice-type dependencies.

Overall, we have proposed a systematic approach to automate the transformation of monolithic source code towards an MSA by detecting and transforming the OO-type dependencies. To evaluate our approach, we have applied our approach on a set of applications to answer three research questions regarding the syntactic and semantic correctness of our approach as well as the performance of the resulting microservice-based application. As a perspective for this work, we will consider other particular properties of certain object-oriented languages (e.g., reflexivity, multiple inheritance, "Friend" concept). Furthermore, we plan to study dependencies and transformation patterns pertaining to applications relying on frameworks. We also plan to study dependencies and transformation patterns in the context of frameworks. Finally, we plan generalize our approach to other languages and frameworks by applying model-driven engineering techniques.

References

1. Allier, S., Sadou, S., Sahraoui, H.A., Fleurquin, R.: From object-oriented applications to component-oriented applications via component-oriented architecture. In: 9th Working IEEE/IFIP Conference on Software Architecture, WICSA 2011, Boulder, Colorado, USA, 20–24 June 2011, pp. 214–223. IEEE Computer Society (2011). https://doi.org/10.1109/WICSA.2011.35
2. Alshara, Z., Seriai, A., Tibermacine, C., Bouziane, H., Dony, C., Shatnawi, A.: Migrating large object-oriented applications into component-based ones: instantiation and inheritance transformation. In: International Conference on Generative Programming: Concepts and Experiences, GPCE 2015, pp. 55–64. ACM (2015). https://doi.org/10.1145/2814204.2814223
3. Alshara, Z., Seriai, A.-D., Tibermacine, C., Bouziane, H.L., Dony, C., Shatnawi, A.: Materializing architecture recovered from object-oriented source code in component-based languages. In: Tekinerdogan, B., Zdun, U., Babar, A. (eds.) ECSA 2016. LNCS, vol. 9839, pp. 309–325. Springer, Cham (2016). https://doi.org/10.1007/978-3-319-48992-6_23
4. Amiri, M.J.: Object-aware identification of microservices. In: 2018 IEEE SCC, pp. 253–256. IEEE, July 2018. https://doi.org/10.1109/SCC.2018.00042, https://ieeexplore.ieee.org/document/8456428/
5. Baresi, L., Garriga, M., De Renzis, A.: Microservices identification through interface analysis. In: De Paoli, F., Schulte, S., Broch Johnsen, E. (eds.) ESOCC 2017. LNCS, vol. 10465, pp. 19–33. Springer, Cham (2017). https://doi.org/10.1007/978-3-319-67262-5_2
6. Baskarada, S., Nguyen, V., Koronios, A.: Architecting microservices: practical opportunities and challenges. J. Comput. Inf. Syst. **60**, 428–436 (2020)
7. Birkmeier, D., Overhage, S.: On component identification approaches – classification, state of the art, and comparison. In: Lewis, G.A., Poernomo, I., Hofmeister, C. (eds.) CBSE 2009. LNCS, vol. 5582, pp. 1–18. Springer, Heidelberg (2009). https://doi.org/10.1007/978-3-642-02414-6_1
8. Chardigny, S., Seriai, A.: Software architecture recovery process based on object-oriented source code and documentation. In: Babar, M.A., Gorton, I. (eds.) ECSA 2010. LNCS, vol. 6285, pp. 409–416. Springer, Heidelberg (2010). https://doi.org/10.1007/978-3-642-15114-9_35

9. Chardigny, S., Seriai, A., Tamzalit, D., Oussalah, M.: Quality-driven extraction of a component-based architecture from an object-oriented system. In: 12th European Conference on Software Maintenance and Reengineering, CSMR 2008, 1–4 April 2008, Athens, Greece, pp. 269–273. IEEE Computer Society (2008). https://doi.org/10.1109/CSMR.2008.4493324

10. Chen, R., Li, S., Li, Z.: From monolith to microservices: a dataflow-driven approach. In: Proceedings - Asia-Pacific Software Engineering Conference, APSEC, pp. 466–475 (2018). https://doi.org/10.1109/APSEC.2017.53

11. De Alwis, A.A.C., Barros, A., Polyvyanyy, A., Fidge, C.: Function-splitting heuristics for discovery of microservices in enterprise systems. In: Pahl, C., Vukovic, M., Yin, J., Yu, Q. (eds.) ICSOC 2018. LNCS, vol. 11236, pp. 37–53. Springer, Cham (2018). https://doi.org/10.1007/978-3-030-03596-9_3

12. Ducasse, S., Pollet, D.: Software architecture reconstruction: a process-oriented taxonomy. IEEE Trans. Softw. Eng. **35**(4), 573–591 (2009). https://doi.org/10.1109/TSE.2009.19

13. Fan, C., Ma, S.: Migrating monolithic mobile application to microservice architecture: an experiment report. In: 2017 IEEE AIMS, pp. 109–112, June 2017. https://doi.org/10.1109/AIMS.2017.23

14. Francesco, P.D., Malavolta, I., Lago, P.: Research on architecting microservices: trends, focus, and potential for industrial adoption. In: 2017 IEEE ICSA, pp. 21–30 (2017). https://doi.org/10.1109/ICSA.2017.24

15. Fritzsch, J., Bogner, J., Zimmermann, A., Wagner, S.: From monolith to microservices: a classification of refactoring approaches. CoRR abs/1807.10059 (2018), http://arxiv.org/abs/1807.10059

16. Gamma, E., Helm, R., Johnson, R., Vlissides, J.: Design Patterns: Elements of Reusable Object-Oriented Software. Addison-Wesley Longman Publishing Co., Inc, USA (1995)

17. Gysel, M., Kölbener, L., Giersche, W., Zimmermann, O.: Service cutter: a systematic approach to service decomposition. In: Aiello, M., Johnsen, E.B., Dustdar, S., Georgievski, I. (eds.) ESOCC 2016. LNCS, vol. 9846, pp. 185–200. Springer, Cham (2016). https://doi.org/10.1007/978-3-319-44482-6_12

18. Jin, W., Liu, T., Zheng, Q., Cui, D., Cai, Y.: Functionality-oriented microservice extraction based on execution trace clustering. In: 2018 IEEE ICWS, pp. 211–218, July 2018. https://doi.org/10.1109/ICWS.2018.00034

19. Levcovitz, A., Terra, R., Valente, M.T.: Towards a technique for extracting microservices from monolithic enterprise systems. CoRR abs/1605.03175 (2016), http://arxiv.org/abs/1605.03175

20. Lewis, J., Fowler, M.: Microservices: a definition of this new architectural term (2014). https://martinfowler.com/articles/microservices.html

21. Mazlami, G., Cito, J., Leitner, P.: Extraction of microservices from monolithic software architectures. In: 2017 IEEE ICWS, pp. 524–531. IEEE, June 2017. https://doi.org/10.1109/ICWS.2017.61, http://ieeexplore.ieee.org/document/8029803/

22. Monaghan, B.D., Bass, J.M.: Redefining legacy: a technical debt perspective. In: Morisio, M., Torchiano, M., Jedlitschka, A. (eds.) PROFES 2020. LNCS, vol. 12562, pp. 254–269. Springer, Cham (2020). https://doi.org/10.1007/978-3-030-64148-1_16

23. Newman, S.: Building Microservices: Designing Fine-Grained Systems. O'Reilly Media, Newton (2019)

24. Nunes, L., Santos, N., Rito Silva, A.: From a monolith to a microservices architecture: an approach based on transactional contexts. In: Bures, T., Duchien, L.,

Inverardi, P. (eds.) ECSA 2019. LNCS, vol. 11681, pp. 37–52. Springer, Cham (2019). https://doi.org/10.1007/978-3-030-29983-5_3

25. Pahl, C., Jamshidi, P.: Microservices: a systematic mapping study. In: Proceedings of the 6th CLOSER - Volume 1 and 2, pp. 137–146. CLOSER 2016, SCITEPRESS - Science and Technology Publications, Lda, Setubal, PRT (2016). https://doi.org/10.5220/0005785501370146

26. Ponce, F., Márquez, G., Astudillo, H.: Migrating from monolithic architecture to microservices: a rapid review. In: 2019 38th International Conference of the Chilean Computer Science Society (SCCC), pp. 1–7 (2019). https://doi.org/10.1109/SCCC49216.2019.8966423

27. Richardson, C.: Microservices Patterns. O'Reilly Media, Newton (2018)

28. Selmadji, A., Seriai, A.-D., Bouziane, H.L., Dony, C., Mahamane, R.O.: Re-architecting OO software into microservices. In: Kritikos, K., Plebani, P., de Paoli, F. (eds.) ESOCC 2018. LNCS, vol. 11116, pp. 65–73. Springer, Cham (2018). https://doi.org/10.1007/978-3-319-99819-0_5

29. Selmadji, A., Seriai, A.D., Bouziane, H.L., Mahamane, R., Zaragoza, P., Dony, C.: From monolithic architecture style to microservice one based on a semi-automatic approach. In: 2020 IEEE International Conference on Software Architecture (ICSA), pp. 157–168 (2020)

30. Soldani, J., Tamburri, D.A., Van Den Heuvel, W.J.: The pains and gains of microservices: a systematic grey literature review. J. Syst. Softw. **146**, 215–232 (2018). https://doi.org/10.1016/j.jss.2018.09.082, https://www.sciencedirect.com/science/article/pii/S0164121218302139

31. Terra, R., Valente, M., Bigonha, R.: An approach for extracting modules from monolithic software architectures. In: pp. 1–8, January 2012

32. Waseem, M., Liang, P., Shahin, M.: A systematic mapping study on microservices architecture in devops. J. Syst. Softw. **170** (2020). https://doi.org/10.1016/j.jss.2020.110798, https://www.sciencedirect.com/science/article/pii/S0164121220302053

33. Zaragoza., P., Seriai., A., Seriai., A., Bouziane., H., Shatnawi., A., Derras., M.: Refactoring monolithic object-oriented source code to materialize microservice-oriented architecture. In: Proceedings of the 16th International Conference on Software Technologies - ICSOFT, pp. 78–89. INSTICC, SciTePress (2021). https://doi.org/10.5220/0010557800780089

A Personalized Code Formatter: Detection and Fixing

Thomas Karanikiotis$^{(\boxtimes)}$ ⓘ, Kyriakos C. Chatzidimitriou ⓘ,
and Andreas L. Symeonidis ⓘ

School of Electrical and Computer Engineering,
Intelligent Systems and Software Engineering Labgroup,
Aristotle University of Thessaloniki, Thessaloniki, Greece
{thomas.karanikiotis,kyrcha}@issel.ee.auth.gr, symeonid@ece.auth.gr

Abstract. The wide adoption of component-based software development and the (re)use of software residing in code hosting platforms have led to an increased interest shown towards source code readability and comprehensibility. One factor that can undeniably improve readability is the consistent code styling and formatting used across a project. To that end, many code formatting approaches usually define a set of rules, in order to model a commonly accepted formatting. However, this approach is mostly based on the experts' expertise, is time-consuming and ignores the specific styling and formatting a team selects to use. Thus, it becomes too intrusive and may be not adopted. In this work, we present an automated mechanism that can be trained to identify deviations from the selected formatting style of a given project, given a set of source code files, and provide recommendations towards maintaining a common styling across all files of the project. At first, source code is transformed into small meaningful pieces, called tokens, which are used to train the models of our mechanism, in order to predict the probability of a token being wrongly positioned. Then, a number of possible fixes are examined as replacements of the wrongly positioned token and, based on a scoring function, the most suitable fixes are given as recommendations to the developer. Preliminary evaluation on various axes indicates that our approach can effectively detect formatting deviations from the project's code styling and provide actionable recommendations to the developer.

Keywords: Source code formatting · Code styling · Source code readability · LSTM · SVM one-class

1 Introduction

Source code readability has recently gained much research interest and is considered of vital importance for developers, especially those working under a component-based software engineering scheme. It is a quite complex concept and includes factors such as understanding of the control flow, the functionality and the purpose of a given software component. At the same time, source code

ⓒ Springer Nature Switzerland AG 2022
H.-G. Fill et al. (Eds.): ICSOFT 2021, CCIS 1622, pp. 169–192, 2022.
https://doi.org/10.1007/978-3-031-11513-4_8

readability is highly related to maintainability and reusability, pillar aspects of software quality.

In this context, the importance of readability is obvious. However, despite the fact that a number of recent research approaches aspired to assess the readability degree of a given component [15,19,20], the proper extraction of features and metrics that could accurately quantify readability still remains a vague process and under heavy debate. Nevertheless, it has been proven that the selection of a correct formatting approach and a suitable code styling can significantly enhance the capability of the developers to comprehend the functionality, the content and the intention of the source code [22] and improve source code readability. On the other hand, the use of various and different coding styles can affect the overall readability [9]. At the same time, the comprehensibility of the source code may be affected by various fields of code formatting, such as the indentation applied on source code.

Several studies have aspired to model code styling and formatting and, mainly, identify styling errors and provide styling fixes or detect deviations from a priorly accepted set of formatting rules [10,11,16]. While these approaches seem to achieve promising results, the majority of them make use of predefined sets of formatting rules, that seem to be globally accepted and can only be turned on/off, without the option to alter any of them or add new. Based on these rules, the aforementioned approaches try to identify pieces of code that diverge from them. At the same time, there is a number of approaches that, focusing mainly on program comprehension, rather than readability from the code styling perspective, aspire to identify changes that could make the code more comprehensible, such as alterations on identifier or method names, code structure or sequence of function calls.

The majority of the aforementioned approaches share the same target; the appropriate modelling and identification of deviations from a commonly accepted code styling and formatting and the ability to help developers apply these common practices into their code. Nevertheless, as teams and individual developers vary in skills, needs, targets and way they develop software, not all styling guidelines can apply to each one of them. Teams may spend a lot of time in order to properly configure the aforementioned approaches and tools into their own needs, which is a quite complex task, especially in cases where there are a lot of developers that participate in the team. Thus, there is a need for a system that can model the desired source code formatting of the team in a completely unsupervised way, based solely on previously developed software. Using this system, the team or individuals should be able to identify deviations from their previously defined code styling and be provided with actionable recommendations about the way to maintain their selected formatting.

In this work, we aspire to overcome the aforementioned limitations by proposing an automated mechanism, which can model the desired code formatting of an individual or team of developers by examining the code styling used in a project or repository in a completely unsupervised manner. Our approach can identify deviations from the global styling that is applied throughout a whole project or repository, without the need of a domain expert. In order to accomplish that, we extend our previous work [7], where we proposed an automated mechanism for identifying styling deviations and formatting errors from a set of source code files. Here, a set of possible fixes to the aforementioned formatting errors is also given to the developers, that can effectively assist them to fix the deviations. In that way, the team can maintain the desired code styling across the whole project or a set of projects, making it easier for them to maintain or reuse certain pieces of code, or cooperate.

Summarizing, the advances of this work with respect to our previous paper [7] are the following:

- The extension of the previous models that identify deviations from a source code styling used in previous projects or files with the use of a scoring function, which can expand the capabilities of our models to detect formatting errors.
- The creation of a fixing mechanism, which, based on the predictions of our models and the scoring mechanism, can identify the best possible fixes to the previously detected formatting error and provide effective and actionable recommendations to the developers.

The rest of this paper is organized as follows. Section 2 provides background information on source code formatting mechanisms and reviews current approaches, while it discusses how our work differentiates from them. In Sect. 3 we present the methodology applied in order to accomplish our goal, the data we used and the models we trained. Section 4 evaluates the efficiency of our formatting errors detection and fixing mechanism against various axes, while in Sect. 5 we analyze potential threats to our internal and external validity. Finally, Sect. 6 concludes this work and provides insight for further research.

2   Related Work

Source code readability is one of the main software attributes that is closely linked to maintainability and reusability, which are considered of vital importance and have gained increased interest in the recent years, since the importance of correct and evolving code is given. Thus, readability has also become a crucial factor of the software development procedure and, in many times, where projects need to be processed quickly while also maintaining a standard level of quality, it is considered a success or fail factor. Additionally, when it comes to large teams of developers that are involved in the software development process and the component-based software development paradigm, a greater emphasis towards source code readability and comprehensibility has been noticed, as it can directly affect multiple aspects of the software development procedure.

While the comprehension and readability degree of a software component is yet to be strictly quantified or even properly defined, it is not arguable that a correct code formatting and a proper code styling can unquestionably ease the developer in the process of perceiving the content and the functionality of a given source code. One attribute that can be of crucial importance in a proper code formatting and can affect the way the developers comprehend the intentions of a given source code in a significant degree is the code indentation. Hindle et al. [5] examined over 200 software projects and carried out a research about the way the indentation shape correlates with the structure of the code block. The results concluded that there exists a high correlation between the shape drawn by the indentations appearing in code and the structure of the given code. This correlation could be proven quite useful for the developers to better perceive the content of the software component. Persson and Sundkvist [22] argue that the readability and the interpretation of source code can be improved, leading to faster understanding of the code purpose and functionality, especially when the source code size increases, by the correct use of indentation within the code.

In the recent years, there have been a lot of tools, which aspire to identify styling mismatches and highlight lines of code that diverge from the globally accepted styling standards, as they are expressed by a set of expert-defined rules. Some of the most well-known tools are *Indent* [3] and *Prettier* [17]. At the same time, Wang et al. [23] aspired to ease the way the developers read, perceive and comprehend the code and its functionality, by splitting a given Java code into smaller segments, each one of which implements a different task. Additionally, Prabhu et al. [16], focused on creating a code editor that can help the developers and can separate the functionality of the source code from the styling and the formatting it appears within the editor. Moreover, the authors provided some additional features, such as auto-indentation and auto-spacing, in an attempt to provide a formatting tool that does not need human intervention. However, although the auto-formatting features can be helpful, they are strictly based on heuristic algorithms developed by the authors, which follow a global styling pattern with no alterations.

Lately, there have been a lot of approaches that aspire to model a globally accepted code styling and formatting and, based on that, identify deviations from that pattern (i.e. formatting errors) and, possibly, provide fixes [10]. Nevertheless, these approaches are mainly based on a set of predefined rules, which the developers can only enable/disable, while they are not able to add their own or alter any of them, in order to create their custom code styling that best matches their needs. It is a fact that maintaining a common formatting across projects or files within a team, especially when the team consists of a large number of developers, can be a crucial factor towards quality code. The work of Kesler et al. [8] supports this argument. The authors conducted an experiment, aspiring to identify the way that no indentation, excessive indentation and a moderate indentation affect the comprehensibility of the source code. It is obvious from the results that there can not exist a perfect indentation style that matches the needs of all teams and individual developers and it constitutes a task that should be carefully examined at each time. At the same time, Miara et al. [12] carried out a study about the most used and popular indentations. The study concluded that, while the level of indentation can be a crucial factor for code comprehensibility, multiple and different indentation styles may be found across programs.

Therefore, there is a need for models that could identify the code formatting that is used across the same project and detect deviations from it.

One of the first approaches towards dynamic adaptation and homogenization of code styling was made by Allamanis et al. [1]. The authors aspired to model the styling used by one or more developers in a single project and, then, detect and identify deviations from it. Their framework, called *NATURALIZE*, could provide a set of recommendations regarding identifier names and styling changes in the given source code, in order to increase styling consistency across the files of a project. The evaluation of the NATURALIZE framework depicted that it could provide accurate suggestions, but it could process only local context and could not incorporate semantically valid suggestions, while it was mainly focused on the use of indentation and whitespaces and not on other aspects of code formatting (e.g. the placement of comments within the code). At the same time, Parr et al. [14] created a code formatter based on machine learning algorithms, which could model the grammar of any given language and, thus, could automatically generate universal code formatters. Although this formatter, called *CODEBUFF*, achieved quite good results, it was based on a trial-and-error trained complex model, with no generalization capabilities. It wasn't also able to handle some (quite common) cases, such as mixed indentation with tabs and spaces or mixed quotes with single and double quotes. Taking these limitations into account, Markovtsev et al. [11] created *STYLE-ANALYZER*. STYLE-ANALYZER is a tool that can provide suggestions about fixing formatting deviations that were previously identified in a given repository, after having modelled its formatting style. While STYLE-ANALYZER achieved pretty good results during the evaluation of the effectiveness the approach appears to have in modelling the code styling of the respective project, the proposed model is quite complex, time-consuming and can only be used with javascript source code. Finally, Ogura et al. [13] created a tool that aspires to maintain a consistent code styling across a software project, helping the developers use their own local formatting style. The tool, called *StyleCoordinator*, creates a styling configuration file upon examining the source code of a given repository. The configuration file is then used to provide consistency in every new file examined within the same repository. However, StyleCoordinator is initially based on a common convention configuration, in order to ensure consistency, and is not able to extract the code styling selected by the user from the ground, while its efficiency is yet to be clarified.

In this work, in an attempt to overcome the limitations introduced in the aforementioned approaches, we propose a generalizable model that dynamically learns the formatting style of a given project or set of files and, then, identifies any styling deviations from it. Taking these deviations into account, our approach aspires to provide actionable and useful recommendations to the developers, in order to fix these inconsistencies. Using our approach, single developers or teams of developers are able to feed their existing source code files to indicate the desired formatting and then use the generated model to format future code in the same styling, by directly applying the produced suggestions into their code. By doing that, they are able to minimize the time and effort needed to comprehend the source code, while the team can maintain a uniform way of developing software. Our approach requires no specific domain knowledge or even rules customisation, which most of the recent linters and style checkers need.

3   System Design

In this section we design our formatting error detection and fixing system, which is shown in Fig. 1. Our methodology is based on two approaches, which aspire to model the formatting of a given source code from different aspects, the generative model and the outlier detection model, and a snippet scoring function that evaluates the purity of code regarding the code styling deviations.

The aforementioned system has been altered from the respective one in [7], in order to incorporate also the snippet scoring stage, as well as the fixing mechanism that can provide possible fixes to the developers, in order to eliminate the styling deviations.

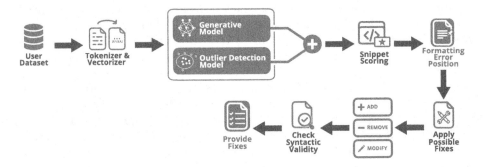

Fig. 1. Overview of the formatting error detection & fixing methodology.

3.1   User Dataset

In the first step of our methodology, the source code files that determine the formatting style adopted by the developers in each specific case needs to be determined. This set of source code files will be used to train the system in the specific needs of each team and model the desired formatting style. This input step differentiates our system from many similar approaches, which make use of a predefined set of formatting rules, in order to identify and highlight styling deviations. Instead, we allow every developer or team of developers to use their own source code files to define the desired code styling. The rest of our modelling procedure simply adapts to the provided dataset and, thus, our system is dataset agnostic.

While our system is dataset agnostic, in an attempt to showcase the performance of our approach in practice against frequently encountered formatting errors that have been found across projects, we make use of the same data used in our previous approach [7] and train our formatting error detection and fixing mechanism on a code writing style that is widely used by developers. Specifically, we made use of the dataset used by Santos et al. [18]. The authors mined the top 10,000 Java repositories and extracted the latest snapshot of the default branch, keeping only the syntactically-valid Java files. In total 2,322,481 Java files were collected.

The dataset collected by Santos et al. [18] contains syntactically valid files that depict the formatting style used in a large variety of projects and by most of the developers. However, we apply an extra step of preprocessing, in which we identify and keep only the source code files that do not diverge from widely known formatting rules, in order to evaluate the ability of our mechanism to identify also commonly found styling deviations. Thus, a set of rules has been defined manually, which describes the occasions when a formatting error occurs. In this context, we made use of 22 regular expressions, in an attempt to detect widely known formatting errors that occur in a single Java file and exclude this file from the rest of our methodology. In Table 1, an example of the 22 regular expressions of our approach is depicted, which identifies a wrongly positioned space that has been inserted before a semicolon, along with a corresponding example of a source code line, in which the regular expression has been triggered. The complete corpus of our 22 regular expressions can be found on our page[1], where the modelling pipeline of [7] is presented. It should be noted once again that the selection of widely known formatting errors is used only for showcasing and does not affect the adaptive nature of our approach, while each developer could train the system with his/her own specific code styling guidelines, just by providing a set of source code files.

Table 1. A regular expression used to identify a space that has been inserted before a semicolon.

Regular expression	" ;"
Source code example	*int myNum = 15 ;*

Using the aforementioned set of 22 regular expressions, we were able to collect 10,000 Java files from the original set of source code files collected by Santos et al., which completely conform to widely accepted coding standards, do not contain any formatting deviations from well-known styling guidelines and, thus, could be used as the basis for training our models.

---

[1] https://gist.github.com/karanikiotis/263251decb86f839a3265cc2306355b2.

3.2   Tokenizer and Vectorizer

In the next step of our approach and before the source code is further processed
by our models, the source code files need to be preprocessed and transformed into
a suitable form. This procedure is widely used in approaches that handle source
code files, is known as *tokenization* and transforms the initial source code into a
set of small meaningful pieces called tokens. Each programming language consists
of a list of all possible unique tokens, which is called vocabulary, and contains
all the possible keywords and operators used by the language. The source code
contains also a set of out-of-vocabulary tokens, which are the variable names,
string literals and numbers used by the developer. In an extra step, these tokens
need to be further processed and they are projected into an abstract form and
represented by the respective token that indicates the corresponding category
the token belongs to (variable, string or number).

In this work, our main target was token differentiation regarding the way
they are placed between the rest of the tokens of the source code. The tokenizer
identifies and abstracts the set of variables, strings and numbers used by the
developer, detects the set of keywords and groups tokens with similar formatting
behaviors and returns the set of tokens identified, as well as the number of
characters each token occupies in the initial source code. Table 2 depicts some
example of keywords identified in the initial source code by the tokenizer and
the corresponding token they are transformed into, as it was originally presented
in [7].

Table 2. Examples of keywords and their respective tokens, as it was originally presented in [7].

Token name	Token symbol	Keywords
KEYWORD	\<keyword\>	Break, for, if, return,
LIT	\<lit\>	Float, int, void,
LITERAL	\<literal\>	True, false, null
NUMBER	\<number\>	123, 5.2, 10, 1, 0,
STRING	\<word\>	"a", "hello",

Each token of the initial source code file is processed by the tokenizer and
categorized into the appropriate token category. An example was originally presented in [7], according to which, whenever any of the words *true, false* or *null*
are identified in the source code, they are transformed and treated with the token
LITERAL. The tokenization of special characters, such as the white-spaces and
tabs, brackets and semicolons, required special attention, since these characters
play a major role for the appropriate styling of the code. In order to convert
source code into a form that is suitable for training our models, a two step procedure is followed. First, the source code is tokenized using the aforementioned
tokenizer and, thus, a set of tokens is returned. Subsequently, this set of tokens

is processed to extract the total vocabulary of tokens used. Each token is then assigned a positive integer index, that will then be used as the input in the following models. Table 3, which was also presented in [7], depicts an example of a full transformation; the initial source code is transformed to a numeric vector that can be treated by our models.

Table 3. The tokenization pipeline from the source code to a numeric vector presented in [7]. The vocabulary indexes for this example are "<lit>" = 0, "<space>" = 1, "<word>" = 2, "<equal>" = 3, "<number>" = 4 and "<semicolon>" = 5.

Source code	int x = 1;
Tokens	["<lit>", "<space>", "<word>", "<space>", "<equal>", "<space>", "<number>", "<semicolon>"]
Tokens lengths	[3, 1, 1, 1, 1, 1, 1, 1]
Vectorization	[0, 1, 2, 1, 3, 1, 4, 5]

3.3   Model Generation

The sequence of tokens generated by the tokenizer from the initial corpus of training files is then used in the model generation section of our methodology to train two different models that aspire to detect a formatting error. Our primary goal in that stage is the approximation of the probability of a token being wrongly positioned among the others, i.e. a formatting error, given a set of tokens that define the formatting style. In order to do so, each token coming from the source code needs to be assigned a likelihood of being a formatting error, as shown in the following equation and was first defined in [7]:

$$P(formatting\_error\_token|context) \tag{1}$$

Each of the two models used in our approach, aspires to approximate the aforementioned probability from its own perspective for every token that appears in the source code. The final probabilities are then calculated by aggregating the outputs of the respective models.

Generative Model. The first model of our approach is the generative model, which, given a series of tokens that have already been identified in the source code, aspires to predict the next token that will be found, from the corpus of the available ones, assigning a probability to each one of them. This model is accomplished using a long short-term memory (LSTM) [6] recurrent neural network model. LSTM neural networks are an extension of RNNs (recurrent neural networks), that resolve the vanishing gradient problem and, thus, can memorize past data easier. LSTMs have been proven really effective in processing source code and predicting the next tokens in a sequence of previous ones [4].

The generative model can play a crucial role towards accomplishing our primary goal, which is the approximation of a function that can estimate the probability of the next token to be identified, given a series of $n-1$ tokens that have been already found in the source code. LSTMs return an array of probabilities that depict the likelihood of the next token to be the respective one. It can be also considered as a categorical distribution of the probability across the vocabulary of all possible tokens. In [7], we originally presented the following equation, which depicts the categorical distribution, i.e. the vector of probabilities given by the LSTM:

$$P(next\_token|context) = \begin{cases} P(< word > |context) \\ P(< space > |context) \\ P(< number > |context) \\ ... \end{cases} \quad (2)$$

Respectively, Fig. 2 (also introduced in [7]) illustrates the way the LSTM predicts the token $< semicolon >$ given the previous tokens from the source code *"int x = 1;"*, as it was originally presented in [7].

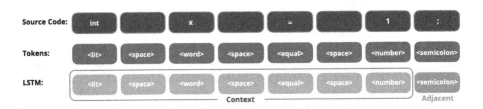

Fig. 2. The LSTM prediction of the adjacent token, given the source code *"int x = 1;"*, originally introduced in [7].

As it has been already mentioned, the LSTM estimates a vector containing the probability of each token of the vocabulary to be the next one to be identified in the series of tokens. Using this probability and inverting its value, we are able to estimate the probability of identifying any other token in the next place of the series, except from the respective one. In other words, inverting the probability generated by the LSTM, we can approximate the probability of the respective token being wrongly placed in the specific position in the source code. In the following equation, originally defined in [7], the probability of the token $< tok >$ being wrongly positioned is depicted, i.e. the probability of any other token to be found next:

$$P(< tok > wrong|cont) = 1 - P(next\_tok =< tok > |cont) \quad (3)$$

where $< next\ tok >$ is the next token in the sequence of the previously identified context *cont*.

The tokens that are generated from the initial source code, using the tokenizer defined in the previous step of our methodology, are fed into the LSTM architecture, in order to calculate their probabilities of being wrongly positioned. It should be noted that, in order for the first n tokens of the source code to be checked also by the LSTMs, we manually added a set of n starting tokens, so the first token to be predicted from the architecture is the actual first token of the code. For the creation of the LSTM neural network we made use of the Keras[2] deep neural network framework, with two layers of 400 LSTM nodes each, parameters that were selected upon testing. The sliding window that was applied to the tokens of the source code in order to create the input vector was chosen to have a context length of 20 tokens, as it was proven to be effective on source code [24]. A window of 20 tokens is selected at each time-step and is given as input to the LSTM network. The model outputs the probability of each possible token to be the next one in the series. We compare these probabilities with the actual next token and, using Eq. 3, we transform this probability into an error probability.

Outlier Detection Model. The identification of a source code token wrongly positioned among the others can also be seen from a different perspective, which is the classification approach using n-grams. N-grams are a set of n continuous tokens from the given source code. Figure 3, which was first presented in [7], illustrates the procedure of tokenizing the source code *"int x = 1;"* and splitting the generated tokens into different n-grams, with $n = 1$, $n = 2$ and $n = 3$.

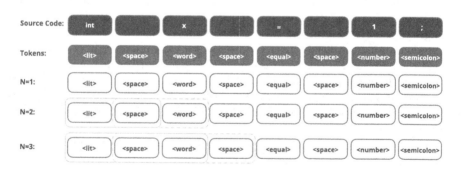

Fig. 3. The n-grams that are produced from the source code *"int x = 1;"* for $n = 1$, $n = 2$ and $n = 3$. For $n = 1$ the unigrams are *"<lit>"*, *"<space>"*, etc., for $n = 2$ the bigrams are *"<lit> <space>"*, *"<space> <word>"*, etc. and for $n = 3$ the trigrams are *"<lit> <space> <word>"*, *"<space> <word> <space>"*, etc. The figure was originally presented in [7].

---

[2] https://github.com/keras-team/keras.

Using the complete corpus of tokens found in the original dataset and transforming these tokens into n-grams, the formatting error detection problem can be approached from the outlier detection perspective, aspiring to identify n-grams in the source code that have not been previously met in the training corpus and, thus, deviate from the developer's code styling. Indeed, if the most of the n-grams a specific token participates in are classified as outliers, then, probably, this particular token has not been previously used in this way and constitutes a formatting error.

The outlier detection model selected to implement this perspective was a *Support Vector Machine - SVM One Class* algorithm, which has been proven successful in outlier detection problems [21]. The SVM One-Class model is trained using only data coming from the original (or "positive") class, this way identifying new data that deviate from the "normal" behavior. In our approach, the model is trained on n-grams coming from the training corpus, which define the developer's preferable code styling, and is then used to detect n-grams that diverge.

During the training of the SVM model, a usual limitation arises, which concerns the fine-tuning of the SVM parameters, i.e. the ν and γ parameters. The process of tuning these parameters usually tends to confine the model, while, in practice, it needs to be flexible and adaptive, since multiple and previously unknown n-grams may be found during the prediction stage of the model. In order to overcome this limitation, we applied the following approach: instead of simply using one single SVM One-Class model, with a certain set of ν and γ parameters, we created a set of SVM models with various ν-γ pairs, that aspire to cover a large area of the fine-tuning procedure. Each model is trained separately and, then, all the predictions are aggregated, leading to the final prediction.

As our primary modelling target is the prediction of the probability of a single token being a formatting error, we cannot make use of the classification of an n-gram into the original or the outliers class. Instead, we take into account the prediction probabilities that are produced by each model. The n-gram is fed into all the different SVM One-Class models, which return their prediction probabilities of the n-gram being an outlier, i.e. the n-gram does not have the same behavior with the ones met in the training corpus. Subsequently, the predictions of all SVM models are being aggregated and the final prediction for the n-gram is made.

Finally, each token coming from the source code is assigned a probability of being a formatting error as the mean probability of all the n-grams it participates. Equation 4 depicts the calculation of the formatting error probability for the token $<tok>$, where *n-grams* is the set of all n-grams the token participates in, *SVM_models* is the set of all the SVM models we used and *context* is the previously identified context.

$$P(< \text{tok} > \text{ being wrong}|context) = \sum_{n-grams} \sum_{SVM\_models} P_{model}(\text{n-gram is outlier}) \quad (4)$$

Models Aggregation. In the final step of our modelling step, we have to concatenate the decisions made by the two separate models, as it is illustrated in Fig. 1. The overall pipeline, from the initial source code that needs to be checked for formatting errors, includes the tokenization of the code and the generation of the respective tokens, as well as the prediction stage, in which the tokens are forwarded into the two selected models, the LSTM and the SVM One-Class. For each token found in the initial source code, the models output their probabilities of the token being wrongfully present in the specific position. In the next step, the two predictions are combined to form the final probabilities of the models. By averaging the probabilities calculated from each model, we were able to fix some ambiguous decisions made by a single model, i.e. a token probably misclassified as formatting error but with low prediction probability from the one model, would be correctly classified with a high probability from the second one.

3.4 Snippet Scoring

Towards optimizing the results of identifying the position a formatting error appears at, an extra step has been added to our approach, as it was originally presented in [7], where a snippet of code is evaluated and a score is calculated. This score reflects the purity of the snippet regarding formatting errors and styling deviations from the ground truth.

A snippet scoring function has been designed that receives a given code as input, transforms the initial code into tokens using the tokenizer described in Subsect. 3.2 and splits the tokens into sets of predefined size, called *snippets*. Each snippet is, then, processed and the tokens are split into bigrams (two consecutive tokens constitute a single bigram), as illustrated in Fig. 3.

We then calculate the frequency of each bigram appearance in the set of training files provided by the developers. The higher the frequency of a bigram is in the training corpus, the less possible it is to be a formatting error. The final score of each snippet is calculated by averaging the frequency of each bigram, normalized based on the number of training files, according to the following equation:

$$Score = \frac{\sum_{bigrams}(1 - norm\_freq)}{\#bigrams} \tag{5}$$

where $norm\_freq$ is the normalized frequency the bigram appears in the training corpus, in the interval $[0, 1]$, and $\#$ *bigrams* is the total number of bigrams in the snippet. A normalized frequency of 0 means that the bigram has not been found in any training file, while a normalized frequency of 1 reflects the fact that the bigram appears in all the training files.

Using the score calculated with the aforementioned equation, the probabilities of the modelling stage of our approach are altered to include the effect of it. Specifically, the probability of each token is multiplied by the score value of the snippet it participates in, as it is depicted in the following equation. Finally, the tokens along with their respective probabilities are being sorted to create a descending order of tokens possibly being formatting errors.

$$Final\_token\_probability = snippet\_score * initial\_probability \qquad (6)$$

where *snipper_score* is the score calculated by the Eq. 5 for the snippet the token belongs to and *initial_probability* is the aggregated probability of the token calculated by the models aggregation stage.

3.5 Possible Fixes

Next, a group of possible fixes for the formatting error needs to be generated. In general, a formatting error appears when a token is misaligned or misplaced and can probably be fixed by modifying this specific token in three different ways [10]:

- Add an extra token in the list of tokens *before* the wrongly positioned one.
- Remove the token that produces the formatting error.
- Replace the wrongly positioned token with another one.

In order to generate the set of possible fixes, the above three cases are taken into account. For the first case, where an extra token needs to be added, the predictions of the generative model, i.e. the LSTM model, are employed. Particularly, the 5 most probable tokens of the LSTM predictions (i.e. the tokens that the LSTM predicted as the actual next ones in the series of tokens) are the potential ones to be added in the series of tokens, just before the token that generates the formatting error. Each one of these tokens is added separately in the series and the prediction is fed to the next step of our system. When it comes to the second case of the possible alterations, the change is quite simple and involves only the removal of the wrongly positioned token. Finally, some possible fixes include the replacement of the formatting error token with another one. Once again, the top predictions of the LSTM model are used as potential substitutions of the examined token.

Having generated a list of possible alterations in the token series, we first need to identify and discard the ones that result in syntactically invalid code. To do so, we employ an appropriate language parser, which in our case is *javac_parser*, in order to examine the syntactical validity of the respective outcome. Obviously, the possible fixes of the previous step that do not produce syntactically correct code are discarded and the remaining ones are given in the next stage, in order to be sorted accordingly.

3.6 Fixes Suggestion

In the last step of our approach, a sorted list of possible fixes is provided as recommendations to the developers. Having verified the syntactical validity of the remaining fixes, we need to calculate a score that reflects the appropriateness of the fix with regard to the user's selected code styling.

In order to accomplish this and calculate a score for each possible fix, the snippet scoring mechanism of the Subsect. 3.4 is once again used. Particularly, for each candidate in the set of fixes, we calculate a score based on the frequency the bigrams it consists of appear in the training corpus. The final score of each possible fix is calculated using the Eq. 5. The complete list of possible fixes is, then, sorted and the top predictions are given to the developer as the best possible changes that will fix the formatting error that was detected.

4   Evaluation

Towards assessing the performance of our proposed methodology in identifying formatting errors and deviations from a globally used code styling and providing fixing recommendations, we perform several evaluation scenarios on various axes. At first and in an attempt to measure the performance of our system, we apply our methodology on the codrep dataset[3]. Additionally, towards the evaluation of the effectiveness of our approach in practice, we apply our system in real-world scenarios, in order to assess its ability of providing actionable recommendations that can be used in practice during development.

4.1   Detection Evaluation

In the first step towards assessing the effectiveness of our system in identifying code styling inconsistencies and pieces of code that diverge from a common formatting, we tested our system against data coming from the *Codrep* competition [2]. Codrep is a competition for applying machine learning on source code. The main goal of the codrep 2019 competition was the identification of the position in a code file in which a formatting error appears. Codrep dataset consists of 8,000 Java files, each one of which contains a single formatting error in a specific character position. An additional file is given, which includes the character position the formatting error appears for each one of the 8,000 files. Figure 4, which was first presented in [7] depicts an example, in which a formatting error appears. In this case, the formatting error is the unnecessary space that appears in character position 30.

```
1 public class test{
2   int a = 1 ;
3 }
4
```

Fig. 4. Example of code file containing a single formatting error in character position 30. This example was originally presented in [7].

---

[3] https://github.com/KTH/codrep-2019/tree/master/Datasets.

According to the codrep rules, the program that participates in the competition should have a single input, which is a file containing Java source code, and output a descending ranking of the characters offsets, according to the probabilities that are calculated and estimate their likelihood of containing a formatting error. The final ranking of the characters is compared with the actual character that contains the formatting error and the evaluation metric is calculated.

For the evaluation of the system's performance, codrep made use of the *Mean Reciprocal Rank (MRR)* metric, which is calculated as the mean value (over all the files given as input) of the inverse of the rank in an ordered list the correct answer is found on for a given file q. Given a set Q of evaluation files of length $|Q|$, for each of which the correct answer is found in the $rank_q$ position in the ordered list of predictions, the MRR is calculated using the equation:

$$MRR = \frac{1}{|Q|} \sum_{q \in Q} \frac{1}{rank_q} \qquad (7)$$

The best possible value of the MRR metric is 1, which depicts that the correct position of the formatting error is found in the first place of the predictions for each file in the evaluation set. On the other hand, an MRR value of 0, which is the lowest possible score, means that the correct position of the formatting error was not found. Table 4 depicts the MRR obtained using our approach only with the generative model, only with the outlier detection model and with both the models combined. In all the cases, the values of the MRR are calculated both with and without the additional use of the snippet scoring mechanism and the table has been altered accordingly from the respective one in [7]. The n-grams we selected to use were 7-grams and 10-grams.

Table 4. MRRs of LSTM and SVM models.

Model	Without snippet scoring	With snippet scoring
LSTM	0.70	0.72
7-gram SVM	0.63	0.63
7-gram SVM & LSTM	0.78	0.79
10-gram SVM	0.57	0.61
10-gram SVM & LSTM	**0.85**	**0.88**

According to the MRR values depicted in Table 4, the combined model, consisted of both the LSTM and the 10-gram SVM, along with the snippet scoring mechanism yields the best results. These values are well above the ones from random guessing the position of the formatting error. Santos et al. [18] calculated that, for a file of 100 lines and 10 tokens per line, the random guessing would achieve an MRR of 0.002.

Despite the fact that we also used the MRR metric for the evaluation of our approach, we refrained from comparing our results with the respective ones from the Codrep competition[4], as the rules of the competition were not quite strict and the participants were allowed to use any possible technique to identify the formatting errors, e.g. using regular expressions, while a training set containing a lot of similar formatting errors was given to them a priori.

However, the MRR is a quite strict and conservative metric and its values can be significantly reduced just by some bad predictions. Indeed, in a case where the correct answer is ranked first 50% of cases and second the other 50%, the MRR value would be just 0.75, despite the fact that this model would probably be considered acceptable. In order to cope with the strictness of the MRR metric, we also calculated the histograms of the position in the ordered list the correct answer was found. Figure 5 illustrates these histograms, calculated both with the snippet scoring mechanism and without it. The height of each bar displays the number of files for which the correct prediction was found on that position. The blue bar reflects the number of files for which the correct prediction was found on the respective position without the use of the snippet scoring mechanism (as it was originally calculated in [7]), while the purple bar reflects the respective ones with the addition of the scoring function of this work.

The results from Table 4 and Fig. 5 show that the correct prediction, i.e. the identification of the formatting error within the source code, is the first one for the most of the times. The combination of the two models, LSTM and SVM, clearly improved the results, while the selection of 10-grams over 7-grams had also a positive impact. The addition of the snippet scoring mechanism also appears to improve the results and enhance the detection outcome.

Towards further examining the performance of the first part of our methodology, regarding the identification of formatting errors and deviations from the globally used code styling, we evaluated our system in the following scenario. From the sorted list of tokens, along with their probabilities of being a formatting error, only the first k tokens are returned to the user, as long as their probability of being a formatting error is above a predefined *threshold*. For these

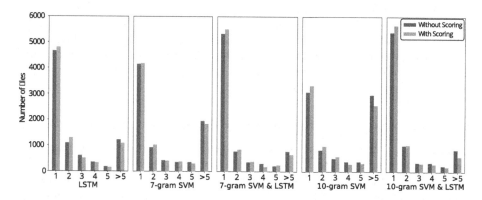

Fig. 5. The histograms of the positions the correct answer was found in.

---

[4] https://github.com/KTH/codrep-2019.

tokens, we examine whether the actual formatting error is included and calculate the metrics *precision@k*, *recall@k* and *f-measure@k*. Figure 6 illustrates these metrics calculated for the best two of the previous models (the 7-gram SVM with LSTM and the 10-gram SVM with LSTM) and using various thresholds in the range 0.9–1.0 and values 1, 5 and 10 for k. The top figures reflect the calculated metrics with the modelling approach of [7] (i.e. without the scoring mechanism), while the bottom ones are calculated using the predictions with the snippet scoring step.

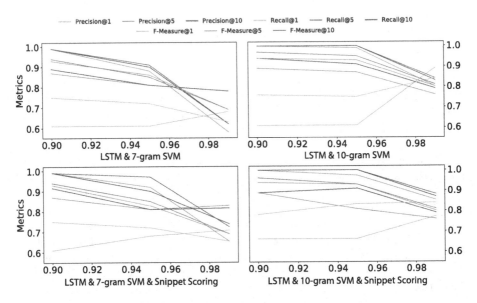

Fig. 6. The precision, recall and f-measure metrics for various k and threshold values.

From the results illustrated above, we can conclude that the 10-gram SVM along with the LSTM and the scoring mechanism performs better with a precision value of 0.9, a recall value of 1.0 and an f-measure value of 0.92 for $k = 10$ and *threshold* $= 0.95$. A system with these parameters could correctly identify deviations from the globally used formatting and provide useful suggestions to the developer about possible fixes.

4.2   Application of Formatting Error Fixing in Practice

In an attempt to further assess the effectiveness of our approach in providing useful recommendations to the developers that can be directly applied on the source code and fix the identified formatting error, we applied our methodology in certain use-cases, in which we aspire to identify the applicability of the formatting error detection system in practice. Thus, we randomly selected some small Java files from the most popular GitHub repositories, in which our methodology would be applied to.

Figure 7 presents the initial version of a randomly selected source code to be evaluated by our system. In this occasion a formatting error is detected in line 12 and concerns the extra use of a new-line character (the character in the red circle). It is obvious that the insertion of just one new character can reduce the overall code comprehensibility, as there is no correct indentation.

```
 1 package com.developmentontheedge.sql.model;
 2
 3 public class AstBeDbmsThen extends SimpleNode
 4 {
 5     public AstBeDbmsThen(int id)
 6     {
 7         super(id);
 8     }
 9
10     private boolean asIs;
11
12     public void  ↵
13 setAsIs(boolean asIs)
14     {
15         this.asIs = asIs;
16     }
17 }
```

Fig. 7. Initial version of file.

Our system is able to identify the formatting error position, while the fixing mechanism evaluates the possible fixes and produces a sorted list of possible fixes. According to them, the fix with the biggest score is presented in Fig. 8. Indeed, the first predicted syntactically-valid fix is the one that a developer would have also applied. The final version of the file is easier for the developers to understand, as the correct indentation can be a valuable guidance towards the code flow comprehension.

Figure 9 illustrates a different example, in which, in the initial source code of the file, the formatting error is detected in line 11 and concerns the extra use of a tab character (depicted in the Figure). Again, the insertion of just one new character alters the way a developer can read the code and understand its content.

Our approach ranks the formatting error first among the set of all possible positions and the fixing mechanism provides a sorted list of suggestions. The first recommendation given by our approach includes the withdrawal of the tab character. In Fig. 10, the final version of the file, the comprehension of the source code follows a natural flow.

Despite these examples seem small and the fixes seem insignificant, they can be quite important in large projects, in which different and various developers

```
1 package com.developmentontheedge.sql.model;
2
3 public class AstBeDbmsThen extends SimpleNode
4 {
5     public AstBeDbmsThen(int id)
6     {
7         super(id);
8     }
9
10    private boolean asIs;
11
12    public void setAsIs(boolean asIs)
13    {
14        this.asIs = asIs;
15    }
16 }
```

Fig. 8. Final version of file.

```
1 package com.developmentontheedge.be5.server.services.impl;
2 import com.developmentontheedge.be5.query.QuerySession;
3 import javax.inject.Inject;
4 import javax.inject.Provider;
5 import javax.servlet.http.HttpSession;
6
7 public class QuerySessionImpl implements QuerySession
8 {
9     private final Provider<HttpSession> session;
10
11     @Override
12     public Object get(String name)
13     {
14         return session.get().getAttribute(name);
15     }
16 }
```

Fig. 9. Initial version of file.

participate with various coding styles. Detecting and fixing these formatting errors could noticeably improve readability and code comprehensibility.

5   Threats to Validity

Our approach towards identifying formatting deviations from the previously selected code styling and suggesting possible fixes to the developers seems to achieve high internal validity, as it was proved by the evaluation of our system in the previous section.

```
 1 package com.developmentontheedge.be5.server.services.impl;
 2 import com.developmentontheedge.be5.query.QuerySession;
 3 import javax.inject.Inject;
 4 import javax.inject.Provider;
 5 import javax.servlet.http.HttpSession;
 6
 7 public class QuerySessionImpl implements QuerySession
 8 {
 9     private final Provider<HttpSession> session;
10
11     @Override
12     public Object get(String name)
13     {
14         return session.get().getAttribute(name);
15     }
16 }
```

Fig. 10. Final version of file.

The limitations and threats to the external validity of our approach span along the following axes: 1) the selected training dataset used as the ground truth and 2) the selected use case. In the first step of our methodology and towards creating the ground truth of our approach, we attempted to define the desired code styling by making use of the dataset Santos et al. [18] created, who mined the top 10,000 Java repositories from GitHub and extracted more than $2M$ syntactically valid files. It is a fact that different projects or repositories could be used in order to train our system with their code styling. However, our methodology can be applied as-is in any repository or benchmark dataset, covering multiple and different evaluation scenarios. Moreover, for the evaluation of our approach the codrep competition was employed, the main goal of which was the identification of formatting deviations from widely accepted coding standards. One threat to the external validity of our approach lies on the evaluation of our approach on different scenarios, i.e. the generalization of our approach on a set of different code stylings. Nonetheless, the selected use case is considered as the most common and necessary one, while it does not differ significantly from the other scenarios.

6 Conclusions and Future Work

In this work, we proposed an automated mechanism, which is able to identify styling deviations from a previously defined code styling and propose fixes to the developer. Our system is based on two algorithms, LSTM and SVM, which aspire to model the problem from different perspectives, and a snippet scoring mechanism that evaluates the purity of the given code regarding the formatting errors. One of the basic contributions of our approach is that it does not need to be pre-trained based on a dataset or based on a set of predefined rules, that allow only minor modifications, but it can learn the coding style used in a project and detect deviations from it in a completely unsupervised manner, without the need of experts or prior domain knowledge. The evaluation of our approach in diverse axes indicates that our system can effectively identify formatting deviations from the coding style used as ground truth, calculate and sort possible fixes and provide effective and actionable recommendations to the developers, enhancing the readability degree and ensuring the styling consistency across the project.

While the use of globally adopted code styling in the evaluation stage of our approach indicates that our methodology could also be used as a common formatter, the main contribution of our approach lies on the unsupervised code styling consistency held across a project or set of files. Should a team of developers apply our methodology across a project, every team member will be motivated to follow the common code styling from the ground, improving the maintenance and the evolution of the software.

Future work relies on several axes. First, the snippet scoring mechanism could be further investigated, in order to create an algorithm that could assess the purity of the given code regarding the code styling and the way the formatting of code under examination correlates with the desired formatting style of the training corpus. Additionally, a thorough evaluation mechanism could be created that could qualitatively or quantitatively assess the performance of the complete system in detecting and fixing formatting errors, as well as the readability improvement achieved. Moreover, we would suggest the creation of a tool or plugin for a set of commonly used IDEs, that would predict the formatting errors, while the developer is typing, highlight these errors and suggest possible fixes. Finally, we could alter the training dataset by using projects with different characteristics and, especially, small projects with developers that use different formatting styles, in order to evaluate the performance of our approach in a small code basis with high formatting fluctuations.

References

1. Allamanis, M., Barr, E.T., Bird, C., Sutton, C.: Learning natural coding conventions. In: Proceedings of the 22nd ACM SIGSOFT International Symposium on Foundations of Software Engineering, FSE 2014, pp. 281–293. Association for Computing Machinery, New York (2014). https://doi.org/10.1145/2635868.2635883
2. Codrep: Codrep 2019 (2019). https://github.com/KTH/codrep-2019. Accessed 27 Sept 2020
3. GNU Project: Indent - GNU project (2007). https://www.gnu.org/software/indent/. Accessed 27 Sept 2020
4. Hellendoorn, V.J., Devanbu, P.: Are deep neural networks the best choice for modeling source code? In: Proceedings of the 2017 11th Joint Meeting on Foundations of Software Engineering, ESEC/FSE 2017, pp. 763–773. Association for Computing Machinery, New York (2017). https://doi.org/10.1145/3106237.3106290
5. Hindle, A., Godfrey, M.W., Holt, R.C.: From indentation shapes to code structures. In: 2008 Eighth IEEE International Working Conference on Source Code Analysis and Manipulation, pp. 111–120 (2008)

6. Hochreiter, S., Schmidhuber, J.: LSTM can solve hard long time lag problems. In: Mozer, M.C., Jordan, M.I., Petsche, T. (eds.) Advances in Neural Information Processing Systems, vol. 9, pp. 473–479. MIT Press (1997). http://papers.nips.cc/paper/1215-lstm-can-solve-hard-long-time-lag-problems.pdf
7. Karanikiotis, T., Chatzidimitriou, K.C., Symeonidis, A.L.: Towards automatically generating a personalized code formatting mechanism. In: Proceedings of the 16th International Conference on Software Technologies (2021). https://doi.org/10.5220/0010579900900101
8. Kesler, T.E., Uram, R.B., Magareh-Abed, F., Fritzsche, A., Amport, C., Dunsmore, H.: The effect of indentation on program comprehension. Int. J. Man-Mach. Stud. **21**(5), 415–428 (1984) https://doi.org/10.1016/S0020-7373(84)80068-1. http://www.sciencedirect.com/science/article/pii/S0020737384800681
9. Lee, T., Lee, J.B., In, H.: A study of different coding styles affecting code readability. Int. J. Softw. Eng. Its Appl. **7**, 413–422 (2013). https://doi.org/10.14257/ijseia.2013.7.5.36
10. Loriot, B., Madeiral, F., Monperrus, M.: STYLER: learning formatting conventions to repair checkstyle errors. CoRR abs/1904.01754 (2019). http://arxiv.org/abs/1904.01754
11. Markovtsev, V., Long, W., Mougard, H., Slavnov, K., Bulychev, E.: Style-analyzer: fixing code style inconsistencies with interpretable unsupervised algorithms, pp. 468–478, May 2019. https://doi.org/10.1109/MSR.2019.00073. https://www.scopus.com/inward/record.uri?eid=2-s2.0-85072331325&doi=10.1109%2fMSR.2019.00073&partnerID=40&md5=1c53eb83d17352bd9e21fc03c40f7ef3
12. Miara, R.J., Musselman, J.A., Navarro, J.A., Shneiderman, B.: Program indentation and comprehensibility. Commun. ACM **26**(11), 861–867 (1983). https://doi.org/10.1145/182.358437
13. Ogura, N., Matsumoto, S., Hata, H., Kusumoto, S.: Bring your own coding style. In: 2018 IEEE 25th International Conference on Software Analysis, Evolution and Reengineering (SANER), pp. 527–531 (2018). https://doi.org/10.1109/SANER.2018.8330253
14. Parr, T., Vinju, J.: Towards a universal code formatter through machine learning. In: Proceedings of the 2016 ACM SIGPLAN International Conference on Software Language Engineering, SLE 2016, pp. 137–151. Association for Computing Machinery, New York (2016). https://doi.org/10.1145/2997364.2997383
15. Posnett, D., Hindle, A., Devanbu, P.: A simpler model of software readability. In: Proceedings of the 8th Working Conference on Mining Software Repositories, MSR 2011, pp. 73–82. Association for Computing Machinery, New York (2011). https://doi.org/10.1145/1985441.1985454
16. Prabhu, R., Phutane, N., Dhar, S., Doiphode, S.: Dynamic formatting of source code in editors. In: 2017 International Conference on Innovations in Information, Embedded and Communication Systems (ICIIECS), pp. 1–6 (2017). https://doi.org/10.1109/ICIIECS.2017.8276008
17. Prettier: Prettier (2017). https://prettier.io/. Accessed 27 Sept 2020
18. Santos, E.A., Campbell, J.C., Patel, D., Hindle, A., Amaral, J.N.: Syntax and sensibility: using language models to detect and correct syntax errors. In: 2018 IEEE 25th International Conference on Software Analysis, Evolution and Reengineering (SANER), pp. 311–322 (2018)
19. Scalabrino, S., Linares-Vásquez, M., Poshyvanyk, D., Oliveto, R.: Improving code readability models with textual features. In: 2016 IEEE 24th International Conference on Program Comprehension (ICPC), pp. 1–10 (2016). https://doi.org/10.1109/ICPC.2016.7503707

20. Scalabrino, S., Linares-Vásquez, M., Oliveto, R., Poshyvanyk, D.: A comprehensive model for code readability. J. Softw. Evol. Process **30** (2018). https://doi.org/10.1002/smr.1958
21. Seo, K.K.: An application of one-class support vector machines in content-based image retrieval. Exp. Syst. Appl. **33**(2), 491–498 (2007) https://doi.org/10.1016/j.eswa.2006.05.030.   http://www.sciencedirect.com/science/article/pii/S0957417406001655
22. Tysell Sundkvist, L., Persson, E.: Code styling and its effects on code readability and interpretation. Ph.D. thesis, KTH Royal Institute of Technology (2017). http://urn.kb.se/resolve?urn=urn:nbn:se:kth:diva-209576
23. Wang, X., Pollock, L., Vijay-Shanker, K.: Automatic segmentation of method code into meaningful blocks to improve readability. In: 2011 18th Working Conference on Reverse Engineering, pp. 35–44 (2011)
24. White, M., Vendome, C., Linares-Vásquez, M., Poshyvanyk, D.: Toward deep learning software repositories. In: Proceedings of the 12th Working Conference on Mining Software Repositories, MSR 2015, pp. 334–345. IEEE Press (2015)

Software Framework of Context-Aware Reconfigurable Secure Smart Grids

Soumoud Fkaier[1,2,3]([✉]), Mohamed Khalgui[1,2], and Georg Frey[3]

[1] INSAT LISI Lab, Carthage University, Tunis, Tunisia
`soumoud.fkaier@aut.uni-saarland.de`
[2] Tunisia Polytechnic School, Carthage University, Tunis, Tunisia
[3] Chair of Automation and Energy Systems, Saarland University,
Saarbruecken, Germany

Abstract. Developing Smart Grids (SG) requires more advanced software engineering tools to keep-up with the growing requirements. Reconfiguration, context-awareness, and security features are becoming necessary for the smart and reliable behavior of future electricity grids. Several software solutions have been proposed to improve the development of such features. However, there is still a need to a software solution that clarify the relation between reconfiguration and context as well as facilitate their development all with satisfying complex needs such the real-time, coordination, and security needs. In this paper, we propose a solution for easy implementation of reconfigurations originated by a context change. We extend an existing software framework dedicated to the development of context-aware reconfigurable applications with mechanisms that handles the contexts in the controller. This paper explores the usage of the said framework as an infrastructure for general purpose SG applications. To show the suitability of the proposed concepts, a formal case of microgrids reconfigurations is conducted.

Keywords: Software framework · Reconfiguration · Security · Context-awareness · Distributed system

1 Introduction

Smart grids are undergoing a large evolution in the offered services to both end-users and producers. The aim behind this evolution is to achieve more reliable, sustainable, and economical power supply [1,2]. This becomes possible thanks to the adoption of modern concepts such as the integration of the renewable energy and storage systems as well as the demand response handling. To satisfy the new requirements, the software governing the system must be strong enough to support such complicated features. In fact, the software needs to provide the awareness about the context [3,4] that the grid behaves within in order to have proper and coherent decisions. It must also allow the use of prediction and intelligence techniques since these techniques are widely used in the electricity field in order to predict the energy production based on weather forecasts

© Springer Nature Switzerland AG 2022
H.-G. Fill et al. (Eds.): ICSOFT 2021, CCIS 1622, pp. 193–217, 2022.
https://doi.org/10.1007/978-3-031-11513-4_9

and/or the consumption rates based on the estimations of users profiles and consumption trends [5]. Further, it is required that the software offers the tools to coordinate with other peers in the system, where collaborations are more and more required [6,7]. More importantly, protecting the coordination between peers against cyber-attacks needs also to be taken into consideration since security is a major concern especially that the modern economy relies heavily on electricity [8]. Moreover, applications need to seamlessly conduct reconfigurations [9], all with checking the aforementioned needs.

Most of the current research in this field is focusing to satisfy each of the mentioned needs in a separate way, although it is generally required to have an application able to perform a set of the requirements simultaneously, if not all of them together. From another side, most the existing works deal with the intelligence and reconfiguration at the control and automation level. This approach has a main drawback: it is generally tied to the considered case. In fact, usually a SG architecture is defined with a set of parameters and assumptions, and even with fixed types of equipment. Also, if we watch the existing works we can notice that the goals are often the same and repetitive functionalities are sought, such as the Demand Response management, batteries operation optimization, Renewable Energy Sources (RES) integration, etc. [11]. Hence, in order to reduce the development time and effort, it is better to create a code infrastructure that can be generic. In this way we can allow reusability by making the main logic as generic code base, which can be extended with systems specificity according to the considered case. In fact, it is of great importance to have a tool that allows to implement applications logic independently from the grid architecture and physical platform (i.e., that can run on top of any hardware). In fact, SG equipment and devices are continuously changing, so it is required to have a software algorithms and business models independent from any restricted platform [12].

Based on the limitations discussed above, this paper proposes to develop the logic of the SG functionalities in the application level using the software framework introduced in the research presented in [13]. This framework is selected because in addition to the ability to develop multiple requirements (security, context-awareness, collaboration, intelligence, real-time requirements), it features the definition of the SG functionalities into services which promotes the generic and reusable aspect of the framework.

In this paper, we demonstrate how it is possible to implement application's reconfiguration scenarios initiated by a context change. For this end, the mechanisms of the controller -which is the central element of the framework architecture that is located in the Context Control Layer- are extended to clearly demonstrate the relation between a context change and a system reconfiguration. A new experimentation with new data-sets is conducted to show the reasoning of the controller face to context changes.

The outline of the rest of the paper is the following: Section 2 reviews the related literature. Section 3 presents the improved framework. Section 4 shows an example of development of microgrids software. Section 5 evaluates the performances of the proposed framework. Finally, Sect. 6 concludes the paper and shows new perspectives.

2   Related Works

This section studies the existing works from two perspectives: First, the relation between context-awareness computing paradigm with regard to the smart grid systems, second the existing context-awareness software frameworks. It finally discusses them and introduces the motivation.

2.1   Context-Awareness and Smart Grids

Given its high potential to bring smartness to the computerized grid, context-awareness paradigm was lately considered by many SG-related works. The work reported in [8] studied the awareness of microgrids in terms of operational and infrastructural aspects. The work layouts a framework for context-aware resilience. The work reported in [14] proposed a context-aware energy management system for smart buildings that relies on IoT and wireless sensor networks. The works reported in [15–17] used the context awareness concepts to create security measures in the energy grid. The work reported in [18] used context-awareness to build an adaptive cognition system for smart homes and smart grids. The work reported in [19] proposed a context-aware traffic scheduling in smart grids. The work reported in [20] proposed a solution for the network of Phasor Measurement Units (PMUs) awareness using the IoT and cloud computing.

From another side, the context-awareness computing paradigm was largely exploited in the smart grids from a communication perspective, specifically the Software-Defined-Networks solutions. Many works have focused on including the contextual awareness to the communication methods due to the high complexity of the distributed entities involved in the smart grid as well as the increasing inter-operability challenges. The research provided in [21] surveyed the main proposed solutions in this direction.

2.2   Context-Awareness Frameworks

The outstanding evolution of sensory and data acquisition technologies has motivated the integration of contextual data in the applications logic. And given the complicated nature of systems relying on real-time decision making, some software frameworks were proposed to facilitate the development of such intelligent software. The work reported in [22] defined a context-awareness framework based on the cloud technology that is dedicated to smart cities. The work reported in [23] presented a context-aware framework for semantic traffic supervising in smart cities. The work reported in [24] introduced a new service-oriented architecture supporting the real-time context-aware services. The contributions were applied to a health care use case.

2.3 Discussion

As it can be seen from the literature overview presented in the previous two subsections, many software solutions in the scope of context-awareness are defined. But despite its importance, we recognized the following limitations:

- From the context-awareness perspective, many context-awareness software frameworks are proposed. But most of them are dedicated for mobile applications and are not suitable for complicated systems like the SG.
- Many software solutions are dedicated to smart grids but most of them focus on inter-operability and coordination issues, such as the wide range of SDN-based works, which do not cover other crucial aspects such as the prediction, reconfiguration, functional constraints, etc.
- Many other software solutions are proposed to leverage intelligence, awareness, and coordination needs, but they are always developed in the automation and control level, and are tied to specific SG architectures.

To overcome the mentioned limitations we propose a new context-awareness framework that enables to develop smart software of smart grids. The framework provides the mechanisms facilitating the implementation of reconfiguration, security, intelligence, coordination and timing needs. The framework is initially introduced in [3,4,13]. In this paper, we extend the controller logic and we show how the framework make the development task more efficient using an example of microgrids case study.

3 Enhanced Software Framework

To design a software architecture for context-aware reconfigurable systems, we need to make the structure simple and clear. In fact, with the increasing complexity of the miscellaneous requirements that need to be involved, the software becomes more and more difficult to develop. This is why, it is important to define the architecture components in a loosely coupled way. The structure of the architecture needs to follow the separation of concerns principle [25] to make every component responsible for a specific role. An analysis of the context-aware reconfigurable systems has led us to define the meta-model presented in [1,26], and based on this meta-model we defined the framework architecture presented in Fig. 1.

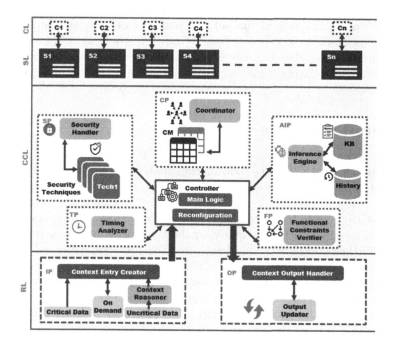

Fig. 1. Framework architecture for context-aware reconfigurable applications.

The framework is defined in [3,4,13] by four layers: RL: the reconfiguration layer, CCL: the context control layer, SL: the services layer, and CL: the communication layer.

3.1 Reconfiguration Layer

This layer is in charge of the communication with the outer environment, specifically ensuring the reading of the inputs of the framework and writing of its outputs. This is done thanks to two pools: the inputs pool IP and the outputs pool OP.

Inputs Pool: The role of the inputs pool is to provide data that are used to establish a context. This pool distinguishes between two types of inputs according to their urgency level, critical and uncritical data, where the uncritical data are processed following a context modeling and reasoning methodology presented in [27]. The context reasoner of this pool produces recommendations of reconfigurations and sends them to the upper layer for further processing.

This pool provides also the reading of measurements/inputs whenever required by the upper layer (CCL).

Outputs Pool: The role of the outputs pool is to ensure the application of the decisions made in the upper layer (CCL). It contains a context output handler that renders the data necessary to change the system behavior. This is done through updating some interfaces to the connected software/hardware components.

3.2   Context Control Layer

This layer is composed of six pools: $CCL = (C, CP, FP, TP, SP, AIP)$, where C is the controller pool, CP is the coordination pool, FP is the functional pool, TP is the timing pool, SP is the security pool, and AIP is the artificial intelligence pool.

The CCL's role is to process the inputs provided by the inputs pool and decides if a reconfiguration is required or the application of the current services must be further continued. This layer uses the upper and lower layers (i.e., SL and RL) where the SL represents the services store. The main logic of applications is ensured thanks to the controller pool C. This pool is the central and major element in the whole architecture since it is the component responsible for the changes of the system behaviors. The controller includes the logic and algorithms that rely on the rest of the pools of CCL.

Controller Pool. The name of the second layer -Context Control Layer- is coming from the fact that this layer, and especially the controller, is responsible for running applications according to a specific context. A **context** is defined as the set of input data that make the system reconfigure itself. The context is created in the reconfiguration layer using the context reasoner methods (see Fig. 1). Thereafter, the controller takes this context entry and processes it in order to determine which configuration to deploy.

Previously the logic of the controller was left to the developers to design and implement. It was offering only the interfaces allowing the interaction with the pools and layers. In this paper, we extend the mechanisms of the controller with more details about the relation of contexts and configurations, and we propose some generic algorithms that could be re-usable in different cases.

Sub-contexts and Sub-configurations. At any instant t of its lifetime, a context-aware application is running according to a well-defined context called the $OperatingContext$ and denoted by OC (see Fig. 2).

The goal of processing the context entry is to make a feasible change of the $OperatingContext$. The OC is given by:

$$OC = (sc_{int}, sc_{ext}) \tag{1}$$

where sc_{int} denotes the internal sub-context that indicates the management of the internal activities of a microgrid and sc_{ext} denotes the external sub-context that indicates the activities that a microgrid performs to interact with the rest of

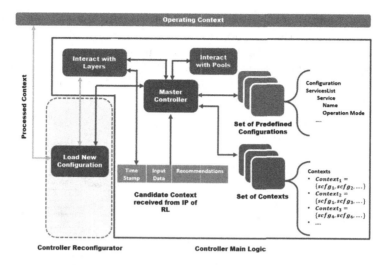

Fig. 2. Context processing by the controller.

the microgrids in the SG such as the trading or the fault recovery. A sub-context is defined by a type and is composed of a set of sub-configurations,

$$sc_i = (T_{sc}, SCFG_{sc}), \ SCFG_{sc} = \{scfg_j | j = 0, ..., m\} \tag{2}$$

where T_{sc} is the type of the sub-context (i.e., internal or external), $SCFG_{sc}$ denotes the set of sub-configurations and m is the number of sub-configurations. A sub-configuration is defined by a set of services such that

$$scfg_j = \{S_i | i = 0, ..., |scfg_j|\} \tag{3}$$

where S_i denotes a service of the services layer SL.

The controller performs two main tasks: processing the main logic and reconfiguring the system (see Fig. 2). Processing the main logic is ensured by a master controller and its function can be summarized as follows: receiving the new context entries, analyzing it using the pools, and then deciding if new services will be added, removed or updated in the $OperatingContext$. In fact, the context entry is considered as a $CandidateContext$, denoted by CC that requires some processing and verification before taking it into deployment.

Adopting the composition of the operating context of internal and external sub-contexts helps to separate the concerns. This is useful to preserve the continuity of services for internal issues. It allows also to tame the complexity of the intertwined events/contexts. In fact, it is required to align with external contexts as maximum as possible but these sub-contexts should not violate the internal sub-contexts. Preferences and priorities of the sub-contexts, and therefore of the services to be deployed, must respect the application goals (which need to be defined by system developers).

The class diagram of the controller is extended with the new proposed elements. Figure 3 shows that in addition to the interaction with the architecture layers and the CCL pools, the logic includes now the processing of the sub-contexts and sub-configurations. The class *SubContextHelper* (*resp. SubConfigurationHelper*)contains the methods that help to handle the predefined list of sub-contexts (*resp.* sub-configurations).

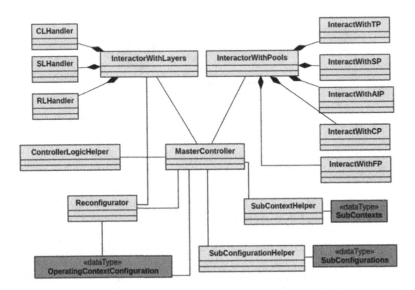

Fig. 3. UML class diagram of the controller.

Reusable Routines. In addition, three generic algorithms that can be used by the master controller are proposed, where Algorithm 1 defines the mechanism to find the match between the context reasoner recommendations and the predefined sub-context, Algorithm 2 defines the process to check a combination of intelligence and functional needs, and Algorithm 3 defines the mechanism of secure coordination among a given microgrid with other peers in the system. The nomenclature used in the algorithms is the following:

- R the recommendations of CC.
- SC is the set of all sub-contexts predefined by the system owners/developers where the sub-contexts must match the set of recommendations defined in the Context Rule Store of the context reasoner of the inputs pool (IP). $SC = \{sc_k|k = 0, ..., |SC|\}$.
- *Reconfigurator* is the controller reconfigurator object.
- PC is the list of possible sub-configurations.
- ps possible services variable.

- irs internal running services.
- ers external running services.

The role of Algorithm 1 is to receive the context entry sent by the inputs pool of RL; from now on, this entry is considered as candidate context CC. Then, it extracts the recommendations from CC if they exist. After, it parses the predefined set of sub-contexts SC and extracts the matching ones.

Algorithm 1. Extract the services of context entry.

$CC = \text{ReadContext}()$;
$R = \text{ExtractRecommendation}(CC)$;
//based on received recommendations, retrieve sub-context from the list of sub-contexts
foreach(sc in SC)**do**
    if $(sc.name == R)$ **then**
        $PC \leftarrow sc$;
    end
end
$ps = GetServices(PC)$;
return ps

Algorithm 2 defines a generic process to check both intelligence and functional needs. In this algorithm, first the AIP is consulted to check the intelligence needs. If the result indicates context conclusions different from the running one, then an update must be conducted. But before executing any updates, we must verify that the changes will not bring the system to an inconsistent state. Thus the functional pool is involved to check for coherence between the new services and the running ones. First, we check if we have completely new services, if yes we need to check whether we have exclusion with one of the existing services. In case there is no exclusion then the service is added, and in case there is exclusion the existing service is removed and the new one is added. In case the new context contains the same services as the running one, an update with the corresponding operation mode is performed.

Coordination among distributed peers requires, in most of the reliable systems, a secure information exchange. For this, we propose Algorithm 3 to enable secure collaboration between peers. The coordination process is based on the predefined coordination matrix of CP. Before sending any messages or transaction in general, the security pool is involved to secure data (hashing, encrypting, etc.), then the transactions need to go through the outputs pool OP. These instructions maybe repeated until a consensus takes place between the peers. The termination condition is use-case dependent. After the peers reach an agreement, then the considered services need to be processed.

Algorithm 2. Check Intelligence and functional needs.

$AIPResult= InteractWithAIP(ps)$;
$\mathbf{if}(AIPResult \neq irs)$ **then**
   $\mathbf{if}(\exists S_i|S_i \in AIPResult, S_i \notin irs)$ **then**
     $FPResult= InteractWithFP(AIPResult, irs)$;
    $\mathbf{if}(FPResult$ is positive$)$ **then**
       $NewServices = \{S_i|S_i \in AIPResult$ and $S_i \notin irs\}$;
       $irs \leftarrow NewServices$;
    else if$(\exists S_i|S_i \in FPResult$ and$\exists\{S_j \in irs|FPExclusion(S_i, S_j) = true\})$ **then**
       $irs \setminus \{S_j \in irs|FPExclusion(S_i, S_j) = true\}$;
       $irs \leftarrow S_i$;
    end
   else if$(\exists S_i|S_i \in AIPResult$ and $S_i \in irs)$**then**
    $rop = GetOperationModes(irs)$;
    $pop = GetOperationModes(ps)$;
   $\mathbf{if}(rop = pop)$ **then**
     do nothing;
   else if$(rop \neq pop)$ **then**
    $opToUpdate = pop - rop$;
    update$(opToUpdate, pop, ps)$; //if different modes, then take the new ones.
   end
  end

Algorithm 3. Coordinating.

repeat
$CPResult = InteractWithCP(ps)$;
$SPResult = InteractWithSP(CPResult)$;
$ss = InteractWithOP(SPResult)$;
$acceptance = AnalyseEfficiency(ss)$; //the efficiency logic is use case dependent.
until$(acceptance = true)$;

Artificial Intelligence Pool. Since modern systems are depending more and more on the artificial intelligence concepts, this pool provides a generic intelligence mechanism that could be used differently according to the use case. This pool provides an expert system composed of a knowledge base, an inference engine, and a pool history. In order to use this pool, developers need to fill the rules and facts bases of the knowledge base and they need to choose which inference type (forward or backward chaining) [13] should the engine use.

Coordination Pool. To allow coordination between distributed peers, this pool uses a matrix of configurations in which the columns represent all the existing peers, and the lines represent the different configurations [13].

Security Pool. Coordination between the distributed peers requires an exchange of data where some of them can be critical. The security pool is a container of security mechanisms such as the algorithms necessary for blockchain-related algorithms, etc. [13]. Since encryption/decryption tools are often used, in this paper we extend the existing techniques with the methods of the crypto-system Elliptic Curve Integrated Encryption Scheme (ECIES) [28].

Functional Pool. With the multiple services that an application can provide, precedence and conflicts could happen between some of them. To overcome the coherence constraint a Functional Exclusion Matrix is created, and to resolve the precedence constraint a Functional Precedence Array is created [13].

Timing Pool. In order to ensure a timing efficiency, a timing pool is created. This pool has the role of temporal behavior analyzer. Analysis helps to check the time feasibility in case of leading reconfigurations [13].

3.3 Services Layer

The services layer, denoted by SL, is defined to store the services to be provided by a system in the form of independent functional units called service and denoted by S_i, hence this layer is defined as $SL = \{S_i | i = 0, ..., n\}$ with n is the number of all services provided by a system. An S encapsulates the necessary operational methods in the form of operation modes denoted by om. Hence a service is defined as the set of operational modes of a particular functionality $S_i = \{om_j | j = 0, ..., m\}$ with m is the number of all operational modes supported by a S_i.

3.4 Communication Layer

The communication layer, denoted by CL, is in charge of presenting the services of SL to the developers. Its role is to expose the necessary dynamics of a certain service. Every communication object represents one unique service.

4   Application

This section presents the use of the framework concepts to develop the software of a smart grid. First, the case study is presented and formalized, then the framework settings are prepared, and finally a scenario is demonstrated.

4.1   Case Study Presentation

Modern smart grids are electricity distribution networks that include an information flow between suppliers and consumers at the aim of guaranteeing more efficient management such as the adjustment of the electricity flow in real-time.

This is achieved thanks to the adoption of software techniques that facilitates the coordination of smaller grids units, optimizing the production as well as the storage of energy in relation with real-time consumption, smoothing the consumption/production peaks, etc. In this paper, we manifest the use of the proposed framework in simplifying the development of such complicated functionalities.

Smart Grid Model and Goals: In this case study we consider a multi-agent model of the smart grid. The grid is considered as the set of distributed microgrids in the field & control level and a network of distributed software agents in the software level (see Fig. 4), where each agent manages one microgrid.

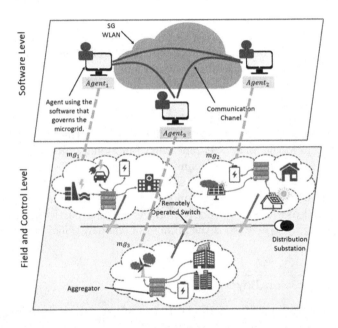

Fig. 4. Smart grid structure.

A microgrid, denoted by mg, is a small scale electricity grid having its own renewable energy sources (RES), loads (L), a storage system (batteries in this example) (B), a switching to utility system a.k.a. remotely operating switches (ROS). Hence the microgrid is given by

$$mg_i = (RES, L, B, ROS) \qquad (4)$$

Microgrids are characterized by the integration of renewable energy sources. So they have the possibility to operate in islanded mode in case of high production and in utility-connected mode in case of shortages. This is why, and given the volatility/intermittence of the renewable energy sources, reconfigurations are always needed to keep the stability and continuity of the offered services. Further, in order to reach better efficiency it is needed to provide the ability to microgrids to reconfigure themselves automatically when changes are happening and new system behaviors are required. This is why context-awareness computing plays a promising role in satisfying such needs. In the considered smart grid, aggregators have the possibility to aggregate electricity from independent producers (i.e., prosumers), to store the collected quantities, and to distribute it over consumers. They work in coordination and consent of microgrids, so the software of microgrids includes also the logic of the interaction with aggregators.

4.2   Settings Preparation

Before starting the development of the software applications, it is necessary first to determine the settings of every layer.

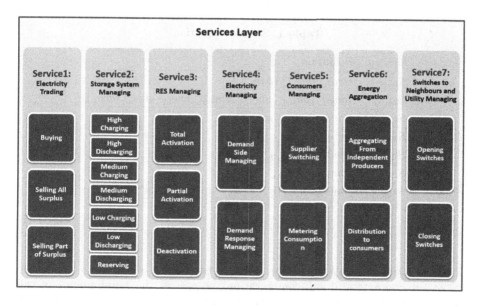

Fig. 5. Service layer schematic presentation.

Service Layer. In the considered example, the microgrid is performing seven services: Electricity trading (ET), Storage System Managing (SSM), Renewable Energy Sources Managing ($RESM$), Electricity Managing (EM), Consumers Managing ($ConsM$), Energy Aggregation (EA), Switches to Neighbors and utility Managing (SNM). Thus the services layer is given by

$$SL = \{S_{1_{ET}}, S_{2_{SSM}}, S_{3_{RESM}}, S_{4_{EM}}, S_{5_{ConsM}}, S_{6_{EA}}, S_{7_{SNM}}\}. \qquad (5)$$

The schematic presentation of SL becomes as depicted in Fig. 5.

Each service has a set of operation modes defined as follows; the first service $S_{1_{ET}}$ provides three operations modes: buying (b), selling all surplus (sas), selling part of surplus (sps). The Storage System Managing service is composed of seven operation modes: high charging (hc), high discharging (hd), medium charging (mc), medium discharging (md), low charging (lc), low discharging (ld), reserving (r). The RES managing service offers three operation modes: total activation (ta), partial activation (pa), deactivation (d). The electricity managing service provides two operations: demand side managing (dsm) and demand response managing (drm). The consumers managing service is composed of two operation modes: suppliers switching (ss) and metering consumption (mc). The Energy aggregation service provides two operation modes: the aggregation from independent producers (aip) and the distribution to consumers (dc). Finally, the switches to neighbors managing service is composed of two operation modes: opening switches (os) and closing switches (cs). Table 1 summarizes the services definition.

Table 1. Services definition.

Service	Definition
$S_{1_{ET}}$	$\{om_{1_b}, om_{2_{sas}}, om_{3_{sps}}\}$
$S_{2_{SSM}}$	$\{om_{1_{hc}}, om_{2_{hd}}, om_{3_{mc}}, om_{4_{md}}, om_{5_{lc}}, om_{6_{ld}}, om_{7_r}\}$
$S_{3_{RESM}}$	$\{om_{1_{ta}}, om_{2_{pa}}, om_{3_d}\}$
$S_{4_{EM}}$	$\{om_{1_{dsm}}, om_{2_{drm}}\}$
$S_{5_{ConsM}}$	$\{om_{1_{ss}}, om_{2_{mc}}\}$
$S_{6_{EA}}$	$\{om_{1_{aip}}, om_{2_{dc}}\}$
$S_{7_{SNM}}$	$\{om_{1_{os}}, om_{2_{cs}}\}$

Context Control Layer. In the lower layer (CCL), we need to define the sets of sub-contexts and sub-configurations as well as the requirements of the pools. Taking the decision to participate in a trading session is not an easy task to perform since many considerations need to be taken into account. Such a decision needs to keep efficiency from a financial, functional, and strategic scopes. Human expertise is required to tell when to buy/sell and with which quantity in order to keep profit. For this, we need the artificial intelligence pool to be involved in right decision making. The rules base is defined as shown in Table 2.

Table 2. Extract from the rules base of the expert system of AIP.

id	Rule
R1	if (BC is medium) & (L is low) & (CSG is high) & (TSG is high) & (MP is high) $\rightarrow$ sell all surplus
R2	if (BC is high) & (L is low) & (CSG is medium) & (TSG is medium) & (MP is low) $\rightarrow$ sell part of surplus
R3	if (BC is high) & (L is low) & (CSG is high) & (TSG is high) & (MP is high) $\rightarrow$ high charging
R4	if (BC is high) & (L is medium) & (CSG is high) & (TSG is low) & (MP is high) $\rightarrow$ high discharging
R5	if (BC is high) & (L is medium) & (CSG is high) & (TSG is high) & (MP is high) $\rightarrow$ sell all surplus

In this table BC: Battery level of charge, L: loads, CSG: Current Solar Generation, TSG: predicted Tomorrow Solar Generation, MP: Market Price.

As mentioned earlier, the sub-configurations match the services with its operation modes, and a sub-context reflects the services that could work together. The following is an extract of the list of sub-configurations. These sub-configurations must be filled in the XML configuration files, so that developers could adjust them "externally"; without the need to change the code of configuration handling of the controller. Of course the added names should match the names of the services of the services layer:

- $scfg_1 = \{S_{2_{SSM}}.om_{7_r}, S_{3_{RESM}}.om_{3_d}\},\ scfg_6 = \{S_{6_{EA}}.om_{1_{aip}}\}.$
- $scfg_2 = \{S_{2_{SSM}}.om_{4_{md}}, S_{3_{RESM}}.om_{2_{pa}}\},\ scfg_7 = \{S_{6_{EA}}.om_{2_{dc}}\}.$
- $scfg_3 = \{S_{2_{SSM}}.om_{1_{hc}}, S_{3_{RESM}}.om_{2_{pa}}\},\ scfg_8 = \{S_{7_{SNM}}.om_{2_{cs}}\}.$
- $scfg_4 = \{S_{2_{SSM}}.om_{2_{hd}}, S_{3_{RESM}}.om_{1_{ta}}\},\ scfg_9 = \{S_{7_{SNM}}.om_{1_{os}}\}.$
- $scfg_5 = \{S_{4_{EM}}.om_{1_{dsm}}, S_{5_{ConsM}}.om_{2_{mc}}\}, scfg_{10} = \{S_{1_{ET}}.om_{2_{sas}}\}.$
- $scfg_{11} = \{S_{1_{ET}}.om_{1_b}\}, scfg_{12} = \{S_{1_{ET}}.om_{3_{sps}}\}.$

Table 3 depicts some sub-contexts (developers could define the sub-contexts as needed in the considered case). For example, in the trading sub-context different combinations of sub-configurations can be used:

Reconfiguration Layer. After having defined the setting of SL and CCL, we move now to define the context model to be used by the RL. In this example, the smart grid ontology takes into consideration not only the environmental facts, but also the entities that affects the trading activity such as the presence of aggregators, prosumers, and the electricity market itself (see Fig. 6).

Table 3. Sub-contexts definition.

Sub-context name	Type	Definition
RegularRoutine1	Internal	$sc_1 = \{scfg_5, scfg_1\}$
RegularRoutine2	Internal	$sc_2 = \{scfg_5, scfg_2\}$
RegularRoutine3	Internal	$sc_3 = \{scfg_5, scfg_3\}$
RegularRoutine4	Internal	$sc_4 = \{scfg_5, scfg_4\}$
Collaborating	External	$sc_5 = \{scfg_9\}$
SellingElectricity1	External	$sc_6 = \{scfg_9, scfg_{10}\}$
BuyingElectricity2	External	$sc_7 = \{scfg_9, scfg_{11}\}$
SellingElectricity2	External	$sc_8 = \{scfg_9, scfg_{12}\}$
Disconnecting	External	$sc_9 = \{scfg_8\}$
Aggregating	External	$sc_{10} = \{scfg_6\}$

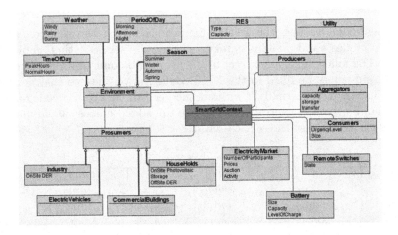

Fig. 6. Smart grid OWL ontology.

4.3 Use Case Scenario

In this paper, we consider a scenario where the context-awareness, artificial intelligence, security as well as functional requirements are needed to lead the proper reconfiguration. Let us assume that the application of microgrid mg_2, is running under the internal context "RegularRoutine2" which reflects that mg_2 is partially activating the solar panels generation, the batteries are making a medium discharge, and that the aggregators are active, and under the external context "Aggregating" which reflects that the aggregator of mg_2 is aggregating energy from prosumers.

$$OC_0 = (sc_{int_0}, sc_{ext_0}) \tag{6}$$

where $sc_{int_0} = sc_2$ is RegularRoutine2 and $sc_{ext_0} = sc_{10}$ is Aggregating.

The last context CR_0 that was created by the inputs pool of RL is given by

$$CR_0 = \begin{cases} i_1 : <o_{ElectricityMarket}.a_{Activity}, false, 0> \\ i_2 : <o_{Environment}.e_{Weather}.a_{Type}, Sunny, 3> \\ i_3 : <o_{Environment}.e_{PeriodOfDay}.a_{Type}, Morning, 1> \\ i_4 : <o_{Aggregators}.a_{Activity}, Aggregating, 1> \\ i_5 : <o_{Consumers}.a_{Size}, low, 1> \\ i_6 : <o_{Battery}.a_{LevelOfCharge}, medium, 2> \end{cases} \tag{7}$$

In the next timer tick (i.e., period of measurements and reads of the inputs pool), the context reasoner detects that some changes have happened, mainly a trading session is becoming active in the electricity market, the level of charge of the batteries becomes high, and the consumption becomes medium. The new context is given by

$$CR_1 = \begin{cases} i_1 : <o_{ElectricityMarket}.a_{Activity}, true, 1> \\ i_2 : <o_{Environment}.e_{Weather}.a_{Type}, Sunny, 3> \\ i_3 : <o_{Environment}.e_{PeriodOfDay}.a_{Type}, Morning, 1> \\ i_4 : <o_{Aggregators}.a_{Activity}, Aggregating, 1> \\ i_5 : <o_{Consumers}.a_{Size}, medium, 2> \\ i_6 : <o_{Battery}.a_{LevelOfCharge}, high, 3> \end{cases} \tag{8}$$

According to the context reasoning process of the inputs pool IP, the Context Rules Store (CRS) must be consulted. We have defined this CRS based on the defined context ontology of Fig. 6 as mentioned in Table 4.

Table 4. Extract from the context rules store.

id	Rule
R1	if (Weather is Rainy) & (Season is Summer) & (PeriodOfDay is Night) → Put off REG
R2	if (Weather is Sunny) & (Season is Summer) & (PeriodOfDay is Morning) → Put on REG
R3	if (Market is Active) & (Battery is Low) & (PeriodOfDay is Midday) → Buying electricity
R4	if (Market is Active) & (Battery is High) & (PeriodOfDay is Morning) → Selling electricity
R5	if (Weather is Sunny) & (Season is Summer) & (PeriodOfDay is Morning) → Charge Battery

Parsing the CRS has resulted in firing the rule R4. Then, the context reasoner creates a new context entry CE_1 with recommendation to "Selling Electricity" and sends it to the controller of CCL.

The controller obtains CE_1 and following Algorithm 1, it extracts the recommendations and checks the table of sub-contexts (see Table 3) to get the type of the sub-context. In this case, it is an external sub-context that changed. So the controller prepares to make the processing with the running external sub-context (i.e., Aggregating).

Then, it starts the processing in order to verify if the recommendation is feasible and in case yes which reconfiguration to lead. Participating in the trading session is not an easy task to perform since many aspects need to be analyzed. Such analysis should include the pricing, current reserve power, future renewable power generation predictions and others. Here the controller calls the artificial intelligence pool to help in decision making. The AIP consults its rule base (see Table 2) and given the facts that the battery level of charge is high, the loads are medium, the current solar generation level is high, the predicted solar generation of the day after is high, and the market price is high, the inference engine fires the rule R5. Thus, the AIP returns the conclusion "Sell all surplus" to the controller.

Now the controller knows that it is a positive decision to participate in the electricity market. So the controller parses the set of possible sub-contexts and picks the sub-context "SellingElectricity1" and prepares the candidate context CC_1 for processing. The candidate context consists of the current running sub-contexts and in addition the new recommended sub-context (sc_6). Figure 7 depicts the XML file of the definition of the sub-context to be added.

```xml
<Configuration>
    <Subconfiguration Name="scfg9">
    <Services>
        <Service>
            <Name>Switches to Neighbours and Utility Managing</Name>
            <OperationMode>Opening Switches</OperationMode>
        </Service>
    </Services>
    </Subconfiguration>
    <Subconfiguration Name="scfg10">
    <Services>
        <Service>
            <Name>Electricity Trading</Name>
            <OperationMode>Selling All Surplus</OperationMode>
        </Service>
    </Services>
    </Subconfiguration>
</Configuration>
```

Fig. 7. XML file of sub-configurations $acfg_9$ and $acfg_{10}$.

The first verification that the controller performs before starting the price calculations and bidding in the market, is consulting the functional pool to see if the addition of the selling activity preserves the functional consistency of the whole system state: the relation of the new services with the other services.

In order to keep coherence of the considered multiple services, FP checks the coherence thanks to the exclusion matrix defining these contradictory relations [3]. Table 5 depicts the defined matrix:

Table 5. Exclusion matrix of the Functional Pool.

	ET	SSM	RESM	EM	ConsM	EA	SNM
ET	X	0	0	0	0	1	0
SSM	0	X	0	0	0	0	0
RESM	0	0	X	0	0	0	0
EM	0	0	0	X	0	0	0
ConsM	0	0	0	0	X	0	0
EA	1	0	0	0	0	X	0
SNM	0	0	0	0	0	0	X

In this matrix 0: false, 1: true, X: not relevant.

In this exclusion matrix, it is stated that the electricity trading service *ET* is in conflict with the electricity Aggregation service *EA*. In fact, performing trading and aggregation in the same time brings a risk in terms of security of supply and it deteriorates the quality of services of energy transfer. This is why, these two services are considered exclusive. Figure 8 shows the implementation of the method that checks whether an exclusion relationship exist between the new sub-context and the running internal one.

```java
public static List<String> Parse(String serviceName, List<String> runningServices)
{
    List<String> result=new ArrayList<String>();

    for(int i=0; i<runningServices.size(); i++)
    {
        String runningService=runningServices.get(i);
        boolean[] relations= CM.get(runningService);
        for(int j=0; j<relations.length; j++)
        {
            if((relations[j]== true) && (GetServiceId(serviceName)==j))
            {
                result.add(runningServices.get(i));
                logger.info("The service "+serviceName+
                " is in exclusion with the service: "+runningServices.get(i));
            }
        }
    }
    return result;
}
```

Fig. 8. Parsing the exclusion checking of the functional pool.

The controller recognizes that the aggregation service needs to be removed whenever the microgrid is selected to be a seller. This condition is known and saved by the master controller, the controller can start to the trading process with all preconditions clear.

Then, it calculates the selling price and prepares a bid (the logic on how the price is calculated is out of the scope of this paper, in fact the aim of this example is to show how the controller works based on a context change). Let as assume that, in order to protect the trading process, the microgrids adopt a trading protocol where the information exchange is secured using cryptography. Thus, every microgrid must encrypt its bid before submitting it to the market using the Elliptic Curve Integrated Encryption Scheme. For this, the security pool SP of the CCL includes the necessary methods enabling the transactions (i.e., bids) encryption. Figure 9 shows the implementation of the key establishment, encryption, decryption methods that are required to participate in the secure trading process.

```
public KeyPair establishKeys(String keysize) throws Exception
{

    ECGenParameterSpec      ecGenSpec = new ECGenParameterSpec(keysize);
    KeyPairGenerator        keyGen = KeyPairGenerator.getInstance("EC", new BouncyCastleProvider());

    keyGen.initialize(new ECGenParameterSpec(keysize));

    return keyGen.generateKeyPair();
}
public byte[] encrypt(byte[] plainText, PublicKey publicKey) throws Exception
{

    Cipher acipher = Cipher.getInstance("ECIESwithAES-CBC", new BouncyCastleProvider());

    IESParameterSpec param = new IESParameterSpec(null, null, 128, 128, new byte[16]);

    establishKeys("secp256r1");
    acipher.init(Cipher.ENCRYPT_MODE, (ECPublicKey)publicKey, param);

    int maxKeyLength = Cipher.getMaxAllowedKeyLength("ECIESwithAES-CBC");
    return acipher.doFinal(plainText);
}
public byte[] decrypt(byte[] cipherText, PrivateKey privateKey) throws Exception
{
    Cipher bcipher = Cipher.getInstance("ECIESwithAES-CBC");

    IESParameterSpec param = new IESParameterSpec(null, null, 128, 128, new byte[16]);

    bcipher.init(Cipher.DECRYPT_MODE, (ECPrivateKey)privateKey, param);
    return bcipher.doFinal(cipherText);
}
```

Fig. 9. ECIES methods implementation.

So the controller calculates the prices and prepares the bids and handover them to SP. The SP encrypts the necessary information and sends it back to the controller. The controller repeats this step as required by its trading algorithm.

In this example, we made the microgrid mg_2 the best bidder, so now it must proceed to the electricity transfer. For this, a reconfiguration is required. So the controller applies the changes mentioned in the recommended context according to Algorithm 2. Hence the new OC becomes as follows:

$$OC_1 = \{sc_{int_1}, sc_{ext_1}\} \tag{9}$$

with $sc_{int_1} = sc_2$ "RegularRoutine2" and $sc_{ext_1} = sc_6$ "SellingElectricity1".

The application runs OC_1 until the energy transfer required by the trading activity is done.

5   Results and Discussions

To show the suitability of the proposed framework we start by comparing it with the existing ones. Then, since the performance of the pools were evaluated and discussed in previous papers, and since this paper tackles the extension of the controller as well as the security pool, we focus in this section on discussing them.

Comparison with Existing Works. In comparison with the work presented in [24], which has introduced an important context-awareness architecture according to the service-oriented approach, our framework provides a more holistic solution. In fact, although it addressed the needs to real-time and distribution of the software of context-aware systems, some other important features such as the intelligence/prediction or the automatic reconfiguration were not considered. Similarly, the work reported in [23] provides an interesting solution to context-aware car tracking that takes into consideration the real-time and prediction needs, however reconfiguration, collaboration, and security needs were not addressed. The work reported in [22] has studied the suitable software framework for smart cities. Although many significant aspects were discussed such as the compliance with the big data concepts, requirements such as the reconfiguration, real-time, and intelligence were not studied. As it can be see, our proposed framework has addressed the lack of a rich and clear context-awareness development infrastructure. Miscellaneous requirements could be easily developed used our framework. Table 6 sums-up the comparative study.

Table 6. Comparison with existing context-awareness frameworks.

Reference	Reconfiguration	Intelligence	Security	Real-time	Coordination
[22]	X	X	X	X	X
[23]	X	✓	X	✓	X
[24]	X	X	X	✓	✓
Our work	✓	✓	✓	✓	✓

Security Pool. Introducing a security pool to be the "container" of miscellaneous security techniques is of great importance. In fact, leaving the possibility to developers to extend the existing techniques with new ones ensures better evolvability to the pool. In this way, the framework could always keep-up with the new and/or personalized security techniques.

However, this approach has some limitations. First, developers need to include/implement new techniques if they need something different from blockchain tools, ECIES as well as RSA encryption. And this requires knowledge in the field of security, so additional effort is needed.

Controller Pool. In this paper, the controller is improved by a refinement of the context usage process. In fact, the controller is able now to distinguish between the internal and external contexts and this shapes its operation, which leads to improve the processing time.

In order to demonstrate this, let us assume that we have an increasing number of services and an increasing number of operation modes in every service. If we check the whole configuration each time we receive a context entry, then a lot of computational time will be required. However, characterizing the sub-contexts as internal and external helps to recognize which scope the context will impact and hence, we don't require to check the whole context.

Let us consider the sub-configuration $scfg_i$

$$scfg_i = \{S_1.om_1, S_2.om_1, S_3.om_1, S_4.om_1, S_5.om_1\} \tag{10}$$

Let us consider these contexts:

- $OC_0 = (sc_{int_0}, sc_{ext_0})$ where $sc_{int_0} = \{scfg_i | i = 0, ..., 2\}$ and $sc_{ext_0} = \emptyset$.
- $OC_1 = (sc_{int_1}, sc_{ext_1})$ where $sc_{int_1} = \{scfg_i | i = 0, ..., 5\}$ and $sc_{ext_1} = \{scfg_i | i = 20, ..., 21\}$.
- $OC_2 = (sc_{int_2}, sc_{ext_2})$ where $sc_{int_2} = \{scfg_i | i = 0, ..., 10\}$ and $sc_{ext_2} = \{scfg_i | i = 20, ..., 25\}$.
- $OC_3 = (sc_{int_3}, sc_{ext_3})$ where $sc_{int_3} = \{scfg_i | i = 0, ..., 15\}$ and $sc_{ext_3} = \{scfg_i | i = 20, ..., 30\}$.
- $OC_4 = (sc_{int_4}, sc_{ext_4})$ where $sc_{int_4} = \{scfg_i | i = 0, ..., 19\}$ and $sc_{ext_4} = \{scfg_i | i = 20, ..., 35\}$.

The time taken by the functional pool to check the exclusion between two services is measured to be 36 milliseconds. Let us assume that the candidate context contains only one sub-configuration which in its turn contains only one service. If we have an increasing size of operating contexts then, the elapsed time will be as mentioned in the following curve (see Fig. 10).

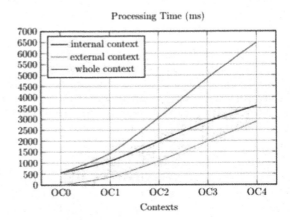

Fig. 10. Computation time of the exclusion checking of the functional pool.

Figure 10 shows that the distinction between internal and external sub-contexts helps to avoid the checking of the whole running context which reduces the elapsed computational time to nearly the half.

6   Conclusions and Outlook

This paper has introduced a software framework for the development of reconfigurable applications based on context change. The framework architecture is composed of four layers reflecting the stages of the context data processing: the first layer, called the Reconfiguration Layer, provides the mechanisms responsible for data collection and context reasoning. The second layer, called the Context Control Layer, provides the possibility to check different aspects of the reconfiguration decision such as the intelligence, timing, functional, coordination, and security issues. This layer relies mainly on a central element, called the controller, which represents the main logic of applications. The third layer, called Services Layer, encapsulates the system functionalties in the form of services. And finally, the fourth layer, called the Communication Layer, is charged by the representation of the system services.

In this paper, we have extended the concepts introduced in [13] by making clear the relation between the context and reconfiguration. The used case study has helped to manifest the decision making of reconfigurations based on context-awareness basis. We have detailed the controller logic and we have developed new cases regarding the case study such as an extended context ontology and different security techniques.

In future works, we aim to study the deployment of the framework applications using the cloud computing resources. Virtualization using cloud computing becomes an interesting alternative that offers promising results regarding the management of IT infrastructures, however some challenges especially interoperability ones need to be further studied.

References

1. Fkaier, S., Romdhani, M., Khalgui, M., Frey, G.: Context-awareness meta-model for reconfigurable control systems. In: Proceedings of the 12th International Conference on Evaluation of Novel Approaches to Software Engineering, pp. 226–234 (2017). ISBN 978-989-758-250-9, ISSN 2184-4895. https://doi.org/10.5220/0006328502260234
2. Abidi, M.G., Smida, M.B., Khalgui, M., Li, Z., Wu, N.: Multi-agent oriented solution for forecasting-based control strategy with load priority of microgrids in an island mode-case study: Tunisian petroleum platform. Electr. Power Syst. Res. **152**, 411–423 (2017)
3. Fkaier, S., Romdhani, M., Khalgui, M., Frey, G.: Enabling reconfiguration of adaptive control systems using real-time context-aware framework. In: 2016 IEEE/ACS 13th International Conference of Computer Systems and Applications (AICCSA), pp. 1–8. IEEE, September 2016
4. Fkaier, S., Romdhani, M., Khalgui, M., Frey, G.: R2TCA: new tool for developing reconfigurable real-time context-aware framework-application to baggage handling systems. In: Proceedings International Conference Mobile Ubiquitous Computing, System, Services Technologies (UBICOMM), pp. 113–119, October 2016
5. Fredj, N., Kacem, Y.H., Khriji, S., Kanoun, O., Abid, M.: A review on intelligent IoT systems design methodologies. Measur. Sens. **18**, 100347 (2021)

6. Naidji, I., Mosbahi, O., Khalgui, M., Bachir, A.: Cooperative energy management software for networked microgrids. In: ICSOFT, pp. 428–438 (2019)

7. Patti, E., Syrri, A.L.A., Jahn, M., Mancarella, P., Acquaviva, A., Macii, E.: Distributed software infrastructure for general purpose services in smart grid. IEEE Trans. Smart Grid **7**(2), 1156–1163 (2014)

8. Mishra, S., Kwasnik, T., Anderson, K.: Microgrid resilience: a holistic and context-aware resilience metric (2021). arXiv preprint arXiv:2106.09640

9. Ghribi, I., Abdallah, R.B., Khalgui, M., Li, Z., Alnowibet, K., Platzner, M.: R-codesign: codesign methodology for real-time reconfigurable embedded systems under energy constraints. IEEE Access **6**, 14078–14092 (2018)

10. Fkaier, S., Khalgui, M., Frey, G.: Modeling methodology for reconfigurable distributed systems using transformations from GR-UML to GR-TNCES and IEC 61499. In: Proceedings of the 16th International Conference on Evaluation of Novel Approaches to Software Engineering, pp. 221–230 (2021). ISBN 978-989-758-508-1, ISSN 2184-4895. https://doi.org/10.5220/0010422102210230

11. Hijjo, M., Frey, G.: Battery management system in isolated microgrids considering forecast uncertainty. In: 2018 9th International Renewable Energy Congress (IREC), pp. 1–6. IEEE, March 2018

12. Karnouskos, S., De Holanda, T.N.: Simulation of a smart grid city with software agents. In: 2009 Third UKSim European Symposium on Computer Modeling and Simulation, pp. 424–429. IEEE, November 2009

13. Fkaier, S., Khalgui, M., Frey, G.: A software framework for context-aware secure intelligent applications of distributed systems. In: Proceedings of the 16th International Conference on Software Technologies, pp. 111–121 (2021). ISBN 978-989-758-523-4, ISSN 2184-2833. https://doi.org/10.5220/0010604701110121

14. Najem, N., Haddou, D.B., Abid, M.R., Darhmaoui, H., Krami, N., Zytoune, O.: Context-aware wireless sensors for IoT-centeric energy-efficient campuses. In: 2017 IEEE International Conference on Smart Computing (SMARTCOMP), pp. 1–6. IEEE, May 2017

15. Santos, G., Pinto, T., Vale, Z., Carvalho, R., Teixeira, B., Ramos, C.: Upgrading BRICKS-the context-aware semantic rule-based system for intelligent building energy and security management. Energies **14**(15), 4541 (2021)

16. Ustundag Soykan, E., et al.: Context-aware authentication with dynamic credentials using electricity consumption data. Comput. J. (2021)

17. Sikder, A.K., Babun, L., Uluagac, A.S.: AEGIS+ A context-aware platform-independent security framework for smart home systems. Digit. Threats Res. Pract. **2**(1), 1–33 (2021)

18. Lugo-Cordero, H.M., Guha, R.K., Ortiz-Rivera, E.I.: An adaptive cognition system for smart grids with context awareness and fault tolerance. IEEE Trans. Smart Grid **5**(3), 1246–1253 (2014)

19. Ahmad, W.S.H.M.W., et al.: Scheduling smart grid network traffic with context-awareness in industrial grade router. In: 2020 1st International Conference on Information Technology, Advanced Mechanical and Electrical Engineering (ICITAMEE), pp. 101–105. IEEE, October 2020

20. Meloni, A., Pegoraro, P.A., Atzori, L., Castello, P., Sulis, S.: IoT cloud-based distribution system state estimation: virtual objects and context-awareness. In: 2016 IEEE International Conference on Communications (ICC), pp. 1–6. IEEE, May 2016

21. Rehmani, M.H., Davy, A., Jennings, B., Assi, C.: Software defined networks-based smart grid communication: a comprehensive survey. IEEE Commun. Surv. Tutorials **21**(3), 2637–2670 (2019)

22. Faieq, S., Saidi, R., Elghazi, H., Rahmani, M.D.: C2IoT: a framework for cloud-based context-aware internet of things services for smart cities. Procedia Comput. Sci. **110**, 151–158 (2017)

23. Goel, D., Pahal, N., Jain, P., Chaudhury, S.: An ontology-driven context aware framework for smart traffic monitoring. In: 2017 IEEE Region 10 Symposium (TENSYMP), pp. 1–5. IEEE, July 2017

24. De Prado, A.G., Ortiz, G., Boubeta-Puig, J.: CARED-SOA: a context-aware event-driven service-oriented architecture. IEEE Access **5**, 4646–4663 (2017)

25. Schlegel, C., Lotz, A., Lutz, M., Stampfer, D.: Composition, separation of roles and model-driven approaches as enabler of a robotics software ecosystem. In: Software Engineering for Robotics, pp. 53–108. Springer, Cham (2021). https://doi.org/10.1007/978-3-030-66494-7_3

26. Fkaier, S., Khalgui, M., Frey, G.: Meta-model for control applications of microgrids. In: 2020 6th IEEE International Energy Conference (ENERGYCon), pp. 945–950. IEEE (2020)

27. Fkaier, S., Khalgui, M., Frey, G.: Hybrid context-awareness modelling and reasoning approach for microgrid's intelligent control. In: Proceedings of the 15th International Conference on Software Technologies, pp. 116–127 (2020). ISBN 978-989-758-443-5, ISSN 2184-2833. https://doi.org/10.5220/0009780901160127

28. Gayoso Martínez, V., Hernández Álvarez, F., Hernández Encinas, L., Sánchez Ávila, C.: Analysis of ECIES and other cryptosystems based on elliptic curves (2011)

A Novel Neural Network-Based Malware Severity Classification System

Miles Q. Li[1] and Benjamin C. M. Fung[2(✉)]

[1] School of Computer Science, McGill University, Montreal, Canada
miles.qi.li@mail.mcgill.ca
[2] School of Information Studies, McGill University, Montreal, Canada
ben.fung@mcgill.ca

Abstract. Malware has been an increasing threat to computer users. Different pieces of malware have different damage potential depending on their objectives and functionalities. In the literature, there are many studies that focus on automatically identifying malware with their families. However, there is a lack of focus on automatically identifying the severity level of malware samples. In this paper, we propose a dedicated neural network-based malware severity classification method. It is developed based on the clustering analysis of malware functions. Experimental results show that the proposed method outperforms previously proposed machine learning methods for malware classification on the severity classification problem.

Keywords: Cybersecurity · Malware severity classification · Neural networks

1 Introduction

Malware programs are becoming more sophisticated and diverse with time [1, 16]. They are developed for different purposes. Some could harm only individual computers and their users, and the damage can be recovered. Some could cause permanent loss to large groups of computers and their users. Thus, the severity of malware programs can vary. The resources of malware defenders allocated to deal with different malware programs should depend on their severity to minimize the potential losses they can cause. To this end, it is crucial to have an AI-based severity classification system that helps malware analysts recognize the severity level of a malware program in a timely manner.

Signature-based methods are the most commonly used kind of malware classification method in commercial antivirus products. If an executable contains a signature that is labelled with a certain class of malware, it belongs to that class. The signatures are crafted by malware analysts through manual analysis of their collected malware samples. The problem with this type of method is that it is limited in recognizing significant variants of existing malware samples or new malware samples since malware authors could avoid the signature while still keeping its functionalities [1, 13, 42]. Therefore, machine learning-based malware classification methods are proposed to identify significant variants of known malware or new malware samples based on the patterns that are recognized from known malware samples [23, 26, 27, 35, 36].

© Springer Nature Switzerland AG 2022
H.-G. Fill et al. (Eds.): ICSOFT 2021, CCIS 1622, pp. 218–232, 2022.
https://doi.org/10.1007/978-3-031-11513-4_10

As a classification problem, malware severity classification is more challenging than malware family classification, while the latter is more intensively studied. One reason that malware family classification is less challenging is that in each malware family, the samples have the same purposes and behaviors, so they are programmed similarly to each other [9,25]. The similarity makes it easier to recognize a new sample of that malware family based on the knowledge of known samples of that family. However, the malware programs at each severity level could present different behaviors and functionalities. Thus, there are many different and independent patterns that can indicate the severity levels of malware programs. This increases the complexity of the malware severity classification problem. The second challenge with malware severity classification is that severity classification is not a normal classification problem in which the relations between all classes are balanced. In severity classification, a higher severity level dominates a lower severity level. In other words, if a program has behaviors at different severity levels, it should be classified as the level of the most severe behaviors. A third challenge is that the malware family classification can be done by analyzing the functional similarity between an unknown sample and a malware family, but severity ranking cannot. When a malware program contains more than the average number of behaviors of programs at a certain level, it should be classified to a higher level, or when most behaviors of a malware program are at a low severity level and only a few behaviors at a high severity level, it belongs to the higher level. For example, when a malware program has multiple Trojan-related functions, it should be classified to a higher severity level than a program that contains only one [21].

The contribution of this paper is a novel and dedicated neural network-based malware severity classification model. It is a neural network extension of the malware family classification model proposed by Li et al. [25], which is based on the similarity analysis of functions of malware samples. Since it is developed based on functional similarity, it will fail the severity classification problems for the reasons we mentioned in the previous paragraph. As artificial neural networks are good at comprehensively capturing the correlation between inputs and outputs rather than just similarity accumulation, we introduce artificial neural networks into the framework proposed by Li et al. [25] for the malware severity classification problem.

The rest of the paper is organized as follows. Section 2 discusses related work. Section 3 formally defines the malware severity classification problem. Section 4 describes our proposed method. Section 5 presents the evaluation of the proposed method. Section 6 discusses the limitations and our future work. Section 7 concludes the paper.

2   Related Work

2.1   Malware Classification

Most existing malware classification studies focus on malware detection or family classification. The former aims to differentiate malware and benign software, while the latter aims to identify the malware family.

Malware classification methods can be categorized as static, dynamic, and hybrid methods [1]. Static methods examine the static content of an executable, and dynamic

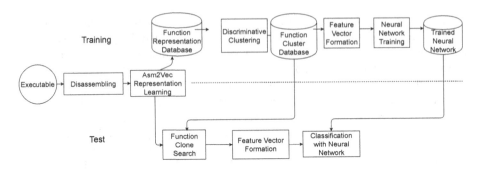

Fig. 1. Workflow of our severity classification model.

methods run it to analyze its behaviors. Common features used by static methods are sequences of bytes [4,17,23,32,35,36], sequences of assembly code [3,4,11,17,26, 27,34], numerical PE header fields [4,6,26,35], PE imports/API calls [6,17,26,29,35, 36], printable strings [20,26,35,36], and malware images [28,40,41]; those used by dynamic methods are memory images [10,19,24], executed instructions [3,4,11,33], invoked system calls or behaviors [2,4,7,10,15,19,20,34]. Hybrid methods use both static and dynamic features for malware classification [4,12,20,34].

2.2   Severity Ranking

The severity level of malware can be defined based on different criteria. In this subsection, we introduce some severity ranking theories.

Malware Rating System. Bagnall and French [5] suggest three criteria to define the severity of a malware program, namely: (1) its payload potential, (2) its proliferation potential, and (3) its hostility level. The payload means the potential of the code to degrade or damage its target. The proliferation potential means the ability to spread itself across the file system or over the network. The hostility level means how malicious the intent is behind the payload. The payload potential and proliferation potential are classified to 10 ratings and hostility to 5. All three criteria considered, there are 5 severity ratings.

Threat Severity Assessment. Symantec Corporation also suggests three criteria to define severity [38]. They are (1) in-the-wild, (2) damage caused, and (3) rate of distribution. In-the-wild measures the extent to which a virus has already spread among computers. Damage caused measures the amount of damage that a given infection can inflict. The distribution component measures how quickly a program spreads itself. It can be seen that damage caused corresponds to the payload potential and the hostility level in the classification criteria proposed by Bagnall and French [5]. Both in-the-wild and rate of distribution measure the spread of the malware program, with the difference being that the former is about the facts of existing spread and the latter is about its ability to spread. They correspond to the proliferation potential in the classification criteria proposed by Bagnall and French [5]. Therefore, both of these two severity level definition systems mainly cover two aspects: proliferation and damage.

Kaspersky Lab Threat Level Classification. Kaspersky Lab uses a tree structure to describe their definition of the severity levels of all types of malware programs [21]. Kaspersky Lab does not provide their specific criteria, but it can be seen that the types of malware that are programmed to wildly spread and that may cause tremendous damage are in the upper part of the tree, and the reverse are in the lower part of the tree. This means that the criteria they use are consistent with the first two systems. Kaspersky Lab suggests that the following principles should be taken into consideration to determine the severity: 1) each behavior is assigned its own severity level, and the behaviors that pose less of a threat are outranked by behaviors that pose more of a threat, 2) if a program can be categorized as a number of different behaviors, it should be classified as the most threatening level of those behaviors, 3) if a malicious program has two or more functions with equal severity levels, which could be covered by Trojan Ransom, Trojan ArcBomb, Trojan Clicker, Trojan DDoS, Trojan Downloader, Trojan Dropper, Trojan IM, Trojan Notifier, Trojan Proxy, Trojan SMS, Trojan Spy, Trojan Mailfinder, Trojan GameThief, Trojan PSW or Trojan Banker, then the program will be classified as a Trojan. These principles make sense not only for their severity classification system, but also for the general severity ranking problem. The last principle also makes this classification problem different from normal classification problems in which the relations between all classes are balanced.

3 Problem Definition

Definition 1 (Malware Severity Classification). *Consider a collection of executables E and a collection of labels L that indicate the severity levels of executables in E. Let exe be an unknown executable that $exe \notin E$. The malware severity classification problem is to build a classification model M based on E and L such that M can be used to determine which severity level the executable exe belongs to.* ∎

4 Methodology

The workflow of our proposed method is shown in Fig. 1. The classification is performed based on the functionality analysis of malware samples. For training the system, we use IDA Pro[1] to disassemble the training samples to get their assembly functions. Then, we apply *Asm2Vec* [14] on the assembly functions to compute their vector representations such that semantically similar assembly functions have large cosine similarities with their vector representations. With the vector representations, we perform a discriminative clustering algorithm to group semantically equivalent assembly functions in a cluster. A feedforward neural network is trained on the vectors representing whether a sample contains a function that belongs to each cluster as input, and predicts the severity

---

[1] https://www.hex-rays.com/products/ida/.

level of the sample. In the test phase, a target sample is disassembled and the vector representations of its assembly functions are computed with the trained *Asm2Vec* model. The vector representations are then used to determine whether the functions belong to a cluster or not. We form a vector representation of the target sample based on whether it has any assembly function that belongs to each cluster. The trained feedforward neural network takes this vector as input to predict the severity level of the target sample.

The disassembling, function representation learning, clustering, and function clone search steps are inherited from the malware family classification system proposed by Li et al. [25]. The feature vector formation and feed-forward neural network classifier are our improvements to that system for the severity classification problem.

4.1 Function Representation Learning

An assembly function consists of one or more blocks of assembly instruction sequences. Assembly functions that achieve the same purpose may appear quite differently when obfuscations or optimizations are applied. Therefore, in its original form, it is hard to directly compare the similarity of assembly functions.

Asm2Vec [14] is a representation learning method for assembly code functions. The vector representations of semantically similar functions have a large cosine similarity so that they can be used to detect clone relations (i.e., similarity larger than a threshold) between different assembly functions. In the training phase, we use the assembly functions of training samples to train *Asm2Vec*, and at the same time, *Asm2Vec* computes the vector representations of the assembly code functions.

The result of this step is the trained *Asm2Vec* and the vector representations of the assembly code functions of the training samples.

4.2 Discriminative Function Clustering

In this step, we put assembly code functions that are semantically equivalent to each other in a cluster. Some clusters are good representatives of certain malware classes since only malware samples from these classes contain assembly code functions that belong to these clusters. They are called discriminative assembly code function clusters. They could be groups of functions related to certain malicious behaviors, such as key logging, proliferation, or corrupting file systems. We identify these clusters with their **discriminative power**. This concept relies on another concept called the popularity of a malware class in a cluster. Let G_i be a cluster, and C_j be a malware class. Let $\|comf(G_i, C_j)\|$ be the percentage of executables in class C_j that has one or more functions in cluster G_i. The **popularity** of malware class C_j in cluster G_i is defined as follows:

$$pop(G_i, C_j) = \frac{\|comf(G_i, C_j)\|}{\sum_{j=1}^{m} \|comf(G_i, C_j)\|} \tag{1}$$

The discriminative power of cluster G_i is as follows:

$$dp(G_i) = \begin{cases} 0 & \text{if } G_i \text{ contains only 1 function} \\ max_j\{pop(G_i, C_j)\} - min_j\{pop(G_i, C_j)\} & \text{otherwise} \end{cases}$$

In plain words, the discriminative power of a cluster is the difference between the popularity of the class with the maximal popularity and the popularity of the class with the minimal popularity in the cluster. The clusters with high discriminative power characterize the malware classes that have large popularity. In other words, when an executable contains a function that belongs to the cluster, there is a large probability that it belongs to the clusters with large popularity in the cluster as opposed to the rest of the malware classes. Therefore, they can be used to discriminate against the classes with low popularity. On the contrary, in the clusters with low discriminative power, the popularity of all malware classes are similar, thus containing a function of these clusters can not bring much knowledge on which malware classes it is likely to belong to.

To get the discriminative assembly code function clusters from the set of assembly code functions of the training samples, we use a discriminative clustering algorithm [25]. The basic is a Union-Find algorithm to gradually aggregate assembly functions to each cluster and its efficiency is optimized by locality-sensitive hashing (LSH). The LSH function family we use is proposed by Charikar [8]. In the hash function, the only parameter is a random vector r, which has the same dimension as the vector representation of an assembly code function. The entries of r are independently drawn from standard Gaussian distribution. The hash value of an assembly code function represented as u is computed as follows:

$$h_r(u) = \begin{cases} 1 & u \cdot r > 0 \\ 0 & u \cdot r \leq 0 \end{cases}$$

Charikar [8] proved that for two vectors u and v, the probability that they have the same hash value is as follows:

$$Pr[h_r(u) = h_r(v)] = 1 - \frac{\theta(u, v)}{\pi} \tag{2}$$

Therefore, the larger their cosine similarity is, the larger the probability that they have the same hash value. Thus, semantically similar assembly code functions tend to have the same hash values. The way we use LSH to group the assembly code functions can be described as follows:

1. We apply a set of LSH functions on the assembly code functions. The assembly code functions that have the same hash values are put in the same bucket. In each bucket, the assembly functions are potentially equivalent to each other. The number of LSH functions should guarantee that in each bucket, the number of assembly code functions should be smaller than a threshold.
2. We apply the Weighted Quick-Union with Path Compression algorithm [37] on the vector representations of the assembly code functions in each bucket to aggregate them in clusters.
3. We filter the clusters with low discriminative power since they are not informative for discriminating samples of a malware class to other classes.

We refer the readers to the original paper [25] for more details about the discriminative clustering algorithm. We keep the same hyper-parameters as theirs for the algorithm. The idea of processing the training executables for clustering is shown in Fig. 2.

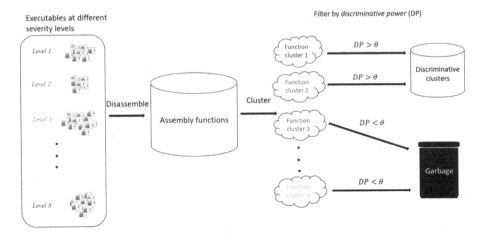

Fig. 2. The procedure to cluster assembly functions.

4.3 Function Clone Search

The classification of a sample is based on its relation to the discriminative assembly code function clusters. The relation of each training sample to the clusters is already known, since the assembly code functions in the clusters are all from training samples. In the test phase, the trained *Asm2Vec* will be applied onto the assembly functions of the test samples to generate the vector representations of the functions. Based on the vector representations, *Asm2Vec* determines whether each assembly function of a test sample is equivalent to an assembly function in a cluster. If it is, the function belongs to that cluster and the test sample is related to the cluster.

4.4 Feature Vector Formation

Let m be the number of discriminative code function clusters that are formed in the discriminative function clustering step. For each training or test sample, we form a feature vector of dimensions m. Each entry of the vector corresponds to a cluster. The value of an entry is 1 if there is at least one assembly function of the executable that belongs to the cluster (i.e., is equivalent to the functions in the cluster) and 0 otherwise.

4.5 Feed-Forward Neural Network Classification

Malware samples in a family are functionally similar to each other. That is the reason that the classification method based on accumulating the functional similarity proposed by [25] could work. However, it would not work for the severity classification problem because similarity does not determine the severity level of a sample. If a malware program contains much more than the average number of functions at a certain level, its severity level is boosted to a higher level. If a malware program contains only a few functions at a higher level and most functions at a lower level, it should still be classified to the higher level [21].

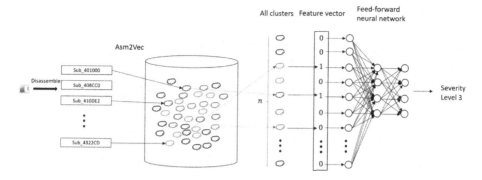

Fig. 3. The procedure to classify an executable.

To solve the aforementioned problem, we replace the functional similarity accumulation-based classification module with an artificial neural network. As is well-known, artificial neural networks are good at pattern recognition for classification. They implicitly learn the patterns that are correlated with each class from the training data. And they can approximate any function to arbitrary accuracy [18]. Therefore, we incorporate a neural network in our proposed malware severity classification model.

The neural network is a feedforward neural network. The input is a feature vector of dimension m formed in the previous step. It is fed to l fully-connected (FC) hidden layers with $Relu$ as the activation function:

$$v_l(x) = FC^l(...FC^1(x)...)$$
$$where\ FC^i(v_{i-1}(x)) = Relu(W_i v_{i-1}(x) + b_i)$$

Then $v_l(x)$ is fed to another FC layer with the output of dimension c, which is the number of classes (i.e., severity levels), and followed by a $softmax$ layer:

$$y(x) = softmax(W_o v_l(x) + b_o) \tag{3}$$

The output $y(x) \in R^c$ is the probability distribution that the query sample is at each severity level. Figure 3 shows the procedure to process an executable and classify it with the feed forward neural network.

In the training phase, we use the feature vectors of training samples and their severity level labels to train the feed forward neural network. We use cross entropy loss as the objective function and Adam [22] as the optimizer with the initial learning rate $1e-4$. The number of hidden layers and the dimensions of the hidden layers are hyperparameters. We consider 1, 2, 3 hidden layers and 256, 128, 64 as the candidate dimensions. We use grid search for tuning hyper-parameters.

In the test phase, we just feed the feature vectors of test samples to the neural network and it computes the probability that the samples belong to each severity.

5 Experiments

In this section, we present the evaluation of our proposed severity classification method. The major evaluation metric is accuracy:

$$accuracy = \frac{number\ of\ correctly\ classified\ samples}{number\ of\ samples\ to\ classify} \qquad (4)$$

We also report the precision, recall, and F1 for each severity level (class):

$$precision = \frac{number\ of\ samples\ correctly\ classified\ to\ the\ class}{number\ of\ samples\ classified\ to\ the\ class}$$

$$recall = \frac{number\ of\ samples\ correctly\ classified\ to\ the\ class}{number\ of\ samples\ belonging\ to\ the\ class}$$

$$F1 = \frac{2 * precision * recall}{precision + recall}$$

5.1 Dataset

Table 1. Statistics of the dataset.

Severity	Training		Validation		Test	
	# of exec	# of func	# of exec	# of func	# of exec	# of func
Level 1	169	67,933	56	23,541	56	21,869
Level 2	724	177,361	216	54,849	216	59,178
Level 3	181	10,066	39	2,952	39	3,126
Level 4	181	6,391	53	2,075	53	1,690
Level 5	96	30,443	19	5,650	19	6,719
Level 6	181	2,223	55	344	55	695
Level 7	31	6,178	7	2,712	7	2,909
Level 8	56	5,934	11	1,478	11	2,238
Total	1,619	306,529	456	93,601	456	98,424

Based on the Kaspersky Lab Threat Level Classification tree [21], we create a dataset of 8 severity levels. There are 1619 malware samples in the training set, 456 in the validation set, and 456 in the test set. We use SHA256 checksum to ensure that there is no repetition between those three sets. The statistics of the dataset is given in Table 1. The types of malware included in our dataset at each severity level are shown in Table 2.

Table 2. Types of malware included in each severity level.

Severity	Malware types
Level 1	Hoax, HackTool
Level 2	Trojan-Banker, Trojan-Downloader, Trojan-PSW, Trojan-Ransom, Trojan-Spy
Level 3	Trojan
Level 4	Backdoor
Level 5	Virus
Level 6	Worm
Level 7	Email-Worm
Level 8	Net-Worm

Table 3. Accuracy of different methods on the test set.

Method	Accuracy
Our method	**91.9%**
Mosk2008OpBi	82.2%
Bald2013Meta	90.4%
Saxe2015Deep	87.5%
Mour2019CNN	27.0%
Li2021Func	73.2%

5.2 Malware Classification Methods for Comparison

In the evaluation, we use the following state-of-the-art malware classification methods to compare with our model:

- **Mosk2008OpBi:** Moskovitch et al. propose to use TF or TF-IDF of opcode bi-grams as features and use document frequency (DF), information gain ratio, or Fisher score as the criterion for feature selection [27]. They apply Artificial Neural Networks, Decision Trees, Naïve Bayes, Boosted Decision Trees, and Boosted Naïve Bayes as their malware classification models.
- **Bald2013Meta:** Baldangombo et al. propose to extract multiple raw features from PE headers and use information gain and calling frequencies for feature selection and PCA for dimension reduction [6]. They apply SVM, J48, and Naïve Bayes as their malware classification models.
- **Saxe2015Deep:** Saxe and Berlin propose a deep learning model that works on four different features: byte/entropy histogram features, PE import features, string 2D histogram features, and PE metadata numerical features [35].
- **Mour2019CNN:** Mourtaji et al. convert malware binaries to grayscale images and apply a convolutional neural network on malware images for malware classification [28]. Their CNN network has two convolutional layers followed by a fully-connected layer.

– **Li2021Func:** Li et al. propose to group assembly functions to clusters, and compute the similarity of a query executable to a malware family based on the comparison of the number of clusters of the family related to it and the number of clusters related to a median sample of the training set in the family [25]. We directly replace malware families with severity levels as the class labels to apply their method to this severity classification problem.

5.3   Experiment Settings

The experiments are conducted on a server with two Xeon E5-2697 CPUs, 384 GB of memory, and four Nvidia Titan XP graphics cards. The operating system is Windows Server 2016.

Our proposed severity classification system and **Li2021Func** are developed with Java 11, and the feedforward neural network is developed with Deeplearning4j [39]. Other baseline methods are implemented with Python 3.7.9. The traditional machine learning models are implemented with scikit-learn 0.23.2 [31], and neural networks are implemented with PyTorch 1.6.0 [30].

5.4   Results

The classification accuracy of different methods is shown in Table 3. Our proposed model achieves the best classification accuracy among all methods. **Bald2013Meta** achieves the second best accuracy, which means the features extracted from PE headers are also informative. However, PE headers only provide peripheral information of an executable, thus, it would not provide as much insight and interpretability as our method since our method is based on the analysis of the malware functionality.

Even though **Li2021Func** is also based on the functionality analysis of malware, it achieves inferior accuracy because of the way it computes the class that a sample belongs to. The severity level of a malware sample is determined by the level of its most threatening behavior, and a greater than average number of behaviors existing

Table 4. Experiment results on each severity level.

Severity level	Precision	Recall	F1-score
Level 1	1.00	0.79	0.88
Level 2	0.87	1.00	0.93
Level 3	0.97	0.90	0.93
Level 4	1.00	0.81	0.90
Level 5	0.83	0.79	0.81
Level 6	1.00	0.95	0.97
Level 7	0.73	0.69	0.71
Level 8	1.00	0.82	0.90
Weighted avg	0.93	0.92	0.92

in one executable boosts its severity level. However, **Li2021Func** would classify an executable to the level of most behaviors because it is correlated to the most number of clusters at that level. This leads to incorrect classification results.

The precision, recall, and F1 of our model on each severity level is shown in Table 4. Our model performs well for most severity levels except severity level 7. The inferior F1 on level 7 is because we have fewer training samples at severity level 7.

5.5 Classification Result Interpretation

Figure 4 shows an example of the interpretation module of our model. On the left, it lists the assembly functions of a query executable and the function "sub_408CF3" is selected. On the right, it shows the assembly functions in a cluster that are semantically equivalent to "sub_408CF3". They are all from the same cluster "level_1_Cluster95", which is a cluster of severity level 1.

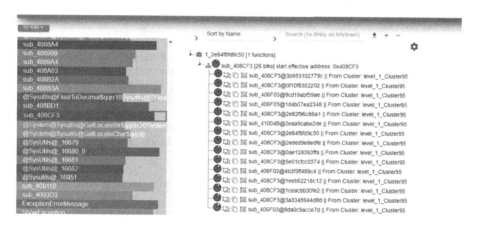

Fig. 4. An example of interpretation for classification results.

6 Discussions

As is shown in the previous section, our malware severity classification model can explain its classification results by pointing out which functions of the query executable and which function clusters contribute to the classification result. This is the interpretability inherited from the method proposed by Li et al. [25]. However, the neural network module is not directly interpretable. This is a limitation since different functions are not equally important to determining its severity level and it cannot explain how much each assembly function contributes to the classification result. One direction of our future work is to improve the interpretability of the severity classification system so that it can quantify the importance of each assembly function related to its severity.

7   Conclusion

In this paper, to classify the severity levels of malware programs, we propose a neural network-based model that is applied on assembly code function clusters. The method has the same interpretability as the method proposed by Li et al. [25] to point out which functions contribute to the classification, and it has a better ability to implicitly learn patterns of functionalities to provide accurate severity level estimation of unknown malware samples. It also outperforms previously proposed methods for malware classification on the severity classification task.

Acknowledgment. This research was funded by NSERC Discovery Grants (RGPIN-2018-03872), Canada Research Chairs Program (950-230623), and the Canadian National Defence Innovation for Defence Excellence and Security (IDEaS W7714-217794/001/SV1). The IDEaS program assists in solving some of Canada's toughest defence and security challenges. The Titan Xp used for this research was donated by the NVIDIA Corporation.

References

1. Abusitta, A., Li, M.Q., Fung, B.C.M.: Malware classification and composition analysis: a survey of recent developments. J. Inf. Secur. Appl. (JISA) **59**(102828), 1–17 (2021)
2. Amer, E., Zelinka, I.: A dynamic windows malware detection and prediction method based on contextual understanding of API call sequence. Comput. Secur. **92**, 101760 (2020)
3. Anderson, B., Quist, D., Neil, J., Storlie, C., Lane, T.: Graph-based malware detection using dynamic analysis. J. Comput. Virol. **7**(4), 247–258 (2011)
4. Anderson, B., Storlie, C., Lane, T.: Improving malware classification: bridging the static/dynamic gap. In: Proceedings of the 5th ACM Workshop on Security and Artificial Intelligence, pp. 3–14. ACM (2012)
5. Bagnall, R.J., French, G.: The malware rating system (MRS)™ (2001)
6. Baldangombo, U., Jambaljav, N., Horng, S.J.: A static malware detection system using data mining methods. arXiv preprint arXiv:1308.2831 (2013)
7. Bayer, U., Moser, A., Kruegel, C., Kirda, E.: Dynamic analysis of malicious code. J. Comput. Virol. **2**(1), 67–77 (2006)
8. Charikar, M.S.: Similarity estimation techniques from rounding algorithms. In: Proceedings of the 34th Annual ACM Symposium on Theory of Computing, pp. 380–388 (2002)
9. Chen, J., Alalfi, M.H., Dean, T.R., Zou, Y.: Detecting android malware using clone detection. J. Comput. Sci. Technol. **30**(5), 942–956 (2015)
10. Dahl, G.E., Stokes, J.W., Deng, L., Yu, D.: Large-scale malware classification using random projections and neural networks. In: 2013 IEEE International Conference on Acoustics, Speech and Signal Processing (ICASSP), pp. 3422–3426. IEEE (2013)
11. Dai, J., Guha, R.K., Lee, J.: Efficient virus detection using dynamic instruction sequences. JCP **4**(5), 405–414 (2009)
12. Damodaran, A., Troia, F.D., Visaggio, C.A., Austin, T.H., Stamp, M.: A comparison of static, dynamic, and hybrid analysis for malware detection. J. Comput. Virol. Hacking Tech. **13**(1), 1–12 (2015). https://doi.org/10.1007/s11416-015-0261-z
13. Demontis, A., et al.: Yes, machine learning can be more secure! A case study on android malware detection. IEEE Trans. Dependable Secure Comput. **16**, 711–724 (2017)
14. Ding, S.H.H., Fung, B.C.M., Charland, P.: Asm2Vec: boosting static representation robustness for binary clone search against code obfuscation and compiler optimization. In: Proceedings of the 40th International Symposium on Security and Privacy (S&P), pp. 38–55. IEEE Computer Society, May 2019

15. Fredrikson, M., Jha, S., Christodorescu, M., Sailer, R., Yan, X.: Synthesizing near-optimal malware specifications from suspicious behaviors. In: 2010 IEEE Symposium on Security and Privacy (SP), pp. 45–60. IEEE (2010)
16. Gandotra, E., Bansal, D., Sofat, S.: Malware analysis and classification: a survey. J. Inf. Securi. **5**, 56–64 (2014)
17. Gibert, D., Mateu, C., Planes, J.: HYDRA: a multimodal deep learning framework for malware classification. Comput. Secur. **95**, 101873 (2020)
18. Hornik, K., Stinchcombe, M., White, H.: Multilayer feedforward networks are universal approximators. Neural Netw. **2**(5), 359–366 (1989)
19. Huang, W., Stokes, J.W.: MtNet: a multi-task neural network for dynamic malware classification. In: Caballero, J., Zurutuza, U., Rodríguez, R.J. (eds.) DIMVA 2016. LNCS, vol. 9721, pp. 399–418. Springer, Cham (2016). https://doi.org/10.1007/978-3-319-40667-1_20
20. Islam, R., Tian, R., Batten, L.M., Versteeg, S.: Classification of malware based on integrated static and dynamic features. J. Netw. Comput. Appl. **36**(2), 646–656 (2013)
21. Kaspersky, L.: Rules for classifying (2020). https://encyclopedia.kaspersky.com/knowledge/rules-for-classifying/
22. Kingma, D.P., Ba, J.: Adam: a method for stochastic optimization. arXiv preprint arXiv:1412.6980 (2014)
23. Kolter, J.Z., Maloof, M.A.: Learning to detect malicious executables in the wild. In: Proceedings of the 10th ACM International Conference on Knowledge Discovery and Data Mining (SIGKDD), pp. 470–478. ACM (2004)
24. Kruegel, C., Kirda, E., Mutz, D., Robertson, W., Vigna, G.: Polymorphic worm detection using structural information of executables. In: Valdes, A., Zamboni, D. (eds.) RAID 2005. LNCS, vol. 3858, pp. 207–226. Springer, Heidelberg (2006). https://doi.org/10.1007/11663812_11
25. Li, M.Q., Fung, B.C.M., Charland, P., Ding, S.H.H.: A novel and dedicated machine learning model for malware classification. In: Proceedings of the 16th International Conference on Software Technologies, pp. 617–628 (2021)
26. Li, M.Q., Fung, B.C., Charland, P., Ding, S.H.: I-MAD: interpretable malware detector using galaxy transformer. Comput. Secur. **108**, 102371 (2021)
27. Moskovitch, R., et al.: Unknown Malcode detection using OPCODE representation. In: Ortiz-Arroyo, D., Larsen, H.L., Zeng, D.D., Hicks, D., Wagner, G. (eds.) EuroISI 2008. LNCS, vol. 5376, pp. 204–215. Springer, Heidelberg (2008). https://doi.org/10.1007/978-3-540-89900-6_21
28. Mourtaji, Y., Bouhorma, M., Alghazzawi, D.: Intelligent framework for malware detection with convolutional neural network. In: Proceedings of the 2nd International Conference on Networking, Information Systems & Security, p. 7. ACM (2019)
29. Onwuzurike, L., Mariconti, E., Andriotis, P., Cristofaro, E.D., Ross, G., Stringhini, G.: MaMaDroid: detecting android malware by building Markov chains of behavioral models (extended version). ACM Trans. Privacy Secur. (TOPS) **22**(2), 1–34 (2019)
30. Paszke, A., et al.: Automatic differentiation in PyTorch. In: Neural Information Processing Systems NIPS 2017 Autodiff Workshop (2017)
31. Pedregosa, F., et al.: Scikit-learn: machine learning in Python. J. Mach. Learn. Res. **12**, 2825–2830 (2011)
32. Raff, E., Barker, J., Sylvester, J., Brandon, R., Catanzaro, B., Nicholas, C.: Malware detection by eating a whole exe. arXiv preprint arXiv:1710.09435 (2017)
33. Royal, P., Halpin, M., Dagon, D., Edmonds, R., Lee, W.: PolyUnpack: automating the hidden-code extraction of unpack-executing malware. In: Proceedings of the 22nd Annual Computer Security Applications Conference (ACSAC 2006), pp. 289–300. IEEE (2006)

34. Santos, I., Devesa, J., Brezo, F., Nieves, J., Bringas, P.G.: OPEM: a static-dynamic approach for machine-learning-based malware detection. In: Proceedings of the International Joint Conference CISIS'12-ICEUTE 12-SOCO 12 Special Sessions, pp. 271–280. Springer, Heidelberg (2013). https://doi.org/10.1007/978-3-642-33018-6_28
35. Saxe, J., Berlin, K.: Deep neural network based malware detection using two dimensional binary program features. In: Proceedings of the 10th International Conference on Malicious and Unwanted Software (MALWARE), pp. 11–20. IEEE (2015)
36. Schultz, M.G., Eskin, E., Zadok, F., Stolfo, S.J.: Data mining methods for detection of new malicious executables. In: 2001 IEEE Symposium on Security and Privacy, S&P 2001. Proceedings, pp. 38–49. IEEE (2001)
37. Sedgewick, R., Wayne, K.: Algorithms. Addison-Wesley Professional (2011)
38. symantec: Severity assessment: Threats, events, vulnerabilities, risks (2006)
39. Eclipse Deeplearning4j: DL4J: Deep Learning for Java (2016). https://github.com/eclipse/deeplearning4j
40. Vasan, D., Alazab, M., Wassan, S., Safaei, B., Zheng, Q.: Image-based malware classification using ensemble of CNN architectures (IMCEC). Comput. Secur. **92**, 101748 (2020)
41. Verma, V., Muttoo, S.K., Singh, V.: Multiclass malware classification via first-and second-order texture statistics. Comput. Secur. **97**, 101895 (2020)
42. Ye, Y., Li, T., Adjeroh, D., Iyengar, S.S.: A survey on malware detection using data mining techniques. ACM Comput. Surv. (CSUR) **50**(3), 41 (2017)

Author Index

Printed in the United States
by Baker & Taylor Publisher Services